In the Sierra Madre

JEFF BIGGERS

In the Sierra Madre

University of Illinois Press

Urbana and Chicago

© 2006 by the Board of Trustees
of the University of Illinois
All rights reserved
Manufactured in the United States of America
c 5 4 3 2 1

∞ This book is printed on acid-free paper.

Library of Congress Cataloging-in-Publication Data
Biggers, Jeff, 1963–
In the Sierra Madre / Jeff Biggers.
p.   cm.
Includes bibliographical references and index.
ISBN-13: 978-0-252-03101-4 (cloth : alk. paper)
ISBN-10: 0-252-03101-6 (cloth : alk. paper)
1. Tarahumara Indians—History.
2. Tarahumara Indians—Folklore.
3. Tarahumara Indians—Social life and customs.
4. Legends—Mexico—Sierra Madre del Sur.
5. Sierra Madre del Sur (Mexico)—History.
6. Sierra Madre del Sur (Mexico)—Folklore.
7. Sierra Madre del Sur (Mexico)—Social life and customs.
I. Title.
F1221.T25B54   2006
972.16004'974546—dc22   2006000328

12/06   32825025

per Carla, per sempre

for Doug, Katie, Keegan, and Logan,
our patron saints in the Sonoran Desert

for Barney and Mahina,
treasures of the Sierra Madre

The treasure which you think not worth
taking trouble and pains to find, this one alone
is the real treasure you are longing for all your life.
The glittering treasure you are hunting for day and
night lies buried on the other side of that hill yonder.

—B. TRAVEN, *The Treasure of the Sierra Madre*

Contents

Preface   xi

Part I: Lost and Found in the Sierra Madre   1

Part II: The Revenge of the Tarahumara   34

Part III: A Devilish Sort of Thing   85

Part IV: The Treasure We Long For   108

Acknowledgments   173

Bibliography   175

Index   179

Preface

I met an extraordinary storyteller in the Sierra Madre of Mexico. To reach his log cabin in a remote hollow, I had to follow the ribbon of a trail along a canyon's edge, ford a creek bed, and then zigzag through the remains of sparse cornfields bordered by boulders and the frontline of a pine forest. I picked up a small rock along the way, which had become a habit, in preparation for the mad dogs of the mountains. Alfonzo had given vague instructions to find his homestead; the Rarámuri in the Sierra Madre have an obscure way of describing their personal geography.

I had actually met Alfonzo outside a Rarámuri village shop a few days before. He was a wiry man; unruly grey hair was tucked under a straw hat. He possessed the weathered face of an outdoor laborer. His eyes engaged with a storyteller's gift of astonishment.

He was expecting me at his cabin; he had probably been expecting me for days. In his two-room abode, which housed three generations of his family, Alfonzo's wife, Maria, offered me a cup of coal black coffee from a pot that had been boiling atop their woodstove. We sat around a small wooden table. There was little else in the way of furniture. A cadre of children hugged the doorway and watched. I could hear dogs barking outside.

"All men do not have a good heart," Alfonzo began, removing his hat.

His words were not as artless as they sounded. He clasped his hands together, staring at me intently, and then recounted his life story.

In the 1970s—the precise date, of course, is unknown—Alfonzo wanted to see how people lived outside of his own remote homeland in the western corner of Chihuahua, in northern Mexico. Carrying only a bag of pinole, roasted corn ground twice into a powdery grain, he walked out of the Sierra Madre, descending canyons, passing the valleys of cornfields and log cabins and the cave dwellings of his Rarámuri people. He finally caught a ride on muleback from a mestizo trader, who took him to the plains of Chihuahua.

With an affable disposition, Alfonzo made friends easily. He had no problems adjusting to adversity; after two years in a faraway boarding school for indigent children, he had spent his youth toiling in the cornfields and forests in the Sierra Madre. He spoke both Spanish and Rarámuri fluently.

Unlike other migrant workers, he had no plans to tuck away his pitiful savings and return home in the off-season. He said he was searching for a different fortune. He found work as a ranch hand in Durango and then as a farmworker in Michoacan. His goal was to move on, see more of the world. He didn't bother with official documents. He crossed borders at night, along rivers, or through the very forests that had made him invisible in the Sierra Madre.

By the time he reached Peru, he had narrowly escaped death at two separate farm incidents. It didn't stop him from jumping a freighter one night in the port of Lima.

"I was a *polizón*," he chuckled.

I shook my head. I didn't know that word in Spanish.

"When someone sneaks onto a boat without permission."

A stowaway. I nodded for him to continue, but that image glowed in my mind with the random process of our journeys.

"When they found me, they had two choices," Alfonzo continued. "They could either throw me overboard to the sharks or put me to work. It took them some days to decide. Then one day a man gave me a mop and told me to get to work."

Alfonzo worked on the freighter across the Pacific. He was given a small stipend when the ship moored in the Chiba harbor. Wandering the streets of Tokyo, the Rarámuri traveler didn't feel like a stranger; he eased into the traffic of the warrens like a bemused apparition. His visit to the gravestones of the samurai at a mysterious temple, all having committed suicide, disturbed his sense of place. He couldn't fathom their ritual act of hari-kari. He found refuge for the night in the gardens of a shrine, where he slept in the shadow of the emperor.

Alfonzo missed his freighter's departure. Hanging around the port for days, he managed to find work aboard a fishing vessel heading to

Vladivostok, where a fellow sailor, who spoke Portuguese and a meager Spanish, described the Trans-Siberian railroad that departed from the Russian peninsula.

He never made it across Russia. After roaming the bitterly cold Siberian streets, he was arrested by the Soviet police. Amid the shouts of linguistic confusion, he was accused of being a spy for Mexico. He spent three months in a Soviet prison until the Mexican consulate was finally informed of his claim of citizenship. It took the direct intervention of President Luis Echeverriá Alvarez of Mexico to gain his release from prison and return to the Central American isthmus.

"I was the first person to speak Rarámuri in Asia," he said, sitting back in his chair.

But the outsiders, in some many countries, amazed Alfonzo with their apparent familiarity with the Sierra Madre.

"They always asked me about the treasure," he said. "I had no idea what they were talking about. So, I told them about my people."

When Alfonzo returned to his village in the Sierra Madre, he was as penniless and starry-eyed for the world as the day he had walked out of the forests. He found his community languishing again in the ravages of a long drought. Many Rarámuri men were readying to depart for migrant labor camps in the plains. The villagers couldn't believe Alfonzo had traveled the world, interacted with the president of Mexico, and not returned a wealthy man. His stories sounded invented; they doubted his newfound vocabulary to match his descriptions.

"'I did not travel for riches,' I told them, 'but rich experiences.'"

He opened his empty, wrinkled hands.

"'You are as poor as we are,' they told me. 'What good are your stories?'"

Alfonzo quieted for a moment. He had choked up a couple of times. I saw him repeating those lines under his breath, as if to remind himself of the value of his journeys. The line had caught me off guard as well; I felt this same sense of conflicting emotion welling up in my own chest.

"So, I claimed a plot of land, built a small cabin, and began to cultivate corn like other Rarámuri," he finally went on.

Born within view of the mission in Mawichi, Alfonzo was both Rarámuri and mestizo, the son of a Mexican lumberjack and a Rarámuri mother.

"Some say I am a *chabochi*," Alfonzo chuckled, using the Rarámuri word for "outsiders." "But the chabochis say I am Rarámuri. I am both Rarámuri and chabochi in my heart."

Alfonzo sipped his coffee, which had not been touched during the course of his story. I saw him struggling to remember the details of his voyages. Over the years, the foreign ports and streets of Tokyo had become faint but vital memories, lingering like the thousand-year-old petroglyphs on the caves near his homestead. But his stories, told and retold in the shadows of gas lamps and fires, were living testaments of other fortunes.

"So, you have finally made it to *la Sierra*," Alfonzo said, looking up with a grin. "You're probably looking for the treasure, as well."

I smiled and took a sip of my coffee. It had become cold.

In the Sierra Madre

Part I

Lost and Found
in the Sierra Madre

The Sierra Madre. No other mountains in the world possess such a timbre of intrigue and wonder. Sure, there are greater chains of snowcapped peaks; I have trekked along the boundless sweeps of the Himalayas, the Swiss Alps, the glaciers of New Zealand, and the Rockies and Appalachians in the United States. Still, only the Sierra Madre in northern Mexico has conjured up a world unlike anywhere else with its labyrinth of canyons and legends.

The range stretches in a network of chasms and rivers that is actually more immense, even more "grand" in its undulating range, than the Grand Canyon on the Colorado River. It doesn't bother with pristine splendor; the *barrancas* of la Sierra loom inaccessible, dangerous, otherworldly.

Despite their inhospitality, these canyons have lured a fabulous procession of prospectors for centuries. Argonauts or accidental travelers, they have all come in search of some sort of treasure, real or imagined, ranging from Spain, Morocco, France, Russia, Norway, Germany, China, Poland, South Africa, Croatia, Italy, and Japan; there have been writers, filmmakers, utopians, Confederates, and Buffalo Soldiers, Boer and Irish war deserters, Mormons and Mennonites, Yaqui rebels and Apache renegades, Chinese laborers and Bohemian missionaries; their ranks have included Antonin Artaud, Geronimo, George S. Patton, Black Jack Pershing, and Pancho Villa.

Like the mercurial American prospectors in John Huston's film version of *The Treasure of the Sierra Madre*, most of these travelers have left the mountains empty-handed but ultimately transformed by their illusive ventures. In the process, the fascinating motives and machinations behind their searches have been forgotten. The very treasure that Alfonzo declared was hidden in the Sierra Madre has been left behind.

Not that the Sierra Madre has ever been uninhabited. Watching over these canyons like guardians, more than eighty thousand Rarámuri (or Tarahumara, as they are more commonly known by Mexicans and outsiders) carry on as the last remnants of a pre-Columbian Mexico spread out over miles of barrancas and mountain forests. They are the second largest indigenous group, north of Mexico City, in North America. Since the first invasion of Europeans in the early 1500s, they have shaped a culture of resiliency, more than resistance. Living on precarious homesteads, with their plots of corn positioned on faraway ledges, they are now dealing with the latest round of treasure hunters wrapped in the guise of mass tourism, drug trafficking, logging, and evangelism. Unlike almost every other indigenous group in the Americas, however, the Rarámuri have somehow managed to ward off the worst of the desperados, absorb the influx of contemporary influences, and continue to cultivate their corn and traditional way of life.

The Rarámuri are not the only indigenous people in the Sierra Madre, of course; smaller communities of the Pima, Tepehuane, Huichol, and Guarojio dot the canyons and lowlands. The question of existence for all of these indigenous communities—the maintenance of their unique ways of living in the twenty-first century—has compelled them to disperse further in the remote canyons, adapting to an even more hostile reality.

Remarkably, the Rarámuri have continued to thrive. I wanted to discover the secrets behind their extraordinary stories of survival. Their interactions with these elusive gold diggers over four hundred years were, as Alfonzo inadvertently noted, personal maps of the unforeseen treasure I sought in another Sierra Madre.

On September 17, 1998, a rather sedate day after the nation of Mexico had clamored into its plazas with the anniversary cry of independence, "Mexicanos, Viva Mexico!" Carla Paciotto, my companion, and

I ventured across the U.S.-Mexico border and journeyed to the Sierra Madre Occidental. We had planned to stay in a Rarámuri village for the school year. In preparation for our sojourn, we had made a quick trip to the region earlier that summer; Carla had toured the area extensively three years before. She was carrying out her field research for her doctoral dissertation on the bilingual education programs of the Rarámuri.

The cornfields on that first day stretched across the canyon basins in withered stalks; the entire region, from the Chihuahuan deserts to the eight-thousand-foot pine ridges of the Sierra Madre, was ailing from the worst drought in Mexico's history.

Nature, of course, always has a way of anticipating our human changes. Mexico was in the throes of a dramatic political and social upheaval, which would eventually result in the toppling of the one-party institution for the first time in over seventy years. As the heart of the logging, drug cultivation, and tourist industries in northern Mexico, the Sierra Madre was embroiled in its own historic period of rapid change. Like the gold diggers in *The Treasure of the Sierra Madre*, pernicious elements in these industries pumped with a voracity for quick wealth. The number of military roadblocks along the way spoke of some mysterious fortune that either needed to be protected or found.

There was an air of uncertainty on *the other side*.

We arrived, like all adventurers, on the Gran Vision. We made a final turn onto a dirt road to Mawichi, a Rarámuri village, leaving behind the paved road that had crawled across the valleys and ridges of the Sierra Madre for the last several hours. The turn seemed symbolic. Winding through the dense forest, bumping over rocks and ruts, we felt as if we had finally entered the backcountry of the Rarámuri, severing ourselves from the zones of transit and commerce of Mexico. As we would learn, the canyons deceived easily.

Completed less than a decade ago, the paved road through the sierra had been optimistically designated the Gran Vision by the Mexican government. The vision didn't refer to the Rarámuri or local inhabitants; it had been shaped to guide the holy trinity of modern-day prospectors—tourism, logging, drug-trafficking—in the Sierra Madre. The vision had simply consolidated the past, paving a loose network of narrow dirt roads, lumber access routes, mule and wagon trails, and foot paths. At each mile marker, I had a vision of *mestizos* (the common term used in the Sierra Madre for "mixed race" people or Mexicans) and Rarámuri work crews on their knees, scaling the mountain for nearly thirty years in a mission to lay over six hundred kilometers of paved road from La Junta to Parral.

The first view of our adopted village broke through the forest with a brilliant patch of blue sky. From there we mounted an overlook of a ridge that peered into the canyon. Bound on either side by towering rock bluffs, with stands of pines etched along the craggy faces, the valley stretched along a narrow creek for over a mile, covered in winding plots of corn. I saw a strand of smoke rising from a chimney on a cabin perched on the side of the canyon walls like a solitary tree. My eyes then shifted to more waves of smoke drifting from a cliff dwelling.

There were so few cabins in view; the apparent emptiness of this "village" had stayed with me since our first visit earlier that summer. Everyone had always spoken of Mawichi as if it were a Rarámuri version of Tenochtitlan, the Aztec capital. Dots on a map in the Sierra Madre made for a wonderful guessing game. As I would learn, a reference to a "village" might only signal a single shop or a mission, or a road crossing.

Following the rough dirt road, which had been carved into the rocky slope of the canyon, we finally saw a smattering of cabins. The village proper was no more than a 250-year-old mission, a boarding school, a clinic, and a cooperative shop, plopped into the basin of a creek-forged valley of steep rock faces. A disparate cluster of a dozen or so log cabins, caves, and wooden chicken coops laced the valley with lines of laundry, which hung from fences and boulders like colorful lines of modernity. A couple of girls herded small flocks of goats by the bend in the creek, where several young women in colorful skirts and scarves stooped, slapping their wash on the rocks. They all stopped their work and stared as our old Bronco rumbled up the road.

"We're home," Carla said, grinning.

Our home was a two-room decrepit log cabin near the mission, which we had arranged on an earlier trip. We felt quite lucky. There were so few cabins and houses in the valley. Most of the cave dwellings had even been claimed.

Our neighbors were an elderly couple, Maria and Bernabé, whose extended family more or less populated the rest of the central valley basin of the village. After building a new adobe home, the couple was using the old log cabin for corn storage. In front of our cabin was a dilapidated one-room stone dwelling, squat and disheveled, which functioned as the *tesguino* corn beer brewery and dirt-floor parlor room in the colder months.

Appearing from behind the cabin, standing with a goat kid in one hand, Bernabé greeted us on our arrival with a gleam in his eyes. In his early sixties, the Rarámuri elder was a short, barrel-chested man, clad in jeans, a buttoned shirt, a straw sombrero, and tire-soled huarache sandals. You realized at once that his soiled hat never left his head.

"Maria is out of the village," he said in Spanish. "Anything I can do for you?" He looked at our loaded Bronco, as if we were missionaries ready to dump our goods.

"We arranged with Maria to live here," Carla said.

Bernabé's expression became blank. Then he recovered, as if recalling an old prophesy of doom.

"Oh, Maria did mention something," he said. "It's her house, I suppose." He widened his grin. "Do you want to move in now?"

The log cabin was in disarray. We immediately started cleaning up the place and unloading our supplies. I could barely stand up straight in the cabin; the low ceilings reminded me of my visits among the ancient cane roof huts of the Danes, which were easier to warm during the rough North Sea winters. Curious and discreet, Bernabé made periodical visits, dropping by an oil lamp and a box of matches. I handed him a dead rat in a shovel, which he took by the tail and flung into the garden. Most of the back room was filled with corn, which would later be fermented and boiled into tesguino.

"Do you know what tesguino is?" Bernabé asked.

We nodded.

"You'll learn soon enough," he said.

We changed the metal pipes of the *calenton*, a barrel that served as a woodstove and heater. We were thrilled to have a pipe of running water. We swept the floors. We stuck rocks and kindling into the most visible holes between the mud-chinked logs. Bernabé returned at one point and took down a fox skin that had been drying on the wall, and then pointed out the stone *mano* and *metate* to grind our corn. He noted that the tables, shelves, wood plates and bowls, and clay pots and cups had all been made by him or other villagers. The invasion of our backpacks and boxes of books and supplies, in fact, along with our computers and solar power equipment, seemed like an intrusion in the sparse cabin that first night.

Bernabé stiffened for a moment of nostalgia. "Four of my kids were born in that corner over there."

I think Carla and I both felt a conflicting sense of welcome and trespassing. Bernabé's natural smile and assistance quickened our intimacy, but it also reminded us how much our residence was going to be an imposition on his own life.

"What's that?" Bernabé said, pointing at a case in the corner. "A guitar?"

"It's similar," I said. "It's a round guitar. A banjo."

"Pancho?" he said, raising his eyebrows.

"Banjo."

"Pancho."

He shrugged his shoulders. My banjo had been renamed.

The novel's (and film's) title was inescapable. B. Traven's *The Treasure of the Sierra Madre* always came up when I spoke to American and European friends about our plans. While more than a few were familiar with sunset images of Copper Canyon, most had trouble imaging the layout of the region. Due to the daily reports on the rebellion in Chiapas, many assumed we were heading to a tropical area. Then they'd adjust the map. "Oh, you mean where that movie with Humphrey Bogart was filmed."

I never got around to mentioning that the film and novel were actually based in the Sierra Madre Oriental, untold miles away. We were heading to the Sierra Madre Occidental. But geography didn't really matter in this respect; the film gave birth to the *Sierra Madre* in our modern vocabulary, real or invented. It placed the range on our literary and film map, that imaginary atlas in the minds of absentee voyeurs and delighted book readers and film viewers. It reminded us that the Sierra Madre was an invention as much as a place.

In the end, like all the rest, we were not heading to Mexico, but to the *Sierra Madre*.

The slow, rhythmic noise of a woman grinding corn on the stone metate outside our cabin woke me the first morning. I rose quietly and watched her from one of the cracks along the front wall. She knelt in a blossoming skirt and top in front of the metate—a huge block of stone—and methodically crushed the kernels of corn with the mano, a six-inch slab of rock. She used both hands until the basin of the block filled with powdered corn, which she then scooped into a wooden bowl on the side.

There was a high-country chill in the cabin. Bernabé had left a small amount of firewood. I made a fire in the calenton to warm the cabin and heat our water. The stack dwindled quickly. I realized at once that wood, after corn, was one of the most important necessities in village life.

Bernabé came by later in the morning, carrying a stack of blue corn tortillas.

"Como amaneció?" he said, quietly.

His morning greeting in Spanish literally means: How did you begin?

"With corn," I said.

Bernabé smiled. He volunteered to escort me to pick up some wood that morning. I assumed he was referring to the sawmill run by the *ejido* cooperative.

"How much do I need?" I asked, standing by the Bronco. I was referring to pesos.

"A few hours," he said, climbing into the passenger's seat of our Bronco.

Bernabé chatted in the truck. Having lost his mother as an infant, he had started herding goats alone at the age of five, deep into the remote canyons. By his early teens, unable to attend faraway boarding schools, he was offered the chance to serve as an apprentice carpenter and jack-of-all-trades through the agency of a Franciscan priest. He eventually ended up in Guadalajara. Bernabé had even considered the priesthood for a short while, until he decided he didn't have the calling. Returning to the Sierra Madre, he found work in the nearby mestizo town of Creel, where he met Maria at a Catholic mass. Fluent in Spanish and the ways of modern Mexico, the two of them formed the most cosmopolitan couple in the village, functioning as a great source of both initiative and controversy.

We left the village on the dirt road, turned onto a logging access road, and climbed a plateau that overlooked the canyon. Our road evolved into a wide trail until the four-wheel-drive jumped into gear and I found myself bushwhacking through the forest, throwing the elder increasingly frantic looks for direction. Bernabé patted the side of our rattling Bronco as it narrowly slid through the tall pines.

"This is much easier than taking the horses," he said nonchalantly. He gazed out the open windows. "Los broncos."

The term *bronco* amused Bernabé.

"That's what the Spanish and Mexicans called us."

For the Spanish intruders, these Rarámuri were "wild, untamable, intractable." They ran from strangers like spooked horses. In keeping with the *caballero*, or horseman-gentlemen, culture of Don Quixote, as anthropologist Jerome Levi has noted, the Spanish never failed from viewing the world from horseback.

"Here we are," Bernabé said, in the middle of a thick forest of pine and some oak. There was very little underbrush. A lightning storm had scorched the edge of the forest on one side, leaving behind a blackened maze of stumps and jagged trunks that looked like burned Joshua trees.

Pulling our axes from the back of the Bronco, we ambled over to a stand of dry pine trunks, more or less the size of old telephone poles. Bernabé didn't say a word. He raised his ax, nodded for me to get out of the way, and then dug into the bark of the trunk with that symbolic first chip and fracture.

I stepped away and inspected my first pine and then prepared my stance. The first crack rattled through my hands as if I had struck concrete. I was stunned, dropping the ax to the ground. Bernabé pretended not to watch. I fumbled with the ax with my numb fingers and tried again, until a bed of chips began to grow at the base of the trunk.

Despite my urban appearances, I was not a tenderfoot to wood chopping. Carla and I had lived in a small cabin for years, fueled only by a woodstove in the high Colorado Plateau forests of Flagstaff. I agreed with Horace Greeley, the legendary editor of the *New York Tribune*, who wrote in his memoirs, "If every youth and man, from fifteen to fifty years old, could wield an ax two hours per day, dyspepsia would vanish from the earth, and rheumatism become decidedly scarce."

My hands were blistered and bleeding by the time I finished felling the first tree. Bernabé was already on his third. I wiped the sweat from my eyes, tucked my glasses into my shirt pocket, and shuffled to the next trunk.

Finding my stride, I eventually looked over at Bernabé, who burrowed deep into the trunk of a pine. We didn't exchange too much, pausing only to catch our breath, look at the other person's progress, then turn back to the gashed trunk. At one interval, wiping his hand across his forehead, Bernabé suddenly announced, "Two people died in the village this month." He paused for a moment, drawing a breath. "But three babies were born and survived." Then he shifted and shattered the final threads of a pine.

Within a couple of hours, the Bronco was stacked as tight as a match box, with most of the trunks hanging a yard or two off the opened tail gate. We bounced down the steep plateau trails, sharing a bottle of water.

Bernabé was chatty, giddy with our quick accomplishment. He spoke about other wood spots, hauling water, working in the cornfields, laboring as a lumberjack in the forests along the plateaus, digging ditches and laying adobe.

"You should play your pancho music at the next tesguinada," he said, adding. "Do you know what tesguino is?"

I nodded.

The more Bernabé chatted, the more I realized that I had passed a certain line of no return in this village. I was in the Sierra Madre, on Rarámuri Standard Time now. I even went by a different name; my own name, difficult to pronounce in Spanish, evolved into "Javier." That name didn't last long. From my interaction with Bernabé, I knew my entire identity in the village would be based on the usefulness of my hands, whether it was with an ax, hammer, shovel, or adobe brick or the nimbleness with which I could toss back a gourd of tesguino. Or my banjo.

"Pancho, do you know Bernabé, my *tocayo* [namesake] on the other side?" the elder said suddenly. "He is a big man with a white beard who has been coming here for years."

The question was asked with the purest intentions; for Bernabé, geography played no role on "the other side," the United States. And he was right. The amazing coincidence was providential.

"Yes," I said. "He's my brother's neighbor."

Bernabé nodded, as if embarrassed to have asked such an obvious question.

Driving the Bronco out of the forests, I tried to hide the palms of my hands, a bloody mass of torn blisters.

"Don't worry, Javier," Bernabé said, as we pulled onto the mountain dirt road, "I'll show you an herb you can put on your hands." He gazed out the window in the opposite direction.

"Andale, bronco."

Our journey to the Sierra Madre began at the end of a dirt road in the *bajadas* of the Tucson Mountains. Skirting columns of saguaros and clusters of cholla and prickly pear cactus, we pulled our Bronco into the clearing of my brother and sister-in-law's guest house. Their place was to serve as our way station, our free loading zone. While Carla returned briefly to her family in Italy, I rounded up our supplies and equipment. I was eager to head into Mexico; the Bronco always looked captive when parked.

9

The desert morning greeted me in a summer fashion, sweat balling under my lower back in bed, the sweet smell of dew-greased creosote wafting after the early monsoon downpour. There was a rare humidity; the clouds in the west were hoary enough to serve as ramadas, while jackrabbits, a kangaroo rat, and a huge colony of quail feasted off the remains of my table scraps.

I saw things in my childhood Sonoran Desert that most visitors would never see: the pocket of rabbits huddling under a prickly pear presidio, a lizard exhumed into the color of his granite rock bed, the withering fruits of prickly pear that had been plucked by woodpeckers, the first line of fungus attached to a palo verde tree, the march of tarantulas after a torrential rain.

This was home, as much as I had ever allowed myself to name such a place. My brother picked up on my restlessness. Doug has been the rooted one, the Tom Sawyer to my Huck Finn.

"Talked to Barney and Mahina lately?" he would often ask.

He was referring to his next-door neighbors, Barney Burns and Mahina Drees. Their home was as close as anyone would ever come to the confines of the rugged Sierra Madre. Their sprawling porch spanned from one end to the other with stacks of wooden plates and bowls, masks, sotol baskets, and even tesguino *ollas*, clay pots shaped by the Rarámuri, Mayo, Pima, and other tribes in the Sierra Madre region. Their house was jammed with more artifacts than most museums.

I tended to visit around sundown, after feeding Katie's horses. I usually returned home several hours later. Their proximity to my brother and sister-in-law's place was an amazing stroke of luck—at times, it seemed like an astonishingly bizarre coincidence. There couldn't have been two people more knowledgeable about the Sierra Madre.

I always found Barney on the porch, using an electric sander to perfect the Rarámuri wooden bowls and forks for American and European tastes. Wearing goggles like a ball cap, with a snow-white Walt Whitman beard nearly reaching his robust chest, Barney was a relentlessly buoyant and curious man in his fifties. He was a combination of scout and bespectacled bookworm, a fearless explorer and outrageous storyteller, a social crusader who had surrendered his own well-being for the sustainability of indigenous cottage industries, and one of the few truly happy souls on this earth who had not given up on the joys of discovery.

No one, not even the woodworkers and artisans, knew that Barney, a PhD-holding trader, professional archaeologist, and "transactional" anthropologist, had worked several hours a day for almost thirty years to sustain a cottage industry in remote indigenous villages in the Sierra Madre. The couple, along with ethnobotanist Gary Nabhan, also cofounded an organization called Native Seeds/SEARCH, one of the most innovative indigenous seed preservation projects in the world. They had spread out seeds on our cabin table in Mawichi, in the shadow of Bernabé and Maria, twenty years before my arrival.

I looked around me. A nearby warehouse swelled with hundreds of carvings, pots, baskets, and artisan work, which Mahina organized and sent out to various shops around the country. An adobe building rested to the side, housing thousands of volumes of books, academic papers, and newspapers. It would rival any university collection in the Southwest.

"You mean you haven't read that book yet?" was a common line from Barney, always blurted out in glee. He would disappear into his dark back room, only to reappear with some rare, out-of-print, dusty volume from the nineteenth century.

It reminded me that a lifetime commitment to a region could not be refashioned in a flurry of study. Barney must have known I was overwhelmed, despite my pretensions of being an insatiable reader and a history buff.

"It's just to give you an idea," he would say.

I asked Barney and Mahina the usual thousand questions of logistics and protocol. They answered them all with a tremendous patience.

"Just hang out and learn to see like you do here," Barney said one evening. "It will take you some time before you're able to spot some wild beans."

That comment haunted me throughout our sojourn; I searched in vain for those wild beans for months, which were apparently growing only a few yards from our cabin.

"Just remember you are traveling in the footsteps of a lot of people," he said, as I prepared to walk home one evening, cradling an armload of books.

Barney smiled and reached for his goggles.

"There are a lot of other people for you to discover," he added. "A lot of other people." He paused for a moment. "But don't get lost down there, and be sure to pack an extra tire."

Walking back to the guesthouse in the evening, I felt like Barney and Mahina, my points of reference in the faraway Sierra Madre, were giving me my marching orders.

In 1927, two years before Marlene Dietrich devastated the screen in *The Blue Angel*, German workers were eagerly awaiting the new novel by the "proletarian" writer B. Traven. His first novels chronicled the lives of American drifters and day laborers caught up in the schemes of greed and cruelty in Mexico and at sea; the author's work was clearly affected by the volatile changes taking place among the country's indigenous communities. The German author's manuscripts appeared mysteriously at the publishing house in packages addressed from Tampico.

Der Schatz der Sierra Madre told the compelling story of three American desperadoes and would-be prospectors in Mexico who become possessed by the golden rule—gold rules. Following a trail unveiled in an ancient story of a gold mine, the trio embarks on a fulsome search for the unattainable: their acceptable share of the treasure.

"Gold is a very devilish sort of thing," declares the grizzled old-time prospector, Howard. "When you have it your soul is no longer the same as it was before."

Before long, the trio disintegrates into conflict and wariness when they indeed discover gold; a stranger who wanders into their camp is killed. The admonishments from the indigenous leaders in the canyons are ignored as a noble soul deplores: "You whites spoil the beauty of life for the possession of gold." After a deluded and war-scarred Fred Dobbs absconds with the collected gold dust, he is killed by banditos, and the precious gold is scattered like sand unwittingly in the process. With a newfound role as a healer, the old prospector vanishes into the canyons of Indians.

It is not the gold, perhaps, but the storytelling about the power of gold that ultimately drives the greedy Dobbs and informs Traven's famous novel. The character Howard is a wizened sage, the oracle who dispatches the characters on their quest and establishes the themes of the novel through a series of stories. Howard's morality tales are steeped in the thinly veiled wisdom of the Indians, whose infallible way of life is at the heart of Traven's novel: "We were the masters of our gold, never its slaves." But to no avail. In their haste to gain wealth, the Americans ultimately fall victim to their vices and the prophecies of the Indian legends.

It took another twenty years before B. Traven's *The Treasure of the Sierra Madre* placed the region on the map for those north of the border. John Huston's film adaptation of the novel, starring Humphrey Bogart, electrified the "Sierra Madre" into a neon-lit household name around the world.

While the film placed the Mother Range on our international cultural maps and multilingual lips, its writer, B. Traven, remained a stranger to all but a few souls, even to this day. Despite selling millions of books in over thirty languages, the elusive author's identity has been one of the greatest sources of raillery and confusion in twentieth century literary history.

B. Traven was simply one of numerous pseudonyms for an author obsessed with privacy. He left behind a web of contradictions and lies that would have fit perfectly in one of his suspense novels. According to one "definitive" investigation, Traven was the Chicago-born son of Norwegian immigrants who drifted with a generation of drifters into the Mexican oilfields and eventually settled in Acapulco. Another writer claimed Traven was an American-born Swede. Biographer Karl Guthke, the first writer allowed complete access to Traven's archives, concluded that the German-publishing author was in fact the Bavarian anarchist and author Ret Marut (most likely another pseudonym). The documents are still contradictory; Traven's will listed his name as Traven Torsvan Croves (while John Huston listed him in the film credits as Berwick Traven Torsvan), and his birth as Chicago, 1890. A secretive Hal Croves appeared on the film set with Huston, claiming to be Traven's business agent; Huston thought otherwise, assuming this was Traven in disguise. Some theorists still believe he was the illegitimate son of Kaiser Wilhelm II, or even Otto Freige, born in Swiebodzin, Poland; others posited that he was actually a Mexican woman writing under a false name.

Traven's books were first published in Germany under the name of B. Traven. If he were really Ret Marut, the author would have participated in the leftist uprising in Munich in 1919, when the Coffee House Anarchists held power and declared Bavaria a free state for an entire week. Led by poets, the new government issued a decree declaring that art was the answer for the starving masses. Toppled first by the communists and then the White Guard, the government fell and widespread executions took place. Rather than follow Rosa Luxemburg's body into the Landwehr Canal, Marut escaped arrest and fled the area, eventually arriving in England, and then Mexico.

Forced to find day labor in Mexico, living in poverty, the story goes, Marut began to write stories in German under the name of B. Traven. Within six years, his work was published again in Germany.

Despite the fame from *The Treasure of the Sierra Madre*, Traven's most important works on Mexico were a series of six meticulously researched novels based in Chiapas. He claimed to have lived among indigenous people in the tropical forests for two years; one of Traven's first books, in fact, was *Land of Spring*, a nonfiction portrait of the Indians in Chiapas. Named "The Jungle Cycle," the novels chronicled the brutal repression, debt slavery, and exploitation of indigenous communities by landowners in a Mexican version of the "heart of darkness" before the Mexican Revolution in 1910. He foretold the future uprisings by the Zapatistas.

Naturalized as a Mexican citizen in 1951, Traven died outside Acapulco in 1969. His ashes were scattered over the Rio Jatate in Chiapas. His Mexican wife and translator declared a few days after his death that B. Traven was in fact Hal Croves, Ret Marut, Traven Torsvan Croves, Otto Freige—all of them. At least as far as she knew.

In truth, the illusory origins of Traven's true identity, a field of its own—travenology—fuel a cultlike following and remain lost like glittering treasure in Traven's homeland of self-invention.

We had only been in Mawichi for a couple of weeks, still feeling our way around the conventions of a culture that seemed so distant and yet strangely familiar at the same time. A younger couple from the village, both fluent in Spanish and accustomed to *chabochis*, or non-Rarámuri (specifically, the Rarámuri word refers to a person with a "spider's web on their face"), had invited us to our first *tesguinada*, the corn beer celebrations of the Rarámuri. We recognized the importance of the ritual; it wasn't just a party, but a practice at the heart of the social and religious structure of this culture. It marked a general acceptance of our tenure among the villagers and a critical step in entering the personal geography of their culture.

Far outside the bounds of towns or cities or daily ghosts, beyond the paved roads and the ruins of shattered glass and concrete, we followed a passage to a rancho along the canyon's edge. The stars guided the stumble of the cadre before us. We took a trail that laced along the slopes of the canyon until it disappeared into the forest. We skirted under the overhang of a cliff, where the ruins of a dwelling littered the path like trail markers.

I tightened my grip on my banjo, which rustled in a leather sling behind my shoulder; the villagers had requested that I bring along my instrument. First a clearing, a cornfield, then a cabin perched on a bluff emerged out of the darkness, where a tiny flicker of light emanated from the cracks in the chinks between the logs. Then we heard unbridled laughter, the thump of a guitar and a fiddle, and the din of a crowd packed into the small cabin.

A smattering of discarded corncobs, tins of sardines, and bottle caps rested in a dirt clearing just to the side of a stone metate and mano. I peeked inside the cabin. Shuffling dancers blurred the dim light from the fire in a woodstove. Howls of amusement rippled through the jammed gathering. In one corner sat a barrel of tesguino, the murky brew fermented from corn. A hand suddenly extended and pulled me inside, casting me toward the corner of the musicians.

Seeking to find a place at the party, I pulled my banjo out of the sling and joined a couple of guitar players and a fiddler. They grinned at my bluegrass accompaniments. They immediately passed me a gourd of tesguino and watched intently as I drained it. The fiddler leaned in fatigue against the exposed logs of the cabin. After a couple of hours of strumming along on Mexican polkas, cumbias, rancheras, and Rarámuri *pascol* dances, I found myself sitting on some sacks of corn in the back corner, cradling the banjo in my arms, taking a rest from the swirl of activity. A guitar player continued one step ahead of the ruckus.

A voice rustled me from any repose.

"Pancho, play another song," an older man said, in Spanish.

A smile swelled on his face; a soiled bandanna held back his mound of gray hair, a wool blanket cloaked around his shoulders, breech-cloth and bare legs, down to his toes; his weathered feet were strapped into tire-soled sandals. Another older man, with silvery hair and a gaunt face, stared at the banjo. His chin was freckled with corn mush. Then he reached out and plucked a string with a cautious finger.

I doodled around the frets, picking a light three-finger rhythm and melody. I was exhausted. I felt tipsy. The burned taste of the homemade brew, including bits of pulp, was on my lips. My fingers were sore from loading wood earlier that day.

"Sing, sing," the first man said.

Smiling, I launched into a bluegrass gospel with a quiet, mournful refrain, pulling all the feeling I could from the English lyrics for the Rarámuri speakers; my abbreviated translations in Spanish were our only linguistic link. I ended with the song's lament:

"They knew not my name, and I knew not their faces. I found they were all rank strangers to me."

Offering me a gourd of the drink as a reward, the men nodded approvingly, and then asked me to play the song again.

"What does it say?" the first man said.

"It's about a traveler from the mountains who leaves and then re-turns to his home," I said, in Spanish, "only to find he doesn't know anyone. Everyone looks like a stranger." I didn't know how to say "rank stranger" in Spanish.

The men nodded some more, offered each other a scoop of tes-guino, which they drained with both hands, and then they turned and spoke in Rarámuri. After a few minutes of discussion, they shifted and told me to play the ballad another time.

"He says he knows the song," the first man told me, glancing over at the gaunt man.

I smiled and played on, but I wanted to ask that elder, tucked into a traditional fiesta that had been part of his culture for centuries, how he knew this plaintive ballad from mountains thousands of miles away. Then I realized, lost in the translation, it was not the actual song, but the meaning of the lyrics that he understood.

"Play, play," the old man beckoned.

Gripping the chords on the banjo's neck, I gently coaxed out the song, as if it belonged in the canyons of the Sierra Madre.

This experience sent me scrambling the next day to reread a pas-sage from French author Antonin Artaud's surreal memoir of his jour-ney among the Rarámuri in the 1930s, *The Peyote Dance*. In a letter to a friend, Artaud wrote that he had been struck by "physical reminiscences so compelling that they seemed to evoke direct personal memories" in the Sierra Madre. It wasn't a matter of déjà-vu; nor was he referring to his constant stream of hallucinations. "Everything seemed to repre-sent," Artaud added, "an experience I had had before." The rock bluffs and huts coaxed undated details of his own rendezvous with history. Any sense of chronology or geography had been altered.

When I first read this passage months before, I had been struck by its insight, but I didn't entirely understand its meaning. I resisted Susan Sontag's admonition: "It would be presumptuous to reduce the geogra-phy of Artaud's trip to what can be colonized." The experience at the tesguinada, singing "Rank Strangers," somehow put the Frenchman's words into context for me.

After settling into Mawichi, I shared Artaud's curious sense of fa-miliarity. Carla and I had actually transferred from one lineal mountain range to another; we had spent a few years living in Flagstaff, Arizona, at seven thousand feet, tucked into the largest ponderosa pine forest in the world. The Grand Canyon was only an hour away. The canyon bluffs in Mawichi surrounded us with the similar embrace of a pavilion. In the early evening, right before the hours of the vespers, I often hiked to the ridge overlooking the village, sitting where young shepherds had passed a solitary day among their goats and sheep. Like Artaud's undated recollections, the daily images in this Rarámuri world—from the dew on the oak plow handle to an old man's grin, a whiff of the woodstove, even the sound of barking dogs—triggered memories from other places and sojourns, the geography long since confused by time.

In the summer of 1936, the French actor, theater innovator, and writer mounted a horse and ascended the narrow trails into the Sierra Madre. He was in search of a mind-altering experience. He had left behind a Europe on the verge of total breakdown. The Spanish Civil War had already been triggered; Germany had marched unopposed into the Rhineland. During the same summer, while eight hundred Gypsies were interned in camps outside Berlin, Jesse Owens was sweeping four gold medals from the grip of Nazi propaganda.

The Rarámuri were the primeval race for Artaud; their use of peyote led the self back to its true sources. He chronicled very little of their actual surroundings, even their own reality. Instead, he insisted their whole life revolved around the "erotic peyote rite."

Artaud had left behind his heroin addiction in Mexico City. He spent the first twenty-eight days in withdrawal, roaming Rarámuri communities for peyote rituals, obsessed by "this heavy captivity, this ill-assembled heap of organs that I was." In the forests of the Sierra Madre, he saw detailed visions of *The Nativity* by Hieronymus Bosch.

The buzz from the peyote shed the clouds of sorrow for the French writer. He claimed they were the happiest days of his life. The poet had stopped tormenting himself. Artaud had not lived a happy life. At the age of four he contracted meningitis and received a bizarre electric shock treatment that would haunt him later in life. By the age of eighteen he had suffered a nervous breakdown, requiring more "cures" and institutions. His departure from France on the eve of the First World War probably saved his life; Artaud was exempted from military service. While the rest of Europe was fractured by combat, Artaud fell victim to an opium addiction at a treatment center in Switzerland.

Moving to Paris after the war, Artaud quickly became part of the thriving theater and nascent film scenes as an actor. In the mid-1920s, he joined Andre Breton and his Surrealist movement, focusing his work on the stage. By the time he broke from the Surrealists for political and personal conflicts, Artaud had already formulated his own theories as a dramatist. His *Theater of Cruelty* treatise appeared in 1931, ushering in concepts of extreme and primordial forms of communication between the spectator and spectacle, but it didn't gain any immediate reception or praise. After the failure of his production of *The Cenci* in 1935, Artaud fell from the favors of the theater world, and set off to travel abroad. He stayed in the Sierra Madre for less than two months.

The writing of *The Peyote Dance* (originally published in French in 1945 as *Voyage au pays des Tarahumaras*) took various forms and years to complete. In 1937, Artaud was imprisoned briefly in Ireland for vagrancy and disruption. Transferred to France in a straightjacket, he began nine years in a series of insane asylums, where he was declared incurably insane. While interned in southern France at the Rodez asylum during the Second World War, barely surviving on wartime rations, undergoing over fifty electric shock treatments that "plunged me into a terror which always lasted for several hours," Artaud finished "The Peyote Rite" segment, which he referred to as "my first efforts to return to myself after seven years of estrangement and total castration."

At the end of the war, in a debilitated state, Artaud returned to Paris and was befriended by a cadre of young poets. He died of cancer within a short time.

According to critic John Stout, Artaud embarked on a "lifelong project of verbal self-reinvention." In essence, he considered the French writer a flawed memoirist who implanted his own personal quandaries on the life stories of other historical and literary figures. Stout's insight was ruthlessly accurate; it applies to every writer who travels. Despite our good intentions, most travelers and travel writers carry more psychological and cultural baggage than the British entourage in E. M. Forster's classic novel *A Passage to India*. Descending into the Rarámuri version of the Marabar caves, we are loaded down with our own stories, experiences, and obsessions. But this self-obsession, for all of its drawbacks, is the most honest aspect of travel writing. There is no such invention as a disinterested or unprejudiced traveler.

Artaud self-imposed his incessant need to see "myself evolve and desire" onto the Rarámuri peyote rituals. He rewrote the dialogue of his travels as if they were plays for the stage, inserting his own words into the mouths of peyote shamans. The Sierra Madre, and the Rarámuri, became Artaud's vehicle for his psychic and spiritual rapture. His stowaway quest. His invented treasure left behind in the Sierra Madre.

There were three ways to view Mawichi those first days: atop the rock bluffs among the shepherds, overlooking the entire canyon; on the roof of our cabin, where I lingered in exhaustion with Bernabé after we had rigged up a frame for our solar panel, affording a view of the nearby cabins, fields, and the mission; or strolling among the villagers around the mission plaza on the weekly Sunday gatherings.

The village name, Mawichi, derives from the Rarámuri phrase "place of eagles." It would take an eagle to range across the entire Mawichi ejido community, which stretches for over twenty miles in a series of hidden canyons and dense forest plateaus. According to a census in the mid-1990s, a little over a thousand people resided in that swath of land.

Despite the Rarámuri name for the area, the village proper was a Spanish invention. The Spanish mission plaza dominated what had become the village center. It was the first and only landmark in the valley when the Jesuits founded the *visita* in 1744, during the reign of the Spanish Crown in Mexico, as part of a policy of *reducción*, or centralization, of the spread-out Rarámuri farms and ranchos. It didn't work. When the Jesuits were expelled in 1767, the mission fell into desuetude until the Franciscans reestablished it in 1791. A Franciscan priest resided at the mission from 1829 until 1859, but he maintained a rather lonely existence. Norwegian ethnographer and explorer Carl Lumholtz declared on his visit to Mawichi in the 1890s that "the purpose of having the Indians remain in the villages has not been accomplished to this day." By 1929, the entire area was incorporated as an ejido, or cooperative village unit, as part of the national land reforms, even though the Rarámuri remained scattered throughout the canyons. In 1978, French researcher Francoise Vatant listed only four families in the central valley of Mawichi: two were mestizo.

When we arrived in 1998, a semblance of a village, with over a dozen cabins, a school, a clinic, a shop, a cafe fashioned out of a broken-down school bus, and a basketball court beside the mission plaza, hushed and depopulated during the week, had emerged.

The haunting vacancy during the week changed on Sundays. This was the day the canyon walls of Mawichi bloomed in women in colorful skirts, legions of children trailed by dogs, and men in their white shirts and sombreros, all cascading down the pencil-thin trails toward the mission plaza. The road to Mawichi was lined with stationary plots of families; many had walked a few hours to reach the Sunday gathering. The division of gender was quite precise. The women sat in piles by the mission walls, shifting babies tucked behind in their rebozos, drinking the weekly Coke, watching as the faithful attended mass, while young men shot hoops at the basketball court between the school and mission and the older men hovered toward the back benches, sitting in an outstretched line of a hundred pairs of huarache tire-soled sandals, waiting for the weekly outdoor meeting of the ejido. Pigs wandered down the road in idle joy, and the dogs fought on cue outside the shop.

Lumholtz loved these Sunday gatherings. His descriptions hadn't varied in many respects from the village a century later. In both periods, families converged from the forest ranchos onto the mission plaza for the mass and the more important judicial assembly that followed. They gathered outside the same mission walls as today; the local governor, or *siriame*, commanded his authority with a similar cane staff. Instead of discussing the ejido and the matters of the police commissioner, the Rarámuri in Lumholtz's time held court over the affairs of thieves and adulterers.

"No supreme court in any civilized community," Lumholtz concluded, "is so highly respected and so implicitly obeyed as were the simple, grave men sitting in front of the crumbling adobe wall and holding onto their canes with a solemnity that would have been ridiculous, if it had not been sublime."

The sensational reality of modern-day cavedwellers has been one of the main tourist attractions in the region for over a century. Still today, tourists cart their digital cameras to the canyon's edge, zooming in on Rarámuri women grinding corn in front of their caves. In 1891, Lumholtz's dispatches of his travels among the cavedwellers in the Sierra Madre beguiled the readers of *Scribner's Magazine*.

"I asked a little kid today where he lives," Carla said one evening, as we were cooking some dinner. Since we went our own separate ways during the day, our early evenings tended to be a period of show and tell. "I'm trying to make a mental map where everyone lives in the canyon," Carla went on. "This little kid answered nonchalantly, I live in that cave over there."

We both attempted to act accustomed to this fact by now, falling silent in the process. Carla accompanied a few children to their homes on the weekends and even spent an occasional night as a family guest. Since many of the kids traveled hours to the village center on foot, the school provided food and dormitory accommodations during the week. Unlike the more severe boarding school policies in the past, which had kept the kids from returning to their parents or homes for months or even years in an attempt to disconnect the children from their native ways, the present boarding school sought to foster a balance between the traditional indigenous culture at home and the Mexican culture and curriculum taught mostly in Spanish at the school. Carla was examining the reality of this bicultural and bilingual approach.

My first contact with some of our cavedwelling neighbors occurred during one of my wood-chopping trips with Bernabé and his son-in-law Chico. After surmounting a steep mesa on a winding road carved into the plateau, a few miles away from our cabin, we stumbled onto Juan Pedro, who lived on the edge of the pine ridge. We offered him a ride in the back of the truck. He made the three-hour walk to Mawichi every Sunday. As a child, he had journeyed in leather-hide sandals his father had carved and tanned from a cow sacrificed for a Virgin of Guadalupe feast.

I returned to visit him on another occasion. From the edge of his fields, which sloped onto a steep bluff, he pointed at the black-eyed caves that dotted the opposite walls of the canyon. They must have reminded the Spanish soldiers of the gypsy caverns visible from the Alhambra in Granada.

"Apache caves," Juan Pedro told me, waving his hands across the valley. He said his father had spoken about the intrusion of the Apaches in the Sierra Madre in the 1880s, after their flight with Geronimo from the Arizona dragoons and reservations. The Apaches and the Rarámuri begrudgingly collaborated and skirmished for centuries. American archaeologists, including Barney Burns, are still trying to track down remnants of living Apache culture in the Sierra Madre.

"Our cave is over here," Juan Pedro continued. Despite his wife's entreaties to return to the cave, Juan Pedro insisted on maintaining a cabin on the ridge during the planting season. They often spent the winter in the cave, which his wife considered to be warmer and more livable. We stumbled down a trail that led to a huge rock overhang in the side of the bluff. More than thirty feet wide and fifteen feet deep, his cave was equipped with stone walls and storage rooms on the side, a mano and a metate, a table, stools made out of branches and cowhide, mats for beds, and a fire pit. A clothes line had been strung from a crevasse to the stone walls. Ceramic ollas, plastic barrels for water, and dozens of dried sotol baskets lined the back chamber, which had been stained black by smoke. I spotted a small radio wedged into a crack in the rock face.

The canyons in the Sierra Madre, especially along the main drainage zones, are pockmarked with a myriad network of caves; rock overhangs and shallow grottoes in the sandstone and igneous bluffs ring Mawichi. A number of Rarámuri still live in caves or maintain a seasonal cliff dwelling near their more distant fields. Many use nearby caves to keep their goats warm in the winter or store their beans. One of our closest neighbors had installed a door and locks on his cave at the basin of our valley and used it as a guest room for visitors and as a storage bin.

Following the thousand-year tradition of Norwegian explorers around the world, Lumholtz made an expedition into the Sierra Madre in 1890 to answer one longing question: Were the present-day cavedwellers descendants of the great pre-Columbian cavedwelling civilizations such as the Anasazi?

Lumholtz first penetrated the Sierra Madre with over a hundred mules and horses loaded down with equipment for a brigade of thirty archaeologists, botanists, geographers, zoological collectors, guides, guards, and Chinese cooks. He had a passport and permit officially approved by the Mexican dictator Porfirio Diáz. He had already published a book, *Among the Australian Cannibals*, about his studies with a supercilious settlement of Aborigines. According to William Dean Howells' review in *Harper's Monthly* in 1890, the intense fear and distrust between Lumholtz and the aborigines had caused the Norwegian to "experience a deep despondency mixed with indifference, from which he had to pull himself together with a strong effort of the will at last, in order to escape from the psychical miasm of their most miserable experience."

Despite registering a profound dislike for the tribal culture, Lumholtz had launched his career as a pioneering ethnographer. In the parlance of the times, he wrote that "the study of savage and barbaric races has since become my life's work."

Raised in the forests near Lillehammer, Lumholtz had studied theology at the insistence of his father. Mirroring Artaud's experience, it led to a nervous breakdown. In the process, he found a job collecting birds and animals for a zoological museum and soon discovered a vocation as a naturalist. He left Scandinavia for a lifetime of travel in 1880 to collect zoological samples in Australia for the University of Christiania; his journeys extended into the remote stretches of the South Pacific, Dutch Borneo, and the Americas. Echoing fellow poet-traveler Arthur Rimbaud's pronouncement in *Une saison en enfer*, Lumholtz scribbled down the motto for modern traveling writers: "It occurred to me what a misfortune it would be to die without having seen the whole earth."

Lumholtz concluded that the Rarámuri may have been one of the last contemporary cavedwellers in the world, but not descendants of the earlier, more complex civilizations that stretched across the Southwest and Mexico and met their demise in the thirteenth and fourteenth centuries. The Rarámuri lacked the architectural skills; their pottery was crude and artistically plain.

Archaeologists later dated burial findings and agave fibers, pottery shards, and manos and metates in some caves in the Sierra Madre back to the eleventh century. Most of the "Apache caves" and *trincheras*, in fact, dated to other inhabitants from 1000 to 1500 A.D. Other archaeological evidence had even suggested inhabitants since the Basketmaker period in 1000 B.C.

Over the next decade, while his own country was fraught in conflict over their final separation from Sweden, Lumholtz spent a cumulative five years living among the Rarámuri and other tribes in the Sierra Madre. The journey was a strange homecoming; it liberated him from the shackles of academia and geographical societies. At the foot of the Basaseachi Falls, he wrote that the "entire scenery, the wild, precipitous rocks, the stony, crooked path, the roaring stream below—everything reminded me of mountains in Norway, where I had run along many a *sater* path through the twilight, alone, just as I was running now."

Sending away the cumbersome expedition party and its official protocol, Lumholtz documented a material culture that remained far removed from Porfirio Diáz's Mexico and its repressive *pan o palo*, "bread or club," economic development policies. Lumholtz noted their daily customs and food, as well as their religious, curing, and corn rituals; he recorded their songs, sagas, and myths on a graphophone; and he made drawings and photos, including a large collection that was lost over the ledge of a steep mule trail. He eventually exhibited samples of Rarámuri hair at the international Colombian Exhibition in Chicago.

References to Lumholtz's groundbreaking work frequently appear in studies and books on the Sierra Madre and the Rarámuri, as well as in studies on the other tribes he examined, including the Huichol, Mayo, and Pima. He published his own chronicle, *Unknown Mexico* (also appearing as *Blandt Sierra Madres Huleboere* in his native Norwegian), in English in 1902 to great acclaim. His writing style in English, as *Harpers'* editor William Dean Howells noted, didn't concern itself with the "literary parade." It was disjointed at times, meandering and unconstrained. Still, Lumholtz possessed an endearing touch, full of humor and respect for his subject.

Unlike his experience in Australia, Lumholtz managed to penetrate the disdain the Rarámuri held for chabochis. The years alone in the Sierra Madre shed his stuffy European pretensions and transformed his perspective from a distant observer to a willful participant. He joined the tesguinadas and learned to sing their songs. He considered many in the indigenous communities his closest companions. He agonized over their future.

Far removed from the demands of his financial supports and international readers, Lumholtz was the first Westerner to value the ways of the Sierra Madre indigenous populations. He questioned his own civilization's rout of another. The treasure he had found, he declared, would soon be erased from this earth:

"It may take a century yet before they will all become servants of the whites and disappear like Opatas. Their assimilation may benefit Mexico, but one may ask: Is it just? Must the weaker always be crushed, before he can be assimilated by the new condition of things?"

When Carla and I made *la marcha* on Sundays, it took a while before I didn't feel self-conscious of our appearance. Chabochis, or outsiders, were not uncommon in the village; it was a rare Sunday when a vanload of foreign tourists didn't arrive from Creel, the nearest town linked to the railroad, disembark en masse, snap photos of the mission and colorful natives, purchase a handmade pot or basket at the shop, and then spin out of the village with a gust of dust on the dirt road. But our waltz around the mission walls, as a couple no less, drew a fair share of grins, raised eyebrows, and the silent exchange of amused and scrutinizing gestures.

Carla was already well known in the village, thanks to the shoeless grapevine of the children at the school and the network of mothers in the nearby canyons. She was a magnet for a cadre of older girls, who kept to her side after school and on the weekends. They were obsessed with Carla's dark curly hair; they pushed her to change into the traditional skirts. They loved to play word games with her in Rarámuri, and Carla, who has a gift for languages and a passion for knitting, eased quickly into the clustered gatherings of women in the nearby dwellings and clearings, threading wool, making clothes or baskets, and chatting about the exploits of children. With the Pope's much ballyhooed visit to Mexico that year, Italy, or at least Rome, while being part of the terra incognita of "the other side," resonated in the minds of the villagers.

My role brought more bewilderment. I split from Carla at a certain point one Sunday. She wandered over to *la junta*, the weekly business meeting of the ejido community, as I strayed over to the basketball court, which was lined with boys, younger men, and other non-property-holding men in the area. Having spent the better part of my adolescence hanging around a playground with a basketball in my hands, I felt an immediate naturalness in this milieu. I stood in the back. My appearance drew only a couple of furtive looks and passed grins, deflecting little from the excitement of the full-court game. The teams ran fast and furious; most players swept across the cracked concrete pavement in huaraches; some were barefoot. Despite the high altitude, the teams didn't let up on a pace that we would have termed "run and gun" at my playground.

The game surprised me with its air of festivity. More Spanish than Rarámuri peppered the banter. When a player made a great shot or a flagrant foul, a round of laughter or cheers was immediate. The players themselves seemed to laugh an inordinate amount, as if they didn't care about the score. They acted unconcerned with fouls or errors or missed shots. An American game, equally as physical, would not have been more competitive, but more serious about winning or losing.

When the game ended, I greeted a couple of younger men, including Bernabé's son-in-law Chico, who lived nearby. Chico, like the other young men, gave me a hip urban handshake, instead of the traditional touch of the finger pads. I suddenly found myself doing the same to a small crowd that had gathered around us, eavesdropping on our exchange. One man was animated; he hissed and groaned while he shook my hand fervently. Then he motioned with hand signals. This was El Mudo, the mute.

Everyone knew I wasn't a passing tourist. Dressed in a cowboy hat, boots, jeans, and a work shirt, I probably looked more like a fair-haired rancher who had gotten lost in the borderlands. The rimless glasses blew that cover, though.

"Do you play?" Chico asked. He grinned. "You're tall."

"Sure," I said. Slightly over six feet, I stood a head above him and most of the other men in the village.

"You'll have to join our team one day," he said.

I overheard one onlooker quip to another, "Que hombre gigante." *What a giant.*

I was relieved I didn't have to play those first days. I wanted to scurry around on the edges of the gathering as an observer. I didn't relish attracting a lot of attention. It wasn't a matter of feeling uncomfortable or singled out; Carla and I had both spent a lot of time in foreign countries and segregated communities as solitary observers and outsiders. I had played basketball in more than one country where I didn't speak the language of my fellow players. I simply wanted to get a first impression, not make one.

The Rarámuri had a certain ease about them that made life comfortable for a chabochi. They were aloof, slightly diffident. They didn't possess any sense of fear or false deference. Very little performance was demanded in public. I noticed that no one confronted me face to face, as would often happen in Creel or other mestizo towns or other countries; an inquisitive soul would saddle up next to me by the basketball court, instead of directly in front of me, if they were interested in slowly easing into a chat. Space seemed to be regarded as much as curiosity.

In fact, at one point I felt like I had blended into the crowd and no one was even noting my existence. I assumed it would have taken longer to meld into village life. This probably added more of a bounce to my step. Foregoing a line at the shop, I walked over to the limbo cafe, the rusted hull of a mini school bus on the side of the road that had been converted into the Cafe de Flore of Mawichi. It was only open on Sundays; I had kept my eye on this marvelous place for days.

I ducked my head at the exit doors and crawled into the back. Stools had replaced the passenger seats, with a counter built on one side. A gas stove sat in the driver's seat. A young woman nodded for me to sit on a stool. There was no one else aboard. Without a word, she turned and then passed me a bean burrito, a bowl of chiles, and a warm bottle of Coke. Again, I felt like I had found a home.

"Hey gringo," Carla suddenly appeared, poking her head inside the exit doors. There were a couple of young girls attached to her skirt; Noreida and Chavela, seven-year-old and thirteen-year-old pairs of inquisitive eyes, would soon become her assistant researchers and companions. "Do you think you can attract more attention?"

I shook my head in confusion, munching on my burrito.

"You should have heard the kids," Carla laughed. "They were shouting, 'That chabochi with a red beard is eating on the bus.'"

When I looked out the bus windows, I realized that half of the Sunday crowd was watching me.

There was no treasure in the Sierra Madre, according to Adolph Bandelier. But he was resurrected by a journey into the canyons, so to speak.

In the spring of 1884, in the southern Illinois town of Highland,

Josephine Bandelier received news of a wire story from Ft. Bowie, near the Mexico-U.S. border. Her husband, Adolph Bandelier, one of the pioneering anthropologists in the Southwest and a scholar on ancient Mexico, had been ambushed and killed by marauding Apaches in the corridor between New Mexico and the Sierra Madre. He had been warned by General George Crook not to travel in the region.

No one was more surprised by the news than Adolph Bandelier himself. Arriving at the gates of Ft. Apache, Arizona, atop a small mule, wearing a "genuine Scotch bonnet with the regulation ribbons hanging at the rear and . . . a Norfolk jacket of rough tweed and knickerbockers of the same material, and heavy English walking shoes," the solitary wanderer had returned from his first and only foray into the Sierra Madre. The discovery of his reported death, in fact, was probably the most extraordinary bit of news in Bandelier's ground breaking but otherwise unremarkable expedition.

Born in Bern, Switzerland, raised as an immigrant in the Swiss community of Highland, Bandelier's independence and autodidactic studies turned him into one of America's leading experts on the American Southwest, Mexico, and Peru. Over the course of his lifetime, he penned his journals in German, French, Spanish, and English. In the 1870s, he became an associate of Lewis Henry Morgan, regarded by many as the "father of American anthropology," who actually nudged Bandelier west. Within ten years, the traveler whose native tongue was German became one of the most widely published American authors on the American Southwest and Mexico.

Bandelier's short journey into the Sierra Madre revealed the first glimpses of cliff dwellings and pre-Hispanic ruins scattered across the canyons and gorges. The trip predated Lumholtz's more celebrated journey by five years. Meeting up later in Santa Fe, the Swiss immigrant even questioned the Norwegian's experience and command of Spanish. The muted tenor of his Sierra Madre report, however, failed to recognize the vast wealth of cultures and history in the region. In fact, it still serves as a reminder that many discoverers and travel writers bring back more fallacies than artifacts. According to Charles Lange and Carroll Riley, editors of Bandelier's journals, "his research in northern Mexico might even be called a setback to science." Despite his month-long travels among the cliff dwellings and dwellers in the Mother Range and the Chihuahuan plains, Bandelier dismissed the treasury of the archaeological sites, including the Casas Grandes trading center. He relegated northern Mexico to a secondary station for further researchers.

Exhausted by the rigorous solo journey into Mexico, Bandelier saw his entire career nearly derailed by his family obligations in Illinois. While he was engaged in the Southwest and Mexico in 1884, southern Illinois's economy had collapsed into a severe depression. Bandelier's father, a banker and financier of coal mines, and his business partners struggled to keep open their bank doors. In 1885, unable to convince Swiss financiers to provide aid to his father, Bandelier returned to Highland to learn that his father had fled the country, his partner had committed suicide, and another partner had left the state, leaving Bandelier as the sole person responsible for the outstanding obligations. Bandelier barely escaped the rage of a local mob; the police threw him into jail in Edwardsville. Released the next day on bail, he caught the late train out of St. Louis and returned to the American Southwest.

The journey to the Sierra Madre, in the end, was a complete fiasco in his opinion. He didn't realize he had opened the door to modern anthropology in the region.

Our first days in the village transpired in a routine fashion. We adjusted to the limited light from our solar panel. We didn't miss the phone; TV had never been a part of our lives. The water was cold but constant; it didn't start to freeze until the winter months. I tuned into the BBC news on our short-wave radio every evening for twenty minutes to catch the world headlines. That need became more sporadic as the year progressed.

The first dispatch of roosters launched the chorus of dogs while we were still in bed. Before we rose, lit the fire in the calenton, and made some coffee and breakfast, we heard the chickens scurrying around the back of our cabin or the banging of the fence as Bernabé walked down to the stalls to let out the goats and cows.

We fell into daily routines quite quickly. Carla set off to the school or to informal meetings with mothers at the scattered *ranchos* in the early morning. I emerged from the cabin a few minutes later, the mountain sun still in the process of lifting the haze from the fields. The dew had burnished rows of corn stalks. At over seven thousand feet, teased by the acrid fumes of woodstoves and open fires, the air was cool year-round in the morning.

Our cabin faced the dirt road, which hugged the creek around the canyon until it disappeared into the forest. In the mornings, clad in my old cowboy boots, a straw sombrero, jeans, and a faded cotton shirt, I either chopped wood down by the chicken coop or helped Bernabé in the fields or on some carpentry project.

Bernabé rarely asked for my help. Every good deed in this culture had to be reciprocated either through labor or gifts of food or tesguino. It took me a while before I realized my volunteering was not seen as a matter of doing Bernabé a favor, but placing him in debt. I finally told him that my work on his behalf was part of the payment for the cabin. He agreed. On the times that he required my help, Bernabé would arrive in the morning, knock on our door, and hand me a fist of wild greens or a plate of blue corn tortillas that Maria had cooked that day. This was the wordless request for my immediate assistance.

One morning I lingered at the far corner of the cornfields, watching Bernabé pull weeds from the rows, clearing the land of rocks. Without a word, as was often our manner of exchange, I strolled out to the fields and joined him, following his lead on a parallel row. Bernabé turned and grunted at me; he never instructed me what to do. There were no operating instructions for the Rarámuri. An outsider, like a child, learned by rote, learned by watching, learned by error in silence.

We were working in view of the road. Every so often a person sprang from around the bend, walking up the road toward the shop in that inimitable stiff gait and short steps of the locals. I would look at the person, then at Bernabé, who never paid any attention to the foot traffic. The passers-by concealed any amusement at my presence.

"Kwira ba," I called out the Rarámuri greeting, if they were men. Protocol kept me from publicly interacting with unknown women.

Without fail, a faint grin crept slowly across their faces.

"Kwira," they responded, then followed with another comment or question in Rarámuri, which I didn't understand, of course, but it generally instigated a round of laughter on Bernabé's part.

Sometimes around twilight, Bernabé and I sat outside and watched the fields age with the darkness and then vanish as the bats fluttered about the roof of our cabin. Our talking had come in spurts earlier in the day, rounds of questions and answers and more questions that tended to move along the mundane tasks. I occasionally plucked my banjo, which Bernabé enjoyed. Chattering, it seemed to me, would have been intrusive. Perhaps the magnitude of the natural surroundings, in areas where the landscape continued to determine history, muted a lot of banter.

Some anthropologists and travelers have confused this with an extreme shyness; the Rarámuri are always noted for their lack of effusive raillery, at least in public. Lumholtz questioned whether the Rarámuri could even procreate without an alcoholic lubricant. He was being facetious, of course, but it certainly spoke as much about the observer as the observed. Like others, he tended to disregard the impact of our imposing presence as chabochis, despite our assumptions of intimacy. Four centuries of conquest contributed to our reception and countenance in the eyes of the Rarámuri, as much as any acts of friendliness and empathy. For starters, I recognized that I physically towered over most men, had stalks of reddish blond hair and a beard, wore glasses, and drove the only four-wheel-drive vehicle in the entire ejido. In the first days, I noted that small huddles of people engaged in conversations often quieted to a hush when I approached.

My own experience as a nonnative Spanish speaker, hardly fluent, added to this equation. With the exception of a few lucky souls and linguists, most people undergo an uncontrollable personality transformation in a second language; your timing, comprehension, and thought processes are skewered. I was an entirely different person in Italian when we lived for several years in Italy. My Spanish-speaking persona in Mawichi was still in progress, which made me empathize with the majority of nonfluent Spanish speakers in the village. In some respects, this language quirk and lack of refinement served in my favor; it gave some the upper hand in a linguistic relationship that had usually served against them among Mexicans and other outsiders.

Instead of a strange shyness, this Rarámuri trait reminded me of some of the cowboys, desert dwellers, and O'odham where I had grown up in southern Arizona. They were not uncomfortable with silence, especially in the presence of strangers. They had different bonds among themselves and with their environment. They raised their eyebrows at the pleonasm of our modern talk show times. They were a sentient crowd with plenty of reasons to distrust outsiders with their words.

My mother once described her own childhood in the southern Illinois hollows in these terms: silence had its own code and secrets. The complex nature of her family's relationship with the townspeople had cultivated a defense mechanism of concealment.

I learned this lesson on our second week in the village. As I was stacking some beams for Bernabé to be used for the roof of a chicken coop, an elderly woman approached the homestead. She had clearly been walking for hours; her legs and feet were covered in dust and mud. She didn't make any eye contact with me, despite my nearby presence. Taking a seat on a large stump in the side yard, she sat down and withdrew a small pouch of pinole and then mixed it into a cup with a bit of water.

"Bernabé's inside," I called out, in Spanish, as I walked by with a beam.

The woman didn't flinch at my comment. She started drinking the pinole. When I returned from the opposite end of the yard, where I had been stacking the beams, I stopped before the woman and announced again, "Bernabé's inside. He's here."

She glanced at me, and then resumed drinking from her cup of pinole, using a finger to scoop out the remains of dissolved ground corn. I assumed she didn't speak Spanish, which was not uncommon for most older women, so I pointed to the door of the house. "Bernabé," I said.

After four more beams, walking back and forth across the yard, I finally smiled at the woman and then walked over to Bernabé's door. I knocked, looking over my shoulder at the woman, who seemed nonplused by my favor. Bernabé answered, peeking outside the door, as if he were flustered.

"I think this woman is looking for you," I said, pointing at her in the yard. "She's been waiting for quite a while."

Bernabé thanked me, and casually walked over and greeted the woman, as if he had been expecting her. Later that day, working together at the stall, I asked Bernabé about the bewildering scene with the woman.

"She looked like she had traveled a long way," I said.

"At least three hours," he said.

"Why didn't she knock on your door?"

Bernabé smiled.

"According to our tradition, you wait until you are greeted," he said. "Only ghosts knock on doors."

Such traditions would have been further evidence of the Rarámuri's primitive and superstitious nature, according to chronicler Frederick Schwatka. He ascended the Sierra Madre trails on muleback in 1888 as part of a flourishing epoch of literary expeditions to reveal the frontier world to magazine readers. This was the golden age of American and European travel writing, which would soon falter to the harrowing trials of the First World War. Like Bandelier, Schwatka's work was both fascinating and disquieting.

Sponsored by the Chicago newspapers *America* and *Herald*, Schwatka swaggered around northern Mexico with an unmistakable presence.

He wouldn't need to knock on any door to sound his presence. He weighed nearly 270 pounds and wore tiny pince-nez eyeglasses. He was an irrepressible alcoholic. The American traveler brought his own cook, whom he had selected on "glowing descriptions of his supposed good qualities."

One of the mythomaniac authors of his times, Schwatka wrote irreverent copy for his popular readership. He aspired, like most travel writers filling the pages in the plethora of subscription magazines and fleeting newspapers in that period, to match the wit of J. Ross Browne's frontier chronicles or Mark Twain's *Innocents Abroad*, usually at the expense of the natives. His racist asides would be insufferable today.

Nonetheless, Schwatka's adventures were daring, and groundbreaking for his forays and mapping in Alaska, the Yukon and the Arctic, and the Mother Range.

This son of Polish descendants drifted to Oregon as a young man. After attending West Point and serving on the Indian frontier across the West, Schwatka settled in his wife's hometown in Rock Island, Illinois. A self-taught spirit, Schwatka earned certification to become a lawyer and a medical doctor while serving as a military adjutant in the western territories. Earning the respect of the Lakota Indians, he was named Gray Wolf. He gained international fame for "Schwatka's Search," which became a commonly used expression for the pursuit of any arduous and nearly impossible undertaking, when he led an American Geographical Society expedition into the Arctic. In search of the remains of the Franklin Expedition, which had disappeared in 1845, Schwatka's party traveled for nearly a year, covering over 3,200 miles on dog sleds, living off the land with the Inuit.

Once again, Schwatka's robust size earned notice; journalist William Gilder turned Schwatka into a celebrity with his book account of the journey, *Schwatka's Search*, adding that "he possesses a very important adjunct, a stomach that can relish and digest fat." In 1883, Schwatka returned north, leading a secret Army expedition to map the interior of Alaska and the Yukon.

By the time Schwatka embarked on his journey into the Sierra Madre, that adjunct—his obesity—had become a heavy burden for the traveler. Attempting the first ascent of Mt. Saint Elias in Alaska in 1886, Schwatka collapsed after nine days, reaching only a summit of 5,700 feet. The expedition, sponsored by the *New York Times*, dissolved into embarrassment; three Inuit guides also died, poisoned by bread that had accidentally been mixed with arsenic. Schwatka collapsed again the following year, leading the first winter passage through Yellowstone Park. An English geographer who accompanied the journey referred to transporting the "eighteen stone" leader as a "quixotic enterprise." This time the expedition, including his humiliated father-in-law, finished without him.

Even in the Sierra Madre, Schwatka's size and ailing health kept him from pursuing the most fascinating objects of his travels: cave and cliff dwellers. He saw at least five to six hundred cliff dwellings on his trip, but never visited one of them. He blamed it on his mules or his provisions, while quietly admitting his physical limitations in scrambling up the rock faces: "I am sorry to say I am not a sailor, a tight-rope performer or an aeronaut."

Regardless of his lack of onsite inspection, Schwatka trumpeted what Bandelier ignored, hailing the Rarámuri settlements and cave dwellings as one of his greatest discoveries. For all of his intolerant colloquialisms of the day, Schwatka couldn't help but flatter the mountain people. "Heretofore the Eskimo of North Hudson Bay I deemed the most modest savages," he declared, "but they are brigands compared with the Tarahumari natives."

Still suffering from alcoholism, Schwatka returned from the Sierra Madre and underwent the Keeley Cure, which included injections of a concoction of morphine and strychnine, among other materials. Despite declaring himself cured, Schwatka's health finally surrendered in late fall of 1892. He was found crumpled at the foot of a doorway at three o'clock in the morning in Portland, where he had been scheduled to lecture. A half-empty bottle was by his side. According to the autopsy, the forty-three-year-old died from an overdose of one of the demons of fellow Sierra Madre traveler Antonin Artaud: laudanum, a tincture of opium.

Schwatka never enjoyed the success of the publication of his collected essays on the Sierra Madre, *In the Land of Cave and Cliff Dwellers*. He left his readers the burden of sorting the facts from fiction, "without knowing the truth," as Edgar Lee Masters wrote in his *Spoon River Anthology*, "or because he is influenced to hide it."

He never knew what he had actually found in the Sierra Madre.

Part II

The Revenge
of the Tarahumara

El Chapareke was not easy to find, even though everyone in our village seemed to have just spotted him whenever I inquired on the sublime Sunday gatherings. I didn't know what he looked like; he had been described as a short man in huaraches, wearing a sombrero, a light shirt, and pants, with a ruddy face and gray hair, which depicted almost every male over the age of forty in the village who didn't wear the *tagora*, the traditional breechcloth. I asked Carla to spread the word among the kids, women, and church-goers while I checked the bus cafe, the co-op store, and the basketball court, where I was recruited for a game.

"Pancho," a few young men called me. "We need another player."

I begged off the offer, shooting a few shots in between matches. Most men were familiar with my presence now. I amused the packed crowd one weekend by playing the role of a giant shot-blocking center in a breathtaking free-for-all. I even risked fate and total alienation by refereeing the games another Sunday, which was relatively easy in a canyon culture that takes seriously the maxim "no blood, no foul." In the early evenings, I sometimes drifted up to the slab of concrete and shot some hoops with the young men who lived nearby; the word spread. I was no longer known as "the chabochi with the red beard," or "Carla's esposo." I had graduated to Javier, or my musical nickname, Pancho.

"I'm looking for El Chapareke," I said to a couple of players.

They giggled.

"Don't you play the pancho?" one said.

"Yes, but I'd like to learn how to play the chapareke," I said.

One of the young men pretended to hold up the instrument, adding out the side of his mouth, "wang, wang, wang, wang." The others laughed, and I was not sure if they were laughing with him or at me.

I had wanted to learn the *chapareke* instrument for weeks. It is one of the last remaining indigenous string instruments in Mexico, perhaps the entire Western hemisphere. Often referred to as a Tarahumara Jew's harp, the chapareke is more dronal as an instrument, strummed as the player sucks and manipulates the wood for a melodic echo. Antonio Camilo, known as "El Chapareke" in our village, was considered the last remaining master.

I had already hooked up with a *conjunto* band in the village, a fiddler and his younger guitar-playing brother. We didn't really tune up; I plucked an open G on the pascol dances, and somewhere in E for the heartbreaking *rancheras* and *norteños*. They strummed along on the bluegrass and country tunes as I called out the chords.

Returning home empty-handed that afternoon, I decided to chat with Bernabé about finding El Chapareke's rancho. He nodded, drawing in the dirt with a stick. His instructions ranged from the clumps of mud to the rocks and pieces of wood.

"He lives over there, somewhere near the waterfall."

I set off the next morning into the dense pinetas and canyons with a bottle of water, my banjo, and a small tourist chapareke. Women at the sparse ranchos and cabins either raced inside and locked their doors when I appeared or simply fled into the forests. The situation probably worsened when I shouted "Chapareke, chapareke," waving my banjo like a pitchfork; they must have assumed a mad tourist was on the loose. They had been warned about ruthless chabochi men or government doctors wielding needles for vaccinations. Lugging my banjo to an overlook of the jagged *barrancas*, I finally happened onto an older woman stationed in front of a loom who was amused at my plight.

"You're looking for El Chapareke," she said. She pointed at a towering ridge, indicating that I needed to surmount it using whatever goat or human trails I could find, and then search for a trail along the backside.

The hike along the canyons was wonderful, despite lugging my instrument. I lost track of the time, distracted by the views from the ridge. A couple of hours later, I located the homestead, but not El Chapareke. Unfinished chaparekes littered the compound. I dropped in front of a pine, drank the rest of my water, and played a couple of banjo tunes for his treacherous dog, and then I made the trek home.

When I returned to our cabin, having walked all day, I found that El Chapareke had made the same hike in reverse, searching for me, since everyone in the village informed him on Sunday that I was interested in learning his instrument.

Antonio came by our cabin the next week, carrying a dried husk of the maguey cactus, his pocketknife, and a small piece of *madroño* wood. He was a small man with sweet eyes and a grin that charmed. We sat down and chatted in the clearing outside our cabin, listening to a recorded cassette of his music, while he carved three perfect pegs from the wood with his pocketknife, poked holes in the cactus husk, hewed grooves for the strings, and tuned the instrument with my banjo strings instead of the traditional skunk guts. My Scottish ancestors had used *thairms*, or cat guts, for their first fiddles. The tuning was not dissimilar to that of an Appalachian mountain dulcimer, with a D bass string and a G tuning on the other two strings.

The origins of the instrument fascinated me. El Chapareke learned from his father and grandfather. He laughed at the claim that the instrument might have been introduced by escaped African slaves who fled into the Sierra Madre.

"This came from our land," he told me, "like our corn."

I watched as he lifted the instrument to eye level, checked out his pegs, and listened to the sound of the first string. He played music the way he raised his corn: the songs were seeds, falling along the steep slopes and craggy plateaus. He churned out and distributed instruments like digging sticks. He didn't appear troubled by where the music took root, as long as it endured. Music was the essence of immortality for the musician.

Traveling around the canyons on foot and as far as the city of Chihuahua, playing at churches, schools, tesguinadas, Rarámuri rituals, and for tourists at regional hotels, El Chapareke had made the survival of the native instrument his mission.

Entangled in the stringing of the chapareke-in-progress, he suddenly looked at my banjo, which loomed like a tank in comparison.

"Where did that thing come from?" he said.

I smiled. Though it hardly resembled its original long flat neck hooked onto a skin-covered turtle shell or gourd, I told him the truth. "The banjo originally came from West Africa and African slaves."

"Africa?" he said, grinning. "Are you from Africa?"

"It was brought over by African slaves to America. To the other side."

"Who taught you? Your grandfather?"

"No," I said, "a friend."

El Chapareke handed me the finished chapareke. It was the size of a dulcimer, a yard long, the strings stretched and wedged in increments like branches. I plucked a few notes, and then I handed it back to him. Antonio grinned, and then played a medley of songs, most with the 6/8 pascol and *matachin* rhythms of the religious dances, drawing over an octave of notes by crinkling his lips on the dried cactus stem of hollow wood. The music was beautiful, crisp, and haunting as a Highlander harp. He stopped abruptly and smiled. He handed me the chapareke.

"The rest is up to you," he said.

I thanked him, staring at the chapareke in my hands, still unsure of the musical steps. I banged at the strings, while wagging my mouth on the wood. I could barely hear the echo.

El Chapareke laughed and rose. He had to make the long walk back to his rancho.

"Africa," he chuckled.

Later that week I asked the guitar player in the village, who knew all of the latest cumbias, norteños, and trio sounds from Veracruz, why he hadn't picked up the chapareke. No one in the village had bothered to learn. Even El Chapareke's son had picked up the fiddle. The guitar player smiled and then shook his head, as if I was joking. He didn't understand why I kept asking these questions about their traditional culture.

"Pancho, the next song is a ranchera in E," he said, nodding at my banjo. "I just learned it off a new cassette." He paused, as if remembering my question about El Chapareke and the old rituals. "This song will be a good one for the dances at the tesguinadas."

The tesguinada was taking place at the stone house in front of our cabin. We had completed a day of communal labor, tending to the fields and fences of a neighbor. A few men lay on the ground outside the hut, quietly drunk from drinking tesguino all day. "Pancho, Pancho," one groaned. I could barely squeeze my way past the fold of people; I ducked my head to avoid a clash with a huge beam, the roof slanting to one side like a lean-to. I clutched my banjo inside my arms to keep from snagging a head or limb of one of the flouncing dancers.

A bedlam of laughing and talking and singing surrounded me; there was not one shy Rarámuri person in this hut tonight. A fire in the corner illuminated part of the room. Women, old and young, twirled in their skirts while men shuffled to their own improvised dance. A row of grannies huddled on a log bench with contented smiles. I saw Carla chatting with a cadre of young mothers. Riddled grins emerged from the darkness; corn-mushed chins swept past my face. Martin and Rogelio played their guitars in a dark corner next to the fiddler, who was replacing one of his strings. Before I reached their circle I felt a grip on my arm. An older man wearing sunglasses and a baseball cap thrust a dripping gourd of tesguino toward me.

"Pancho, drink," he said, struggling to keep his balance.

El Mudo, the village mute, wobbled toward me, grunting out his laughter, clapping his hands for me to drink more.

Drinking tesguino (referred to as *sugui* in Rarámuri in our village), more than anything else, was the prime determinant of our acceptance by the villagers. They watched me closely as I held the gourd. They monitored how quickly I drained the cup, and how often I accepted another round. They knew that for one intoxicated period we relinquished our baggage to join their ancient ritual, on their terms.

The act of drinking and getting drunk on tesguino remains one of the most critical aspects of Rarámuri life. Tesguino accompanies virtually every work project, celebration, or ritual in the village. It determines family and friendship networks and religious patterns. Given their isolated and dispersed lives in the canyons, it has traditionally served as the conduit for community exchange and interaction. For anthropologist John Kennedy, who lived in a traditional and non-Christianized community in the late 1950s, the "tesguino complex," more than any other element, defined the Rarámuri social structure.

The brew confounded the first missionaries in the sixteenth century, and it still confounds some outsiders today. Most people find it hard to accept that the corn brew serves as anything more than an alcoholic drink. All cultures, of course, have conjured up their own mind-altering beverages, my ancestral Scots in particular. For the Rarámuri, the fermented beer is a sacred gift from Onoruame, their mother-father God figure, and drinking it ensures the constancy of the stars, seasons, and cycles, as well as a good time. Originating from the cornfields, tilled and watered by their own sweat and labor and hope, it is the very lifeblood of their way of life.

Within a short time, I found a role at the tesguinadas: I played along with the other musicians. I belted out improvised versions of country tunes in Spanish, mixed with a few words of Rarámuri. "Going Down the Road Feeling Bad," became "Drinking Down the Tesguino and Feeling Good." The crowd would shout for more. The Irish ballad, "Oh, Peggy Gordon, you are my darling, come sit ye down upon my knee," became, "Oh, Catalina, you make such good tesguino, come dance around the room."

"That's an Irish song," I would say, grinning to the other musicians. "That's my old people. They have their own tesguino. It's called Guinness."

At one tesguinada, one woman tugged at my sleeve and told me to play my banjo, "but don't sing." She took the center stage of the dirt floor party, raising her hands. As I picked a spirited rhythm, she started to improvise her own song. Everyone cheered. When she finished, another man signaled for me to continue, and he blurted out his lines to the spit-flying belly laughter of the others.

I strummed along until the last singer crooned. Martin and Rogelio, tired of the Rarámuri bluegrass karaoke treadmill, launched into a round of cumbias. I made the chord changes and played on.

"What does it mean to be Rarámuri?" I asked Bernabé one evening.

We were sitting outside the cabins on some logs, drinking coffee. El Chapareke was visiting. Bernabé laughed. He had watched my interest in the indigenous instrument with amusement. I think he misinterpreted my question as if I were asking how I could *become* Rarámuri.

"Javier, no," he said, lifting up my arm and placing it next to his. "You're white. Your grandfather didn't come from here."

His line reminded me of the tale of the illusory Indian chieftain recounted in *The Treasure of the Sierra Madre*, who declares to the Spanish doctor, "Your heart is different from mine, and your soul is not like mine. God has made us that way."

One of our visitors during our journey did have grandparents from the Sierra Madre. Author of several books of prize-winning poetry and an acclaimed memoir of gang life in Los Angeles, Luis J. Rodriguez provoked a real discourse on the issue of identity and heritage, and what it meant to be indigenous, during his visit.

Luis grew up in the barrios of East Los Angeles. His mother spoke only Spanish; her family came from Chihuahua. Her mother was the daughter of a young Rarámuri woman who had descended from the Sierra Madre to seek work as a servant in the home of a Mexican family. Luis had ventured to the Sierra Madre in search of a cultural inheritance that continued quietly in his mother's home; she still retained knowledge of traditional herbal remedies. Then living in Chicago, Luis also participated in a Native American spiritual group. He felt a profound and living connection with his ancestral heritage in the Americas. There was a longing about Luis that I understood: an urgent desire to know the meaning of what we had lost.

Because of Luis's trip and familial quandaries, I asked several villagers about their own family histories; I was curious to see if there was any concept of family trees or clans. It was the most basic but elusive question, French writer Andre Malraux once declared: the agnostics believed we would all be asked at death, "Where do you come from?" Most Rarámuri could not go back further than their grandfathers, which reminded me of Carla and her Italian friends. Few Italians cared about their ancestry beyond *la nonna*, or grandmother. Unburdened by the American immigrant's displacement and subsequent quandary for roots, they considered themselves indigenous to the Mediterranean.

Linguist Don Burgess, who was then residing in Creel and had spent more than three decades living and working in the Sierra Madre, once suggested that ancestry among the Rarámuri sometimes mixed into legends of animals. As with other tribes in the Southwest, this could have been an indication of ancient clan names associated with animals. No such clan names have endured.

Their own name for themselves, Rarámuri, has often been translated as "light-footed" or "fleet-footed ones" due to a fanciful interpretation by Lumholtz. The commonly used Tarahumara is a Spanish corruption of Rarámuri. The Norwegian was fond of their kickball races and phenomenal running marathons and stamina. Burgess suggested that the name might have originated from the Rarámuri word *rayena*, or "sun." Among the Rarámuri I would ask, the term *Rarámuri* now functioned in self-identification only. It designated "the people," in the way *diné* and *o'odham* indicate "the people" among those tribes, Navajo/Apache and Pima/Papago.

Beyond word games, the meaning of names often underlines the roots of our family experiences. On a closer look, I found it also offered a glimpse of the old conflicts at play and the clashing differences inferred by Traven's tribal chief in *The Treasure of the Sierra Madre*. Unlike Luis Rodriguez, I had no blood connection to the region, of course. But like most Americans from older immigrant families, my family roots had entangled into the traumatic events and parallel experiences that had shaped the reality of indigenous people on our continent today.

My father's surname, Biggers, originated from Lowland Scots; *biggar* had been associated since medieval times with the trades of builders or masons. According to one genealogist, my mother's paternal surname, Followell, originated from the middle English *falwe*, from the old English *fealg*, or "cultivated land," and *wella*, meaning "spring or stream."

In the 1670s, after the plague and the Great Fire had laid waste to London and with Scotland in economic turmoil and torn by bloody conflicts over episcopacy and presbyterianism, my ancestor William Bigger joined the ranks of other indentured Scottish servants and settled in New Kent County, Virginia. He lived at the center of Nathaniel Bacon's rebellion of the colonists in 1676. The future Americans were not only outraged by English taxes, but also by the Crown's efforts to stop them from attacking and taking more land from the Native Americans. Their bitter declaration accused England of "having protected, favored, and emboldened the Indians."

The Rarámuri had already endured a hundred years of encroachment by the Spanish settlers by then. As noted by Spanish conquistador Cabeza de Vaca in the narrative of his travels across Texas and Mexico in the 1530s, Spanish slave raiders had been sweeping the plains and inhabited lower river valleys in northern Mexico for years. By 1589, Spanish miners, along with their African slaves, had penetrated the Rarámuri uplands around Chinipas. When silver strikes occurred in Parral in 1630, Rarámuri men were rounded up like wild broncos and impressed into slave labor in the mines. Others sought refuge among the Jesuits, who counted over four thousand in the ranks of the supposedly protected and baptized in 1645.

The "missionization" of communities in the lower *bajadas* of the Sierra Madre intensified a growing clash among the Rarámuri. Breaking into baptized and nonbaptized factions that linger even today, they failed to unite in any rebellion against the Spanish. While thousands of lowland groups quickly converted under the Spanish policy of "reduction" into clustered villages centered around a mission, most Rarámuri abandoned their scattered ranchos in the more fertile lower valleys and retreated to the highlands.

The Rarámuri were never reported as warring or hostile. Even their rebellions, as chronicled by Jesuit Padre Jose Pasqual in 1651, resulted from desperation: "In the three wars we have had with the Tarahumara nation, they have never acted treacherously, they have never ambushed us, nor have they set out to rob and kill as have other nations. Rather the Tarahumaras have only defended what they consider theirs and have revenged themselves on Spaniards who have harmed them."

After an attempt to ally various tribes faltered in 1648, the outrage of the nonbaptized and some embittered baptized Rarámuri exploded in the 1650s. The Jesuits, who had introduced the metal ax, saw it come back to haunt them. Led by Teporaca, a fiery orator and baptized leader with the nickname of El Hachero, or "Woodsman" (a strict translation would be "the ax-man"), one of the first acts of the rebellion was to crucify a Jesuit priest (a Belgian who had Hispanicized his surname in order to serve in Mexico) at the mission of Papigochic. Two years later, another Jesuit, a Neapolitan who had "begged to be sent to take his place," according to Jesuit historian Peter Dunne, "hoping no doubt [he] too at some future might be able to achieve martyrdom," met the same fate on the cross. Despite Teporaca's ability to raise an army that numbered in the thousands, the Spanish troops brutally suppressed the raids. Betrayed by a group of Spanish-supporting Christian Rarámuri, Teporaca was finally captured and executed in 1652.

Toward the end of the seventeenth century, after a decade of European diseases had ravaged indigenous settlements, rumblings about a new rebellion were revived in the Sierra Madre. Finding a hoard of poisoned arrows and corn, and in anticipation of a new revolt, a Basque commander beheaded thirty Rarámuri and posted their heads on the road to Cocomorachic as a warning to the rest of the indigenous communities in 1696. He repeated this gesture in the mission village of Sisoguichic, spurring a bloody period of raids and attacks that terrorized the region for two years. In the end, large segments of the Rarámuri never surrendered, but fled deeper into the labyrinth of the Sierra Madre.

By the time the first mission in Mawichi was established as a *visita* in the 1740s, the Rarámuri in the region had fully embraced the metal ax, plow, and domesticated animals. Until their expulsion from Mexico in 1767, the Jesuits even reported gains in baptizing and grafting Christian ceremonies, such as the matachin dancing and Semana Santa (Holy Week), onto the traditional indigenous rituals. With the Jesuits' banishment from the country for the next 133 years, the Rarámuri were left alone for the most part by the weaker Franciscan missionaries and ephemeral Spanish and Mexican governments. In the highlands and isolated canyons they readapted the rituals and their agricultural ways to the rugged slopes and remnants of their traditional cultures.

At the same time the Jesuits were leaving the New World, my Biggers family drifted west with the Indian wars. After crossing the Appalachians, Macon Bigger died in Maysville, Kentucky, on the Ohio River in 1811, the same year the Shawnee leader Tecumseh sought to unite the Cherokee and other tribes against the American settlers. The Ohio River Valley had erupted into one of the bloodiest centers in the Indian wars; Daniel Boone, who ran a tavern in Maysville, had already become a living legend.

At this point, my ancestors added an "s" to their name; Biggers was also found on the slave owner schedules from 1840 to 1860. Earlier that century, a distant relative had been killed during a slave-raiding expedition. A slave auction near Maysville prompted Harriet Beecher Stowe to write *Uncle Tom's Cabin*. Trapped in the volatile and divided Kentucky borderlands during the Civil War, my branch of the Biggers family abandoned their successful hemp farms, split with their Confederate brothers, crossed the Ohio and Wabash rivers after the war, and finally settled in southern Illinois as castaways. They lost a child to illness within a year.

The Biggers were not the first in my extended family to cross into the dense Shawnee forests. By 1804, Stephen Stilley, my great-great-great-great-grandfather on my mother's maternal side, followed the tradition of the Jesuits and became the first Baptist missionary to penetrate the dangerous forests on horseback, preaching to various tribes. He also served in the War of 1812 on the opposite side of Tecumseh and his bands of Native Americans that aligned with the British.

Mirroring Teporaca's campaign, Tecumseh's attempts at uniting the Native American tribes ultimately failed. He was killed at the Battle of the Thames in 1813. The rest of the Shawnee in the Ohio River Valley either surrendered or dispersed into small bands. After Congress passed a bill in 1830 calling for the removal of all Native Americans living east of the Mississippi, the Shawnee and Miami bands were rounded up with members of over fifty other tribes and relocated to the western territories. They did not have the vast reaches and canyons of the Sierra Madre at their disposal.

The Stilleys eventually built a family log cabin in the craggy and steep hollows of Eagle Creek in the Shawnee National Forest, also known as the Illinois Ozarks. The name of their dispersed community—Eagle Creek—echoed the translation of the Rarámuri name of Mawichi, *the place of eagles*. This became my mother's family homestead for nearly two hundred years. Nature provided its own defense; the family retreated into a woodland solitude. They worked the land, the mills, and drifted into the coal mines. Bordered by the Wabash and Ohio Rivers, the terrain was as difficult to farm as the canyons in the Sierra Madre. The woodlands also possessed one of the most diverse biomes in the region, featuring a mix of oak, maple, gum, beech, and dogwood trees.

My forefather Stephen Stilley most likely rode his horse to the Ohio River in the winter of 1838 and watched as thousands of ragged Cherokee and other tribes crossed into southern Illinois at Golconda. The procession became infamously known as the Trail of Tears.

My family represented the quintessential experience of the American frontiersmen, dating back to the earliest colonies. We were as transient as the next wagon party; we moved through imaginary frontiers with each generation, reinventing our identity and heritage along the way. The family homestead in Eagle Creek was as close as we ever came to claiming any homeland in the country. Its existence was made possible only because of the Indian Removal Act of 1830, one of the most important but unremembered pieces of legislation in American history.

Viewed in this respect, history put a slight damper on any genealogical nostalgia. The hard clash of conquest rattled my modern sensibilities; it was an irreversible component of my heritage. I couldn't just dismiss it as vague sketches of history that were unrelated to my personal experience. Living among the Rarámuri in the Sierra Madre compelled me to examine it with a contemporary eye. Our family history had become a living reminder of the choices each generation faced, including my own, in the name of progress and expansion. This included the life and death of other cultures.

Given the four centuries of onslaught and invasion in the Sierra Madre, it carried a haunting relevance to the indigenous reality today. In Mawichi, I was struck by the question of our modern society's lack of acceptance of the indigenous way of life, as if it were still an affront to our march for advancement. Has our attitude really changed much since the winter of 1830, when Andrew Jackson unveiled his plan before the United States Congress? Jackson declared:

> Humanity has often wept over the fate of the aborigines of this country, and Philanthropy has been long busily employed in devising means to avert it, but its progress has never for a moment been arrested, and one by one have many powerful tribes disappeared from the earth. What good man would prefer a country covered with forests and ranged by a few thousand savages to our extensive Republic, studded with cities, towns, and prosperous farms, embellished with all the improvements which art can devise or industry executes, oc-

cupied by more than 12,000,000 happy people, and filled with all the blessings of liberty, civilization, and religion?

This quandary lurked in the back of my mind when I had asked Bernabé, "What does it mean to be Rarámuri?"

His answer seemed appropriate now.

"Javier, no," he repeated, "you're white, your grandfather didn't come from here," as if our histories, despite our modern bridges and entreaties, would be forever irreconcilable.

Maria's return was unmistakable. I heard a clamor outside the cabin one morning, about a month into our sojourn. Then came the knock. I rose to answer the door. We did not have a lock, but a board that latched into wooden hooks on either side like medieval barricades. Our neighboring landlady and sixty-year-old companion to Bernabé stood in the doorway, a four-foot eight-inch rotund figure with a piercing gaze or glare and silvery hair, clad in a traditional flowery skirt and scarf, a Miami Dolphins jacket, and Nike sandals. She reminded me of a Rarámuri Mother Jones, the bantam heavyweight matriarch of union leaders in the United States who was both revered and reviled by many. There was a sweetness in her grin, though, as compassionate as any grandmother.

"Where's Carla?" she said. "I want to speak with Carla."

This tended to be a comment I'd hear often around the canyon settlements, especially if I appeared at a tesguinada alone or visited some of the neighboring cabins and caves by myself. "Where's Carla?" Our connubiality—not necessarily the state of being married but living together, given that many Rarámuri didn't celebrate any formal religious or civil union—was critical to the community. With me in the village, at least in the eyes of the women, Carla was not a wandering threat, someone who could steal their men. She had to return home and reckon with her own man each night, which meant I was accounted for, as well.

This situation was serious enough that my appearance was required at some of Carla's interviews with the younger fathers in the village. I would linger out in the fields, or on a nearby ridge, always in view, in order to assuage the concerns of the village.

Maria was watching me intently at the door.

"Where's Carla?" Maria said again.

"Come in," I said. "I'll wake her." I hummed a bar of "The Bramble and the Rose."

The cabin belonged to Maria because it sat on her ancestral land.

Her family was one of the first Rarámuri to settle in the Mawichi valley near the mission. Even in the late 1970s, the central area that had become today's "village" was virtually an unpopulated dominion of a mestizo who controlled the ejido like a cacique. That mestizo had since been expelled from the ejido for corruption. This made Maria and her few siblings the eldest keepers of the land.

"We farmed the first fields around the creek," she said later that day.

Once she became accustomed to my presence, we would chat sometimes in the mornings behind the cabins, where the fields sloped down toward the arroyo. Her presence outside, slapping the wash, feeding the chickens, and grinding corn, had altered the routine of my wood-chopping mornings.

"What does your father grow?" Maria asked.

"Oranges," I said, "and some lemons."

I knew the purpose of this common question referred as much to my origins. The citrus, in my mind, and in my parents' (a retired teacher and an attorney) front yard in urban Tucson, designated the desert and hot climate for me. European friars had introduced citrus, especially the now popular limes, in the lower canyons of the Sierra Madre.

"On the other side?" she said.

"Yes, la frontera," I said. "The desert."

"Carla is from the same place of the Pope," Maria said.

She grinned, standing only a few feet away from three yard-high crosses staked to the ground and a shrine for the Virgin of Guadalupe that rested under a towering willow tree to the side of the cabin.

Maria was a deeply religious woman. She had roamed this canyon and creek as a child until she was literally picked up and hauled away at the age of eight by Jesuit Padre David Brambila, a scholar who produced one of the most important Rarámuri-Spanish dictionaries. A mestizo woman had told the priest that Maria was wild and unattended to. Arriving in the mission center of Sisoguichic, she studied under the auspices of nuns until her early teens, at which point she traveled to the central Mexico city of Puebla to serve as a maid at a convent.

Just like Bernabé, Maria eventually eschewed the life of the nunnery to return to the Sierra Madre; she found work in Creel as a maid. After meeting and marrying Bernabé, they returned to her family's land in Mawichi to raise corn and a family. While he tended to her land, Maria eventually took a job as a cook at the local school and other schools in the area.

I occasionally heard Maria grinding corn on the metate or the upright metal grinder in the mornings. In the evenings, Carla and I would help her round up their goats and cows or weed her garden. These household chores were only the beginnings of her responsibilities in the community. As one of the very few women of her generation who was fluent and literate in Spanish, Maria had become the main reference point for government officials in the area. She spoke at conferences and attended regional and national meetings. When President Luis Echeverria arrived in Creel in the 1970s, he selected Maria to escort him into the Rarámuri communities. During our sojourn, the state politicians were courting her participation in the first ever "congress" of indigenous women in the Sierra Madre.

"I don't like the term *gringo*," she said one day as I was helping her weed the garden. "It has too many bad meanings." She and I slowly moved down a row, throwing invasive plants to the side. "But the word *indio* is even worse," she went on. "Who are indios? I am not an indita. I am indigenous. I am Tarahumara. Rarámuri, as we say." She gazed at me with her probing eyes, clearly monitoring whether I understood her point.

The appellation of *indios* reappeared in a few of our conversations. Maria detested the contemporary use of the old term and its indication of secondary status. Despite the growing blitz of tourism in the Sierra Madre, the reference continued to be a commonly heard slur for the Rarámuri and other indigenous groups by hotel and tourist operators and a large number of the Mexican *serranos* (mountaineers): in some minds, the Rarámuri were still indios, savages, uncivilized.

Within days I realized that women such as Maria and her two daughters largely kept the villages in orbit in the Sierra Madre. In Mawichi, for example, a women's cooperative (led by Maria) had launched the village shop. They made and sold handicrafts locally and at regional fairs; they monitored the schools and teachers and took care of the children. They worked in the cornfields with the men, and they tended the homes and domestic needs. They hauled the water. They also made the tesguino. Only the ejido administration (or day jobs in the migrant fields or construction sites) and the sawmill, which functioned erratically, seemed to be the dominion of men, though it also employed women.

Maria enjoyed a certain leverage of power, which had brought her respect, envy, and resentment in the village. With access and knowledge of the government programs and international aid projects, she was the person who turned in the handwritten requests. Within the last five years, she had cultivated the first vegetable garden supported by government aid, received grants for chemical fertilizer, and had running water installed at her house. The outside walls of her adobe house were even used for an experiment by the government to demonstrate environmentally sound ways to preserve adobe walls with a lime-based plaster. Many of her canyon neighbors, simply in need of food and blankets, looked on in awe and bewilderment, as if from another history.

This power had not always gone in Maria's favor. Her mercurial personality had led her to be banned from speaking at the Sunday community meetings. But these controversies bored Maria. During our first week together, she was obsessed with talking about fresh eggs.

"We need more eggs in the community," she told me one morning, scurrying around her chicken coop. I stayed outside the bounds of a miserable tethered dog inside the coop, whose sole mission in life was to guard the chickens from foxes. "At the tienda, the cooperative store here, we sell eggs from the outside," Maria went on. She glared at a cluster of cocks. "From the outside," she shouted. "Why can't we raise enough eggs so people don't have to buy eggs from the outside?"

We marched around the cabin toward the front side of her house.

"Right here," Maria said. "This is where we're going to build the chicken coop for the women's cooperative."

A stack of adobe bricks, shaped from the creek bed and left in wooden frames to be dried by the sun, rested to the side. Another pile of beams and tree trunks sat to the side like a broken-down barn.

"Fresh eggs," she said, pointing at the stack of cracked and fraying adobe. She looked back at me with a glimmer of excitement. "Bernabé and some other men will start working tomorrow, if you're still around."

"We've already started," I said, holding out my torn hands.

I had actually stacked the adobe blocks with Bernabé and another man earlier that week. Maria stepped back, looked at the bricks and wood, and then grinned, still staring at the mounds of materials. They appeared to be ruins. I could imagine their depiction in one of Adolph Bandelier's first archaeological reports on the Sierra Madre, which I had recently read: worthless, inconsequential remains. Instead, as I looked at the ruins now, I realized that Maria had given those mud bricks and pine logs meaning, longing, even roots.

We heard the rattle and the roar from the truck's loudspeakers long before the vehicle came into sight. Dropping into the canyon on the road carved along the creek bed, the truck blasted norteño tunes off the bluffs as if rallying a valley of polka dancers.

The dirt road into Mawichi never saw much traffic. Logging trucks descended from the high plateaus, occasional tourist vans arrived from Creel, Coca-Cola and packaged food vendors shuttled their deliveries to the village co-op shop with the fanfare of Pony Express runners, and on Sundays, two vegetable trucks converged on the village gathering, blaring out norteño on competing sound systems.

We watched this new truck jostle into view from the side of Bernabé's house. It looked like an old furniture moving van. I was laying the beams for the roof of the women's cooperative chicken coop with Bernabé and another villager, Pedro.

"Machine guns, machine guns!" screamed a nasal voice, strangled by the muzzle of the sound system. "The revenge of the Tarahumara! So much violence!"

I looked at Bernabé, who was covered in a veil of wood chips and dirt, holding one of the beams in place, while Pedro straddled the roof above with a hammer in one hand and a mouthful of nails. Pedro watched as the truck wound past a clearing and parked near the mission. Bernabé withdrew his sombrero, wiped the sweat from his face, and then grinned.

"The movies are back," he said.

"Machine guns, violence, la india Maria!" the loudspeaker whined.

According to Bernabé, the cinema-on-wheels had come to the village every summer for years. Their screaming sound system inspired a cacophony of roosters, dogs, and fleeing pigs, and spooked horses and cows. The muzzled voice spewed out movie previews like threats, until the speaker coughed and opted for the recorded um-pah-pah of norteño.

"The revenge of the Tarahumara," Pedro laughed, pounding nails.

Two men assembled the cinema on the side of the old mission walls. A black carnival tent rose, with a screen propped up at one end. Rickety wooden chairs were lined up in uneven rows on the ground.

I was curious to see the turnout. So few people lived within listening distance of the loudspeakers, even if the noise screeched far into the canyons with relentless tunes and announcements. "Only two hours to go! Machine guns, violence, the revenge of the Tarahumara!" With the exception of Sunday, when the bluffs came alive with streams of families maneuvering down the steep trails in their Sunday best, including women and young girls draped in their colorful dresses and scarves, there were rarely more than two dozen souls in view in the village.

We received knocks on our door before dusk, counter to ghostly customs.

"Pancho," one young man asked me, as I stood at the door. We had worked together on a ditch for a new cabin. "Can you loan me ten pesos?"

Marco, a clever ten-year-old neighbor, followed. "My papa needs ten pesos for some food. Can you give it to me?" He paused for a moment, adding in a whimper, "Korima."

Carla and I agonized over shelling out pesos. We knew our comparative wealth made us commodities, whether we handed out or hoarded our resources. We decided prior to entering the community that we didn't want to become the village bankers. The requests came quite rarely, however, and usually under desperate circumstances. We had fudged on our promises to provide a few loans out of despair. In truth, it was an uncommon custom for the Rarámuri to ask outright for money in the Sierra Madre. Women brought by their pine needle baskets or clay pots; men quietly dropped by the cabin with a wooden doll or a chopping block they carved. There was no discussion of their need for funds; their trips were infrequent enough that we understood their situations. Nor was there ever any discussion of the price.

"How much do I owe?" I would ask.

"Whatever you want to give," they would respond.

While the act of *korima* (loosely translated as gift-giving or sharing among one more fortunate person to another) existed in the village, it had traditionally been related to instances of those who had fallen on remarkably bad times, such as crop failure, death, or illness. In these cases, according to Bernabé, it was not seen as an act of charity but sharing. In extreme situations, the indigent person might work around the rancho of a more established person, grinding corn, fixing fences, or doing whatever was required, in order to receive a gift of corn and beans.

This tradition of korima had been skewered in recent times. Rarámuri mothers and children now lined street corners as beggars in Chihuahua City and Ciudad Juárez; brigades of children had even emerged in Creel, roaming from restaurant to restaurant, beseeching the tourists with outstretched hands. They invoked the magic word openly. In response to the lingering impact of the drought, a number of Mexican and international organizations had appropriated the term in their "korima benefit" drives for food and blankets; a Korima Foundation based in Texas had institutionalized the concept.

When I was in Creel once with Maria, picking up some supplies at the store, I watched from across the street as she spoke with some of the children who were begging. She was as stern as ever. They eventually scattered. Shaking her head in apparent dismay, she shifted in my direction, caught off balance at my stare. We both felt awkward on the drive back to Mawichi. We never said a word about the incident.

Marco's ten-year-old appeal for korima in the name of the movies came as the latest contemporary spin.

Without electricity, the kerosene-lit village rarely saw illuminated nightlife, outside of bonfires set for the tesguinadas. Inside the school sat a broken-down generator, which on rare occasions jump-started the video player for the kids. We knew when the kids had seen a video; the next morning they would practice karate kicks or chase each other with pistols carved from wooden sticks.

Carla and I arrived late for the first showing in the evening. The movie had started minutes before, the rattle of machine gun fire blasting through our cabin walls, as if a war was taking place in the front yard. The tent was already packed with at least fifty people, most wearing sombreros, caps, or scarves. Even El Mudo, the village mute, gazed at the screen. A lot of the kids had escaped from school, straddling the towering mission walls for a precarious peek above the tent confines. They couldn't afford, like most people, the ten-peso (roughly $1) charge. The average daily salary in the sawmill was forty-five pesos.

A reel-to-reel projector snapped the images onto the screen from the side of the truck. The maximum volume compensated for any blurriness. Settling onto our chairs, saluting everyone in the crowd, their heads cocked upward and their backs and shoulders slightly withdrawn, as if to dodge the overflow from the violent duels, we readied ourselves for the drive-by theatre.

"The Revenge of the Tarahumara" was about a Yaqui in Sonora who looked Italian. His son, with more Swedish than indigenous features, had been kidnapped by the evil Mexican grandfather who didn't want his daughter, a plump Julia Roberts, to commingle with the Yaqui anymore. In the end, the father rescued the boy, escaped to his sister's hacienda—she was a dead ringer for Jane Russell in deer hides—and scurried the kid back into the mountains, annihilating the grandfather's goons in the process. The father took a few ceremonial bullets, but he survived.

The crowd cheered at the end of the movie. Kids fired off their wood pistols from the mission walls.

The next movies revolved around the *narcotraficantes*, who had reached legendary status for some filmmakers and music groups. In fact, the truck blared some narco-norteo tunes before the show, glorifying the drug dealers and their wealth and power. In the films, one cartel fought another, with a plot centered around a lot of threatening, drinking in opulent mansions, big-breasted women who glared at the camera in a sort of indifferent sophistication, and enough polyester suits and firing of machine guns to force Scarface into retirement. Pure unadulterated machinations of deceit, debauchery, and greed that made *The Treasure of the Sierra Madre* look like a Disney film.

At the end of the night, worn down by the neck-craning battles, the villagers vanished into the darkness. Many followed the trails up the bluffs and through the forests, making their way back to their distant cabins.

The films relayed the facts and artifacts about the outside world. Was it any different than the images we received about Mexicans and indigenous peoples in Hollywood portrayals? Was it any different than our perceptions of Mexico, still based on the black and white images of *The Treasure of the Sierra Madre?*

I asked Pedro the next day what he thought of the movies. He had sat in the front row.

"They were so-so," he said, lifting a beam. "But *la India Maria,* which is tonight, is a lot better."

"You mean you've seen it before?" I asked.

He nodded. "About ten times. Some of those movies are ten years old. I've seen *The Revenge of the Tarahumara* many times."

"But the movies are so expensive."

"Oh, I didn't pay," he said, grinning. "We sneak in through the back." He paused for a theatrical moment. "The revenge of the Tarahumara."

One film about greed, gold, and the glory of indigenous people would never be shown at the Mawichi cinema-on-wheels. Starring Upton Sinclair and Sergei Eisenstein, two of the world's most widely recognized writers and directors in 1930, *Que Viva Mexico! (Da zdravstvuyet Meksika!* in the director's Russian) heralded the making of the "greatest film ever." Conceived as a paean to the rebirth of indigenous cultures and the revolution in Mexico, the film turned out to be the silent film industry's most calamitous miscarriage. In the process, the tragicomedy of errors behind the making of the film, which would rival the intrigue of some of the narco films, nearly destroyed the careers of both men.

Sinclair couldn't restrain his own ideas for the film; the "Rank Stranger To Me" ballad could have been on his soundtrack. In a letter to Eisenstein, he proposed the story, more or less, of Alfonzo's journey out of the Sierra Madre, where a young man, "raised on Indian superstitions," leaves the mountains for a trip to see the world and comes in contact with modern science and ideas, only to reject them and return to his native home, "a sadder and still more uncertain man." According to Sinclair, "to portray an Indian boy coming into contact with the new currents in Mexico and shrinking back from them bewildered, will be about as safe a theme as you can choose."

By the time Eisenstein arrived in Mexico in 1930, the cinema had been part of the country's entertainment for over thirty years. The first series of short films, made and introduced by Frenchman Gabriel Veyre in 1896, included *The Breakfast of Indians*. A collaborator with the Lumiere brothers, Veyre and fellow Frenchman Claude Bernard presented the new invention to the Mexican dictator, Porfirio Díaz.

The Mexican silent film industry produced scores of adventure and romantic films over the next few decades, including those by Guillermo "El Indio" Calles, a man who claimed to be of indigenous origins from Chihuahua. Dating back to 1913, Calles acted and directed in over sixty films with an indigenous bent, including *The Yaqui Indian*, *The Aztec Race*, and *The Bronze Race*.

First lured to Hollywood to make pictures for Paramount, the Latvian-born Eisenstein had become world-renowned in the 1920s for his film direction genius in the Russian masterpieces *Strike* and *The Battleship Potemkin*. His groundbreaking film editing "montage" techniques—cross-cutting between images to heighten emotions—remain a lasting influence in cinema today.

Eisenstein's obsession with Mexico was launched in the theater. In 1921, he designed the scenery and costumes for the Moscow production of *The Mexican*, a play based on a short story by Jack London. A few years later, Eisenstein met the celebrated painter and muralist Diego Rivera, propelling "a burning desire to travel" to Mexico.

After making a lecture tour through Europe, including stops in Berlin, Paris, Zurich, and London, Eisenstein arrived in Hollywood in the spring of 1930 and signed a contract with Paramount. Despite his fame and prestige among the Hollywood denizens, the Russian director's more oblique film concepts never suited the commercial expectations of the American producers; numerous ideas and scripts were either rejected or fell through, including Eisenstein's scenario for a film based on Theodore Dreiser's *An American Tragedy*. By October 1930, Paramount publicly terminated Eisenstein's contract.

So close to the Mexican border, Eisenstein refused to allow the Paramount debacle to force his premature return to the Soviet Union. Prompted by Chaplin, he contacted Upton Sinclair, who had long been a Socialist supporter of the Soviet Union. By 1930, Sinclair, then living in Pasadena, had become one of the most widely translated American authors. In that same year, over 525 titles of his work appeared in thirty-four countries.

Always one to take up a good cause, Sinclair and his wife agreed to serve as the producers and fundraisers of the film in Mexico. They summoned Sinclair's brother-in-law Hunter Kimbrough, a Southern stock salesman, to serve as the onsite general manager of the film in Mexico. Kimbrough maintained a self-professed "dislike for artists." As a sign of things to come, teetotaler Sinclair begged Kimbrough on the day of departure to "promise not to drink" in Mexico.

Having thrown out a casual figure of $25,000, Eisenstein and the Sinclairs agreed to a contract that would have "no strings attached," with the expectations of the film taking three to four months to shoot.

Eisenstein had no plans at the beginning, other than naming the film *Da zdravstvuyet Meksika!* His reception in Mexico City was nothing less than royal. His photo graced the front pages of the Mexican newspapers. He soon remade contact with Diego Rivera and other Mexican artists, as well as the American writer Katherine Anne Porter, who later beguiled the literary world with her fictional portraits of Mexico in *Flowering Judas* and *Pale Horse, Pale Rider.*

Two weeks later, the Mexican police arrested Eisenstein and his party for seeking to disseminate Bolshevik propaganda. The whole affair ended as a blunder for the Mexican government, which issued an apology to Sinclair, by the secretary of foreign relations, within a few days.

Sinclair had immediate problems in raising money in an economy that was still feeling the tremors of the stock market crash. He also faced the objections of the head of the Russian film division in the States. The Soviets cringed at the status of Eisenstein as an artist freed from the control of the state apparatus.

After a month of "listening to the heartbeat of Mexico," Eisenstein still possessed no storyline. In the meantime, the authorities summoned him again, though this time by mistake; the chief of the central police department of Mexico confused Eisenstein with Albert Einstein, realized his error, and then released him. For Sinclair, the fundraising details had become an albatross around his writing career, forcing the cancellation of lecture trips to Europe and the Soviet Union.

Wary of Eisenstein veering from proscribed policies on film topics, themes, and styles, the Soviets demanded that he clarify his scenario in writing and submit it to their own film division. Instead, beholden to illness and the rainy season, Eisenstein wrote to Sinclair that he would not be able finish the film for $50,000. The Sinclairs, at their wit's end on raising funds—Mary Sinclair had mortgaged some of her properties—suddenly realized that the once informal agreement had unraveled. During a moment of panic, they even sought to sell the rights of the entire project. Sinclair approached officials in the Soviet Union in a deal that would exchange the royalties on his books for $25,000 to be invested directly in the movie.

At this point, tempers were unleashed in the teeming exchange of letters and telegraphs between Sinclair, Eisenstein, and the rest of the party in Mexico. In need of film, Eisenstein obstinately declared that he could not finish the project for $50,000. The fundraising lagged from dismal to an outright crisis.

In July, the film party made headlines again when one of the actors, a boy who played a bandit, took a loaded pistol from the set and accidentally shot and killed his sister. (Forever the creative genius, Sinclair later pitched the story as a film promo for a leading magazine.)

Finally, in August, Eisenstein sent Sinclair a complete outline of *Que Viva Mexico!* However, Sinclair, on the verge of a nervous breakdown and suffering from delaying a hernia operation, dismissed the outline and beseeched Eisenstein to modify the film to meet the original budget. Outraged by the suggestion, Eisenstein saw his relationship with Sinclair and Kimbrough shift from bad to worse.

At one of the worst ebbs in the correspondence, the Soviet film division announced their interest in following up on Sinclair's proposal to invest $25,000 in the film. In September, in the midst of negotiations, both Sinclairs were rushed to the hospital—Mary Sinclair for ptomaine poisoning, and Upton for exhaustion and a kidney infection.

Despite the relatively positive negotiations with the Soviets, Sinclair began to express his resentment at Eisenstein's lack of correspondence to match his daily notes. He pleaded, "Germany is likely to declare herself bankrupt any day . . . and if that happens, it means quite certainly that the Bank of England will have to close." Sinclair concluded, "This is the situation upon which you propose to go on spending money without limit."

Unaware of the internal politics in the Soviet Union and their film bureau, Sinclair pursued the investment negotiations in a concrete fashion. By November, however, one of Eisenstein's enemies in the film division took control and dismissed the Soviet negotiator in the States. As a foreshadowing of the purges to come, the Stalinist forces launched a chain of events to discredit Eisenstein's name.

The Mexican censors in the Los Angeles consulate suddenly halted the venture, insisting on reviewing the new footage before it was handed over to Sinclair. The consul objected to scenes depicting horses ridden by ruthless landlords and their hired guns, trampling the heads of half-buried peasant boys.

These tremors of controversy paled compared to a chilling cable sent directly to Sinclair by Joseph Stalin: "Eisenstein loose [sic] his comrades confidence in Soviet Union . . . he is thought to be deserter who broke off with his own country."

Sinclair responded with a long and detailed defense of Eisenstein, addressing the letter to Comrade Stalin. Fearful of alerting Eisenstein and risking any emotional tailspin, Sinclair wrote letters in search of a conclusion to the film, to which Eisenstein responded that the film would be an "absolute flop" unless he received more money.

At this point, Sinclair received notice that the Soviet Union was contemplating a complete withdrawal from any investment. It considered Eisenstein's intent to remain in Mexico a breach of faith. (The Soviets must have had a premonition: Leon Trotsky, with the aid of Diego Rivera, eventually accepted asylum in Mexico in 1936.)

By the end of 1931, the exchange between Sinclair, Eisenstein, and Kimbrough deteriorated into accusations and counteraccusations. At odds over the accounting of the budget, Eisenstein and Kimbrough referred unabatedly to each other as liars. Kimbrough accused Eisenstein of hiring an assassin; Eisenstein claimed Kimbrough was a drunk who had been tossed in a Mexican jail for a raucous episode with prostitutes; Kimbrough countered that Eisenstein was "some kind of a pervert" and a homosexual. The Sinclairs, meanwhile, "argued for days and nights," according to Sinclair. While Sinclair attempted to salvage the Soviet connection, he plunged over $20,000 from the film rights of his own novel *Wet Parade* into Eisenstein's project, relieving his wife of any financial responsibilities.

In January 1932, rebuked by the Soviet Union, which reneged on its promise to invest, and with his own life in shambles, Sinclair wired to Kimbrough to "permit no further shooting . . . come home immediately . . . bring party." Stunned by the news, all members of the party, including Kimbrough, attempted to make up their differences and continued shooting until the end of the month. In a disingenuous attempt to stay in the country and finish his project, Eisenstein cabled the Soviet authorities that he was bound by his contract and government restrictions to remain in Mexico.

Feeling betrayed by Eisenstein's delaying tactics, Sinclair advised the Russian director that he took no responsibility for his relationship with Moscow. He urged the film party to return at once. On February 17, having driven from Mexico City, the party arrived at the Texas border, only to be detained by customs officials. Eisenstein and his Russian assistants were held for days until Sinclair could convince several senators to issue a short-term visa. Given the delay, Sinclair agreed that Eisenstein should return to Moscow and cut the film, instead of returning to Hollywood.

Despite his letters of intent to ship the film to Moscow for Eisenstein's editing, Sinclair went into a final tailspin of his own in the spring of 1932. Instead of heading home directly, Eisenstein lingered in New York, outraging the Soviet officials as well as Sinclair and his investors. Meanwhile, Sinclair was also shown numerous boxes of "obscene" drawings by Eisenstein, taken from his personal belongings, which depicted sexual acts between various religious figures. Finally, Eisenstein attempted to charge Sinclair for the cost of his travel back to the Soviet Union, when he had already been given $4,000 by Paramount for the return trip home.

Sinclair snapped. Writing a lengthy letter about his relationship with Eisenstein, addressed to the Soviet authorities and even Comrade Stalin, Sinclair detailed the numerous crises with the film director. He declared his intention to keep the film in the States and allow another editor to carry out the final cut. The disclosure incensed Eisenstein, the Soviet authorities, virtually every director of note in Hollywood, and the Communist Left in the States, which had been following the entire filming process in the press. With only his notebooks and drawings, Eisenstein boarded a ship for Europe.

On May 10, 1933, the world premiere of *Thunder Over Mexico* took place in Los Angeles at the Carthay Circle Theatre. The production of the film had been handed over to Sol Lesser, then with Principal Pictures, who later went on to fame and fortune by producing the *Tarzan* films; he won an Academy Award in 1951 for *Kon Tiki*. Sinclair, bitterly assailed over the year by both leftists and artists as a sellout, appeared briefly on the stage after the screening. He declared, "The man who directed this film is rated by many as the greatest director of our time." At another showing in New York, the police provided Sinclair with a police escort. The *New York Herald* declared it "the most controversial film in the world."

The actual film was only a fragment—the dramatic story of a peon who is abused and then brutally murdered by prerevolutionary feudal lords—of the planned six stories by Eisenstein. Lesser eventually carved the nearly twenty thousand feet of film into *Thunder Over Mexico* and *Death Day*, which chronicled a religious festival and a bullfight. Another company purchased the remaining footage, producing a series of "educational shorts" called *Mexican Symphony*. In 1954, after long negotiations, the Museum of Modern Art bought the bulk of the footage and created a series of "study films."

It wasn't until the 1970s that Eisenstein's assistant, Grigori Alexandrov, had the opportunity to edit the remains of the film in Russia according to Eisenstein's notes and drawings. This version was finally released as *Que Viva Mexico!* Part documentary, part visionary travelogue, part dramatic epic, the brilliant images and composition in the silent film—set to an often overly dramatic score—are a romantic and loving tribute to the evolution of Mexico from a pre-Columbian paradise to the struggles against the Porfirio Diáz dictatorship to its revolutionary mix of indigenous and modern ways.

Eisenstein never saw the final results of his work. He returned to a volatile Soviet Union, and due to a series of problems did not direct again until the late 1930s. While one film was banned for political reasons, he made two other films, including the celebrated *Alexander Nevsky*, which received the Stalin Prize.

Eisenstein died of a heart attack in 1948, not long after his fiftieth birthday. *Que Viva Mexico!* always remained a tragedy for him, but his time in Mexico, he wrote, was a moment "of highest creative excitement . . . which nourished all subsequent work."

For Sinclair, who stirred the country in his run for the California governorship in 1934, his newfound friendship with Sol Lesser was "the best thing that we got out of this whole experience."

The novelist Alfredo Vea and his wife Carole Conn arrived for a visit a week after *The Revenge of the Tarahumara*. They had taken the train to Creel from the Los Mochis coastal area, on the other side of the Sierra Madre, not far from the Rio Yaqui, the homeland of Alfredo's grandfather.

Unlike the Rarámuri, the Yaqui engaged in direct and bitter warfare with the Spanish and Mexican intruders for over four hundred years. Their resistance to Diego de Guzmán's slave-raiding incursions in the Yaqui river valley in 1533 impressed the Spanish chroniclers enough to record the fierce Yaqui military acumen.

"There are eight Yaqui cities along the river," the Yaqui grandfather explains to his young grandson in Vea's first novel, *La Maravilla*, "and you, Beto, are from Cocorit; your blood, tu sangre, is from Cocorit." The scene, which takes place at a peyote ritual, includes a Yaqui-Rarámuri character living in the States.

Yaqui blood spilled in Cocorit in 1887, when the disputatious Yaqui leader Cajeme—"he who does not drink"—was executed, launching nearly half a century more of armed conflict. Cajeme, who had served in the Mexican Army as a captain, actually fought against the French occupation in the Valley of Mexico. As part of the campaign to control the Yaqui, the Mexican government resorted to deporting Yaqui men and women as serfs to plantations in various parts of the country. The brutality under the Díaz dictatorship mirrored the dramatic scenes of the indigenous peasants being trampled by the feudal lord's horses in *Que Viva Mexico!* By 1908, hundreds of Yaqui had fled across the border to seek refuge in the States. After the Mexican military occupied Yaqui territory again in 1926–27, thousands more Yaqui followed the railroad ties through Sonora, as if they were an iron river of freedom, until the Sonoran railway linked into the Southern Pacific.

"Most of us found jobs with the Southern Pacific railroad," the grandfather, Manuel, says in *La Maravilla*. "My father worked on the gangs that laid down the first iron in many places."

While bands of the Kickapoo, Cherokee, and Black Seminole tribes had fled the States and filed for permanent residence in Mexico, the Yaqui petitioned the United States for status as political refugees. In 1978, they finally became a federally recognized tribe, living on the fringe of Tucson and Phoenix in the Sonoran Desert.

In the 1950s, Buckeye Road in *La Maravilla* spiraled southwest of a rising Phoenix for thirty Sonoran Desert miles until it arrived in the settlement of its namesake, Buckeye, Arizona. The backwash of western migrations and good intentions littered the road. It was lined with fields of cotton and barley, abandoned homesteads, tar-paper shacks, and crumbling adobes, and the lives and cultures of those who had fallen off John Steinbeck's *Wayward Bus*.

In one of the best-kept secrets in the Western states in those same years, Upton Sinclair lived in anonymity in Buckeye, Arizona, with his ailing wife, coolly sitting out the McCarthy years while keeping up his correspondence with some of the great minds of this century. Only a few years prior, Sinclair had won the Pulitzer Prize for *Dragon Teeth*, part of the Lanny Budd adventure series that he completed while living in Arizona. By the time he reached Buckeye, Sinclair's literary reputation was reduced to the rubble that surrounded him in the desert. Beholden to his buoyant socialism, Sinclair would be remembered more for his radical crusades than his pioneering literary work on immigrant families, cultural dislocation, and the stories of the dispossessed.

On the other end of Buckeye Road, Vea came into the world in 1950 to a thirteen-year-old mother and was raised by his Spanish grandmother and Yaqui grandfather, who were locked in a religious battle over the child's soul. Looking "out" into the city with the eyes and wisdom of his Yaqui grandfather, Vea's world could have been a backdrop for one of Sinclair's proletarian tracts. Instead of a teeming urban jungle, however, the squatters on Vea's Buckeye Road, composed of his bickering grandparents, Okies, Irish, Pimas or O'odham, southern blacks, Chinese grocers, the Holocaust-surviving Jewish Fuller Brush man, well-endowed prostitutes, disinherited farmworkers, and a busload of haute couture transvestites, churned up a glorious dust devil of cultures connected by extension cords. In a lyrical prose akin to that of Mexican writer Carlos Fuentes, a transcendence to a world of myriad possibilities and hopes occurs.

Fuentes once noted that Mexico was a land of happy children and sad old men. On Vea's Buckeye Road, just as in our Rarámuri village, old men somehow transcend their anger and grief into whiskey-tinged (or tesguino-tinged) wells of joy. For Vea's nine-year-old protagonist, Beto, indigenous people, immigrants, and the inheritors of folk cultures, in spite of their labors, become the very fountains of the American experience.

Set on the edge of the Sonoran Desert, *La Maravilla* could easily be transplanted into the forests and canyons of the Sierra Madre. The conflicts of the young Beto, Vea's alter ego, struggling to understand his indigenous heritage in a mestizo world, mirrored the conflicts of the Rarámuri kids living in a *narco* film world of fulsome affluence that had arrived on the big screen in Mawichi.

Beto's Yaqui grandfather tells him in *La Maravilla:*

"Yes, you are American, but not in the gringo sense. You are Spanish and Yaqui, you are a mestizo from Aztlan, this land, right here where the Nahua people began." He stamped his foot into the packed earth. "That is what a Mexican is. But you were born here in America, *también*, and that's what a Chicano is. You don't become nothing. It's only the gringos that become! They are Xipe," he said, referring to the ancient god of new growth beneath the old, the god the Aztecs distorted into the God of the Flayed Skin. It was Manuel's word for those people on earth who do not know where they belong . . . "You do not become American, no, no. Shit, no. America becomes you, *mijo*."

Sinclair would have benefited from a chat with Alfredo's grandfather. Despite his perennial campaign to change America, Sinclair became an ambulant radical who drifted out of the American chronicles, as if he no longer belonged to literary history. His demise on Buckeye Road, during the same period of Vea's residency, fascinated me; Alfredo and I even searched once for Sinclair's unknown home in the Sonoran Desert.

Buckeye unfolded onto the Main Street town of Mom and Pop stores and restaurants, boarded-up storefronts, and gas stations. We followed signs to the town library, though we knew it was probably closed on Sunday. It was; I started canvassing the neighbors.

"Christ, honey, talk to this guy," a man clad in a T-shirt, holding a beer, and sporting a meatpacker build, shouted behind his screen door. As his wife approached I heard him mumble, "Asking about some house of sin or something."

"Upton Sinclair doesn't live here anymore," she said, smiling behind the screen door.

Sinclair wrote over eighty books. He worked on his autobiography down the street from the Buckeye high school. From this desert hamlet, he also maintained a relentless correspondence and chronicling of his own life story, as if obsessed with ensuring his immortality.

Sinclair's house was unmistakable, ringed by an imposing seven-foot-high brick wall. It was a small bungalow on the corner of a tidy residential street. It was a long way from Sinclair's New York City highrise or southern California villa or the utopian farm he founded in New Jersey. We entered a yard strewn with beer cans and spare auto parts. A cage of fowl sat in the corner. We knocked on a cracked front door. A torn and discolored sheet was draped in the front window. We had no luck in stirring the ghosts.

We called more teachers, librarians, and barbers. We knocked on more doors and interrupted Sunday dinners. Sitting on their living room sofa, one couple invited us into their home and described their own attempt to unveil the mystery around Sinclair's Buckeye residence. Their son once took up an English teacher's extra credit assignment, for fifty points, and interviewed Sinclair's doctor and tracked down the house. He found no records or articles or interviews in the local paper, not to mention a street sign or Upton Sinclair Day at the library or a display at the school. The deed of the house was in the name of Hunter Kimbrough, the in-law scion from the film debacle.

"The town thought he was a Communist," the couple told us.

In his Nobel Prize nomination on behalf of Sinclair in the 1930s, co-signed by Bertrand Russell, Albert Einstein, John Dewey, and numerous others, George Bernard Shaw spoke of Sinclair's unique literary role in altering history rather than any stylistic triumph. Few other authors in American history could lay claim to writing a novel that so dramatically altered the way we lived. President Theodore Roosevelt personally attributed the impact of *The Jungle* to the passing of the Pure Food and Drug Act of 1906. Not quite ninety years old, Sinclair returned to the White House to witness President Lyndon Johnson signing the Wholesome Meat Act of 1967.

Yet, few other writers of Sinclair's worldwide fame have been so easily forgotten. I found this a cruel irony for someone like Sinclair, one of the literary world's great self-promoters and a man so concerned with his immortal place in literature and society that he maintained a prolific correspondence with some of the greatest historical figures and recorders in his century.

As we drove out of town, Vea noted the signs of better times when Buckeye Road wasn't overlooked or considered the transit zone between two dead ends.

"It's almost as if Upton Sinclair wanted to lose himself out here," Vea said.

Beto's grandfather forewarns his grandson of such a displacement of the soul:

> To lose yourself is the greatest mutilation . . . Mexico is an old word, *mijo*. It means the navel of the moon . . . to the gringo immortality means from today forward, *mijo;* each gringo wants to live forever. That's what they want from their God, that's what they want from their medicine. To a Yaqui immortality can also mean from today backward to the beginning. The future is no longer than the past.

They are the same distance no matter where you stand. The Yaqui people have lived forever.

We returned from felling a truckload of trees, chopping the trunks into blocks to haul back to the village. I had become Chico's *compañero* in the wood-chopping business that fall. He was Bernabé and Maria's thirty-two-year-old son-in-law and the only man in the village who owned a gas-powered chainsaw. His "muscles bulged like iron hoops on a whiskey barrel," as poet Don West wrote of another sawyer. With large round eyes and a quick laugh, Chico spent a lot of his time telling jokes and laughing at my blunders. He maintained the dry Rarámuri sense of humor that pervaded in the village. No work project or ritual, even the most serious, transpired without a grin and a hilarious one-liner, as if humor was as vital to the Rarámuri as corn.

I volunteered with delight on his wood-chopping expeditions. Compared to the other times with Bernabé, when we simply drove our axes into the trunks of the old pines until our hands bled and our brute strength willed the timber into submission, this was a cakewalk. Up on the plateau, Chico toppled the trees with his saw while I hoisted the body-long beams onto my shoulders and grunted up the slopes to the truck.

Chico was amused that I sang while we worked. He loved norteño, *musica romantica*, and even the Gulf Coast Playboys' cassette I brought along one day; the cajun and zydeco tunes, driven by the accordion and creaking violins, shared some of the same roots and rhythms of the Mexican polkas. All the songs possessed the same plaintive lyrics of the Celtic and Appalachian reels and ballads: love and betrayal, paeans to hard work and hard drinking. Hard living. Like the ballads in all of these places, the people shared an understanding about the struggle for survival and dignity.

I hadn't done so much physical work in years, not since a summer haying on farms in the Virginia Blue Ridge and deeper into West Virginia's Appalachian range on the New River. As in Appalachia, I dropped into bed exhausted every night. I would spend most of the day wood-cutting with Chico, or loading adobe to build a chicken coop for a women's cooperative, or fixing walls and fences or fields with Bernabé, or carting lumber and beams for new cabins. My role as a volunteer pack mule and farmhand deepened my connection to the villagers.

After working on the railroad and the Gran Vision highway through the Sierra Madre, Chico forsook the wiles of the Mexican slums and returned to work his wife's land in Mawichi. His acceptance in the community had been tenuous. Raised in another Rarámuri community on the other side of Copper Canyon, which had acculturated to mestizo ways of life, he could not speak his native language. Some considered him a chabochi. This linguistic conflict was shared by a number of spouses in the community. Many brides and grooms in Mawichi opted for partners outside the perimeters of their dialect. Considered part of the Uto-Aztecan family, the Rarámuri language has fissured into half a dozen variants among its eighty thousand speakers. In effect, Rarámuri speakers from opposite sides of Copper Canyon would have great difficulty understanding each other. This was not insurmountable; we met several couples who had learned the language variants of their spouses, as well as Spanish. But many had not.

Armed with his saw and truck, two rare possessions among the locals, Chico supported his family as a woodcutter. He also tended a small plot of corn and beans. His wife, Anna, ran a small shop out of their house and cultivated one of the few vegetable gardens in the village, which were supported by a Canadian aid organization.

"Come here," Chico called me one day. He noticed the evening before that I had used newspaper and fine wood chips for kindling to start the fire in our calenton. Kneeling by a trunk that had been severed by lightning, he brushed off the cinders to reveal reddish-brown heartwood. He took out his knife, cut out a stick the size of dynamite, and then told me to sniff it. It had a sappy, oleaginous texture that exuded a perfumed smell of oil.

"Use this to start your fire," he said. "It's ocote."

The word had originated from the Nahuatl of the Aztecs; the *ocote* pine could be found throughout the Central American isthmus. When lit with a match, ocote sticks sparkle, and the oils burn long enough to inflame the rest of the logs.

We arrived late from the mesa that afternoon, stinking like people who lived with animals and dirt floors, bathed weekly in limited cold water, and soured like spoiled fruit in work clothes. There was no such thing as staying clean in the natural world. The tesguinada that evening had been thrown for the beginning of a religious holiday, and it coincided with a collaborative work project in the fields.

We climbed up the hollow to the cabin, a wood structure with more holes than seals, where women pulled yarn from lamb's wool and made tamales while their babies peered out, attached to the backs or breasts. The men were out in the fields repairing the stone fences that snaked around the furrows and canyons like Hadrian's Wall. Perched on the side of a ridge, the cabin afforded a breathtaking view of the creek, where women slap-washed their clothes and children bathed beside the plots of corn that had been forged from the slopes and floodplain of the valley. Chico and I then delivered a truckload of wood.

Drinking breaks occurred with precision. The singular gourd was dipped into the plastic barrel and passed on; I serve you, you serve him, on and on. No sipping. No wiping the saliva. By the time I arrived there was a crust of culture on the rim of the gourd that kissed back like a layer of dried sap.

A calm air of repose and satisfaction lingered around the cabin. The drinking here, like at most of the tesguinadas we attended, was not chaotic or full of despair, but tempered by the collective pleasure in working and being together. It functioned as a reward, not a habit. The laborious weeklong process of making tesguino, as well as the investment of valued corn, negated any casual drinking at home. No one in the village ever produced tesguino for private, solitary consumption. In fact, the tesguinadas, in my experience, generated the most productive times in the village. Chico said they were the only way to accomplish most tasks.

"People prefer to work for tesguino, not money," he told me.

It wasn't quite dusk. *Tonari*, or plain goat meat, boiled below on the ledge of the canyon, watched over by children, who threw amused and veteran smiles at their quietly besotted parents. The kids tossed rocks at the goats and sheep to get them into the corrals for the evening.

Chico moved me along the line of men, sanding our fingers in greeting, and then he introduced me to the village *hombre-mujer*. The man-woman had surrendered his masculinity and social role for women's clothes and tasks; he had been accepted by the community in this new role. The hombre-mujer, an aged man who lacked teeth but not timidity, smiled and held out his hands to dance. Everyone egged him on. There was no malice in their teasing.

Three men were inside the cabin, playing the high-pitched drums, which had been stretched with goat skins and tuned with a piece of cord like a snare drum.

After making the rounds for a couple of hours, Chico and I, picking up Carla and Anna, took off for another tesguinada in a nearby hollow, the ever-ready *alla*. This was one of two directions for everything and everyone in this village—either *alla* or *abajo*, over there or down there. Anna and Carla were quiet. As we walked away, Carla quietly mentioned in English that Anna had just found out, on a rare visit to a nurse at the clinic, that a doctor in Creel inserted an IUD-like birth control device into her without informing her eight years ago. She considered herself lucky. Numerous indigenous women were still sterilized without their knowledge by doctors in the Mexican towns. Anna had two kids before the incident.

There was a sober resignation about her, the same resignation that had forced her to look for work in outside mestizo communities only to realize that the sacrifice and parsimony of living among her family in Mawichi, without electricity or plumbing or consumer goods, was more favorable than dwelling in poverty amid Mexican want.

The issue of disparity bewildered younger Rarámuri like Chico and Anna. They had seen what modern Mexico had to offer and they were beguiled by its charms. They spoke Spanish, listened to Mexican music, drank beer, and longed for electricity and a TV crowded with *telenovelas* from the urban world of Mexico City. Their place in that mestizo world, however, was not as Rarámuri; they became chabochis in their mind. Sometimes, when they returned from a day in the Mexican town of Creel, they said they felt like strangers in their own homeland.

Rosa, another woman at the tesguinada, had mentioned a similar dilemma of assimilation. Members of her family had weathered the slums of Chihuahua and Ciudad Juárez. One of her sons was actually working as a laborer in Los Angeles without a passport or work permit. Their goals were the same: they all longed to return to the Mother Range one day. No one had left willingly.

"It's one thing to be without things here, where everyone is dirt poor," Rosa said, while her husband handed me a gourd of tesguino. "But it's another thing when you are so poor in a world surrounded by so much food and things and people with money. You are not only poor. You are miserable."

Our friend Alfredo Vea, when he visited us in Mawichi, recognized this conflict. In his novel *La Maravilla* he had raised this concept of acquired poverty through the young narrator's Yaqui grandfather in their Arizona community:

> To say his family was poor would be accurate enough but not really true. In Spanish *pobre* would be true but, in his mind, not very accurate. In Yaqui to be *kia polove* is to be without desire for "things." There is no concept of "poor" for a noncomparative, communal society. A Yaqui is only poor when he deals with the whites or the Mexi-

cans. When he is forced to pay taxes on land he has always lived on or when the laws of Arizona require that he buy a tombstone, then he is poor. Then he must reach outside his language for the word.

When Carla and I had visited Rosa's cabin earlier that week, I noticed that Rosa's husband and two boys were slaughtering one of their few sheep. They had run out of corn. Rosa had no idea how they were going to manage during the months of hunger.

She had smiled, looking around at her younger kids in the corner of the cabin.

"We'll manage. We always have. At least we are here, among our family, our land, and our people."

They were not going to leave Mawichi and enter the stream of Mexican migrant workers. Being Mexican called for the surrendering of the Rarámuri identity and their separate history to the whims of those who had colonized their land and vilified their culture as backward.

Chico and Anna and Rosa, perhaps even the hombre-mujer, despite their preoccupations about their own futures in Mawichi, were not ready to surrender being indigenous.

After one religious ceremony, while most villagers were trickling to their neighbors for tesguinadas, Carla and I joined a group of young Rarámuri friends at a cookout on the other side of the Gran Vision road. Our expedition was curious. We packed up our Bronco, leaving behind the quiet and lovely confines of our canyon, and drove out of the village and down the paved road for about fifteen minutes. Following our friends, we pulled off the road and parked at the concrete ruins that had once housed the road service brigades, as if we were Mexican tourists passing through the area.

Javier, the leader of our group, waved us in. He had come by our cabin earlier that day and announced they were having a *convivio*, invoking the phrase of Dante and his call for a gathering. Javier was a happy-go-lucky man in his mid-to-late thirties, and one of the few Rarámuri I met who reveled among the Mexicans and tourists in a jocular fashion. He worked at the Muki Sekara shop and as a carpenter in the village.

"This road was one of my first paid jobs," Javier told me, pointing at the Gran Vision.

The ruins of the road service brigades were littered with beer cans and broken glass. Plastic bags and toilet paper wrapped into the bushes at the foot of the pines. While Javier scurried to set up a fire pit for the cookout, the rest of us lounged under the towering pine trees and listened to *norteño* tunes blasting from the boom box.

Javier had grown up in an *amestizado* Rarámuri village and then moved to Mawichi when he married one of the local women. He did not speak much Rarámuri. Like the men in this group, he dressed in the Mexican attire of jeans, boots, T-shirts, and baseball caps; the women wore T-shirts, pants and baggy clothing, and tennis shoes. They danced to musica romantica and norteño and drank beer. A plastic bottle of tesguino sat to the side like a reminder of what was transpiring in the other canyons.

If the Rarámuri were symbolists, then the Gran Vision that traversed the Sierra Madre was the symbol of our times and our modern longing for treasure. But how "grand" or encompassing was that vision? Along with the railroad, it had mounted the final penetration into a remote culture that had largely determined its own contact with the outside world. It had distorted the old concepts of geography; the "other side" was arriving on the doorsteps of the Rarámuri now, whether they sought it or not.

Legions of tourists emerged from buses out of Creel. Lumber trucks stacked six high with virgin forest pine passed the traffic of narcotraficantes, who played cat and mouse with the military battalions. Coca-Cola trucks were as common as Virgins of Guadalupe. Rarámuri hitchhikers, who had adopted the English word "ride," lined the roadsides like aspen among the pine.

"It used to take an entire day to walk to Creel," Javier told me, sitting back against a pine. We could make it now in twenty minutes or so. "It took days to get to Guachochi." That town on the other side of the sierra could be reached in three hours.

Less than ten years old, the Gran Vision had made inroads with apostolic zeal. It paved the way to schools, clinics and pharmaceutical remedies, and outside labor opportunities. It had also carried in the rest of the world with the backwash from commercial trends. I made notes of the imports and cultural changes, from the baroque-era Jesuit-introduced Spanish language, plows, axes, missions, and domesticated animals, to the contemporary Mexican polyester shirts and pants, porno comic books and sombreros, ranchera music cassettes, boots, coffee, tequila and beer, and toilet paper, to today's American basketball, Chicago Bulls ball caps, gas-powered saws, Maruchan instant soup, candy, packaged cookies, cans of sardines and even corn, batteries and boom boxes, high-top sneakers and bras—and the pervasive spirit of Coca-Cola. I was always in a hurry to point out the abrupt revisions in Rarámuri life: what they had lost.

At times, Carla and I became exasperated with this obsession; we also recognized our hypocrisy. Unable to get over that hump of aversion to the worst of American and Mexican imports in the face of a battered indigenous culture, we were the first in the village to install a solar panel, pull on our socks and leather shoes and down jackets, and climb into our Bronco to purchase Mexican items in Creel. We saw the convenience in plastic containers over ceramic pots and ollas. The issue, of course, wasn't maintaining the drudgery of poverty in any culture; my mother, who had grown up without electricity or running water in the hollows of southern Illinois, had often reminded me of the bane and exacting toll of such an existence.

On this picnic, this particular cadre of friends represented a very small but growing elite of young Spanish-speaking Rarámuri villagers who functioned as cultural brokers. While still on the margins of typical village life, they were becoming increasingly involved in the trends and decision making in Mawichi. Unlike most of their peers, they had attended middle school in the mestizo towns or villages. The majority of village kids today still dropped out of school after the third grade.

As Carla found in her research, these Spanish-speaking Rarámuri viewed Mexican education for their children as a way to climb the Mexican socioeconomic ladder in the wage system, while most other Rarámuri parents considered their children's brief experience at the school as a way of equipping themselves with the skills needed to defend their families and community from outside exploitation.

This bicultural quandary underscored Carla's research in the school. It forced her to examine whether the progressive-sounding bilingual-bicultural government education policies had dragged "education out of its native elements," as Rabindranath Tagore had warned under British-occupied India, or connected with the community. In truth, courses using the Rarámuri language were held only in the first two grades, as a transitional program into Spanish. Tagore had denounced a similar policy in colonial India: "The regime of our mother-tongue is confined alone to elementary education: in other words, it is worthy of an infant education, that is, the vast concourse of a people who have no opportunity of learning any other tongue must forever be treated as infants concerning their right to education."

I wondered whether, despite their well-meaning intentions, were the schools ultimately introducing a Mexican curriculum and modern way of life that disengaged the village children from their native language, customs, diet, material culture, music, rituals, and agriculture? Could such a school foster cross-fertilization of the cultures?

This *convivio* (signifying a "sharing" in Spanish), however, startled another concept in my mind: the colonization of a culture, like an individual, was never one-sided. These few Rarámuri might have jumped aboard foreign vehicles on the paved road of conquest, but they had not cast off their own grand vision or Rarámuri values. Nor had they stopped transforming the Sierra Madre, and the incoming Mexicans, in the process.

Javier's use of Dante's phrase was telling; despite the dominance of another culture, we were all bringing something to the convivio, the banquet. The presence of that untouched bottle of tesguino, as if it were an icon as holy as the Virgin of Guadalupe, was noteworthy.

This gathering compelled me to consider my own family and ancestors and country, and the often-ignored backside of colonization: what *we* had lost in the process of conquest, or rather, what we had exchanged with Native America and transformed into our own immigrant American culture. I thought of our so-called Old World cuisine: tomatoes, green beans, potatoes, squash, tobacco, cotton, and so many other products that originated from the native people of Mexico and the Americas. We tended to forget that the corn we grew—those spikes of wild teosinte plants that had mutated into the first ears of maize—was a Native American gift that had generated a midwestern and southern culture of its own in the United States. Corn had defined and transformed the early American immigrant experience, and it had spawned the making of the great American heartland of my ancestors.

And then what? The collapse of the family farm in the Midwest or my own southern Illinois, the quintessential symbol of the American heartland, marked the rise and fall of a subculture in such a tragically short historical period. It wasn't a matter of changing: these rural cultures, like that of my mother's family, were gone. Only a tiny remnant remained. The average American farmer today is sixty years old. As their offspring, we had all fled for the cities and suburbs, assuming an urban culture and language with ease.

What could I bring to the convivio from my grandparent's land-based culture? Or better yet, what could I bring to the convivio from my ancestors' Scotland? The answers to those questions, as for most people in my generation, were hauntingly empty.

Javier and his cohorts, on the other hand, may have embraced some Mexican habits, but they had made the ultimate decision to spurn the Mexican towns and return to their native homeland and Rarámuri social structures.

"Why would I want to live in a town, with people on top of each other?" Javier told me. "Here, we all have our own fields. We have our families."

In the end, these amestizado Rarámuri had refused the fundamental doctrine of the Spanish policies and modern Mexican society: reduction, or centralization into urban clusters, dependent on wages, paid utilities, and mechanized services. They still maintained their isolated and scattered ranchos and their corn culture and rituals. They may have changed their dress, even their language and choice of beverage, but the rhythm of this indigenous life and its cycles, unlike our own, remained largely the same.

The Rarámuri were not the only dwellers in the Sierra Madre region struggling with the viability of their agricultural traditions and religious beliefs. No one understood the question of loss and transience better than the Mennonites, a hermetic religious community that had roamed across the earth in search of Mexico's valleys.

When we returned to the border once to renew our visa permit for the Bronco, I was amazed to see a Mennonite man in the waiting line at the Mexican customs station in northern Chihuahua. I recognized him. I had met Franz earlier that year in Creel, where he sold yogurt, cheese, butter, and salami out of the back of his truck on Saturdays. With stalks of blond hair tucked under his soiled Chicago Bulls ball cap, clad in cowboy boots, tight jeans, and a buttoned plaid shirt, the forty-something Mennonite cut a towering and unmistakable presence in the line of Mexican travelers and American tourists.

We smiled, nodded our recognition of the moment, and moved on.

On our way back to the Sierra Madre, Carla and I took the western road, passing through the red desert plains, arriving an hour later in the agricultural communities around Cuahtemoc. The downtown streets and shops were packed with blond Mennonite families. While older men sported overalls, young men had switched over to the western look of Mexican cowboys. The black-brimmed hats of the old days were mostly gone; many wore American ball caps. The women, however, remained in their traditional homespun dresses and heavy black shoes.

"By remaining agricultural and isolated," Franz had told me before in Creel, "the most conservative Mennonites think they can keep their old traditions."

His words resounded as an eerie parallel with the Rarámuri. Those old traditions included the Old Colonists' belief in their calling, or *berufung*, as "tillers of the soil."

Franz's people originated from Flemish Mennonite congregations that had moved to Danzig and western Prussia. They established a colony in southern Russia in the eighteenth century. From there the strict religious community continued east in the late nineteenth century, seeking land and autonomy in the Manitoba province of Canada. At odds with both the Canadian government and a breakaway sect, which had sought to modernize, a large portion of the Old Colony Mennonites headed south.

When the Mennonites arrived in 1922 in thirty-six chartered trains, Chihuahua was still reeling from the bloody end of the revolution; Pancho Villa was gunned down in Parral one year later. Signing an agreement that exempted them from paying taxes and taking part in military service and allowed them to educate their own children, the Mennonites turned the valley into the breadbasket of the region. Over forty thousand Mennonites now lived on thriving orchards, dairy, oat, and corn farms. Their presence in Cuahtemoc was remarkable.

"Mennonite cheese, Mennonite yogurt," screamed a Mexican vendor in the open market.

Carla and I headed straight for the stalls to buy our reserve of cheese and some bulk foods. With the best agricultural equipment and irrigation systems in the region, the Mennonites had traded in their horses and buggies for Ford trucks and John Deere tractors. Given their high-tech acumen, some of their farms felt more like Illinois than Chihuahua. Only a tiny holdout of the Old Colonists remained on horse and buggy.

We drove down the back warrens of the numbered campos for a visit, where pioneer homes with wooden porches and shade trees had been carved into perfect plots. Our welcome at the Mennonite farm was professional. Hustled into a home by a German-speaking host, we found ourselves sitting at a long bunkhouse table with a few other wide-eyed travelers. Steps echoed across the clapboard floors. Young women in plain homemade dresses, their hair wrapped in dark scarves, stomped into the room with the savvy of truck stop waitresses, passing out plates of biscuits, cheese, salami, jam, and butter. A smaller girl filled our glasses with coffee and lingered by one woman visitor, clearly enthralled by her ornate silver earrings. The child's mother then appeared at the door and motioned for her to leave.

A slight sense of trepidation hung in the air. While the Mennonites had hooked into the ecotourist market, it didn't appear that they cared to expose their children to outsiders, as if they shared the Rarámuri's contempt for chabochis.

Another woman entered the room with her embroidery.

"For sale," she repeated in three languages.

When we wandered over to a barn that had been set up as a shop, one father dismissed his two younger boys. With just enough of a Spanish vocabulary to register the cheese and cut and price, an older man packaged our order. The kids eyed us from behind a tractor.

After two generations in Mexico, the Mennonites were going through their own cultural conversion. According to a Mennonite plumber I had met earlier in Creel, who married a Mexican woman and left behind his community, many young men were no longer content to work on the farms or remain in the closed, German-speaking settlements.

"I wanted to go to the dances," he said.

We left the Mennonite farm and headed back up the road to the mountains. The remnants of northern Europeans dotted our route. We passed plots of land formerly held by the American tycoon William Randolph Hearst, and then the San Pedro hacienda, which remained mired in Nazi lore about notorious German conspiracies during the Second World War; a portrait of the Fürher still allegedly hung in one of the chambers. American hysteria over Germans in Mexico dated back to the First World War. The intercepted "Zimmerman telegram" in 1917, which had been sent from Germany to Mexico, proposed an alliance between the two countries—Mexico was to receive Texas, Arizona, and New Mexico, after an invasion of the United States—was supposedly one of the issues that prompted President Woodrow Wilson to declare war. For the Second World War, some historians claimed Nazi general Erwin Rommel studied the military strategies of General Pancho Villa, who had eluded General John Pershing's American army, in which George Patton served.

We finally climbed the winding Gran Vision road, arriving a couple of hours later in the town of Creel. It had changed in recent days. A new restaurant was being added alongside more shops and hotels-in-progress. Three-wheeler off-road vehicles, topped with tourists, raced down the main drag. Tourist buses from the States were parked on the sides of the plaza. Groups of American tourists roamed the streets for souvenirs.

Then we spotted Franz's truck at a nearby hotel. He had arrived before us, just in time to catch the Friday night dance at a hotel discotheque.

One of our visitors from the other side terrified most of the village. Erik Bitsui, who had worked with me in Flagstaff, was a twenty-something member of the Dinetah, or Navajo Nation. Towering over the smaller Rarámuri, sporting a waist-long pony-tail—most Rarámuri men preferred short bowl-topped haircuts and bangs—Erik trudged around the back trails and along the mission walls in black boots, black jeans, and a black heavy metal concert T-shirt (usually Metallica, though I once spotted Ozzy Osborne). The Navajo guitar player joked that his long hair was not really a matter of adhering to his Dine roots but a gesture to his heavy-metal idols. The Metallica and Megadeath T-shirts in the Rarámuri community shocked him; I was amused that the evangelical American church groups that distributed the secondhand clothing had Satan-worshipping head-bangers among their members.

Most of the villagers weren't aware of the Navajo, the only indigenous group larger than themselves in the western United States–northern Mexico region. But their ancestors had first-hand experience with the Apache, and given that the Navajo and Apache share distant Athapaskan origins and languages from Canada and the Arctic, we simplified matters and told everyone in advance that an Apache friend from the States was coming to town.

That reference didn't particularly extricate a gush of excitement. The last Apache raid in the Sierra Madre occurred within the lifetime of some of the elders. Erik's heavy metal appearance, however, struck a chord of fear and silence.

"He looks like one of the narcos in the movies," one young man whispered to me.

"He looks like one of the drug agents in the movies," another countered.

When we did *la marcha* through the community gathering on Sunday (author Luis Rodriguez was with us as well), entering the mission plaza, where the elders congregated for mass, rounding the chain of women in rebozos along the mission walls and passing the stands of watchers and children around the basketball court, I felt like we were walking the runway at a modeling show for the next narcotraficante film. I could hear some catcalling and giggling from Chico and the other young men at the ball court.

Erik wasn't pleased with his Apache appellation. He became aggravated when he heard my introduction, in Spanish, "Apache" being the only word he recognized.

"I'm not Apache, dude," he would pipe up.

The cat was already out of the bag. I continued to introduce Erik as an Apache just to see the reaction. El Mudo shook his head and walked away. Alfonzo inspected Erik, sized up his youth, and then grinned and walked away. One older man came up to me and asked if he could "shake the hand of the Apache leader." Erik, who had perfected the Rarámuri greeting, sliding the pads of his fingers across the hand of the other person, was surprised by the man's muscular grip. The older man sauntered away in a contented fashion, as if he had faced down death and won.

We took Erik and Luis to what were referred to as the Apache ruins. One day, some of our closer friends, Tomas the police commissioner and his wife Jorgina, escorted our party to his traditional homeland in Tejaban, on the rim of Copper Canyon. Tomas had taken up my habit of introducing Erik as an Apache, which impressed his extended family members, who cast Erik wary but knowing grins. Within minutes, they led us to the pre-Columbian ruins that dotted the caves and canyons in the area. The villagers proudly announced they were Apache cave dwellings or forts and encouraged Erik to enter the ruins of his ancestors. Erik posed agreeably for photos. As Lumholtz observed a hundred years before, most of the ruins probably dated back to other indigenous cultures around the 1300s. More than likely, the confusion over the settlement of the ruins has been a result of both the power of the contemporary Apache legends to weave themselves into any landmark befitting a fugitive, and the far chance of a brief occupancy by roaming bands of Apaches in the late nineteenth century.

The journey among the Rarámuri affected Erik; it was part of his own pilgrimage for an understanding of an indigenous past. This was his first trip to Mexico and among indigenous populations outside of the States. He saw some loose parallels in the community organization and rituals; Erik had herded flocks of sheep and goats as a kid. "It smells like the rez," he said, repeatedly. The lifestyle in Mawichi reminded him of the images in his grandmother's stories. The stone metate and mano in front of our house, regularly used by our neighbors, were the same as those in the Four Corners area. His own community, while not mountain dwellers, farmed corn at higher altitudes, wove their own blankets from wool (sheep having been introduced by the Spanish), and fashioned clay pots. As a participant in peyote rituals at home, Erik was intrigued and probably disappointed by the lack of peyote use among the Rarámuri in the highlands. On the most intimate occasions he would reveal a sack of corn pollen that accompanied him as a source of power on all of his journeys. He obtained a sack of pinole and a chapareke to take back to the States.

But not all the locals were star-struck by Erik's appearance. Taking Erik and Luis on a short jaunt near our cabin in Mawichi one day, we descended from a hillside trail and straggled onto the dirt road that was used by the loggers. Coming in the opposite direction was a young Rarámuri couple. Both were carrying tequila bottles in one hand, their other arms wrapped around each other's waist. This was the first display of romantic affection among villagers that I had ever seen in public, outside of the drunken tesguinadas, where physical contact was both accepted and rampant. The three of us passed grins; we were impressed by the license of the couple in their early twenties.

Breaking their revelry, the couple had a completely different view of us. We must have looked like three alarming giants: a tall blond Viking, a tall Apache with hair to his belt buckle, and a robust mestizo in a baseball cap. Lumholtz actually recorded a Rarámuri legend that dealt with giants near Mawichi. "They were as big as pine-trees and had heads as big as bowlders [sic] . . . the giants were fierce, and ravished the women while the latter were under the influence of the moon." The Rarámuri made a lethal concoction of corn and bits of *chilicote* tree and the giants died.

The young couple had another idea. Within twenty feet of us, they stopped and set their bottles on the ground. I slowed our pace for some odd reason. I watched the young man pull back his shirt and reveal a revolver. He braced himself, as if readying for a duel. Choreographed by his inebriation, the young man swaggered with the exaggeration of a roguish gunfighter in a Mexican action film.

Luis, as a one-time veteran gang-banger from East Los Angeles, stood quietly in place and watched the man. I raised my hands, as if it was a hold-up, and started naming all the neighbors and fields where I had worked in the vicinity. I was not sure what I intended to achieve, other than keeping that gun from shooting a hole through me. Erik gazed around, as if admiring the various pines and birds.

"Pasale," the young man finally said, waving his hand.

We passed to the side of the couple, who scowled at us, and continued walking down the road. I had never seen either of them before.

Luis never said a word, maintaining his pensive expression as we continued down the road. I looked over my shoulder. The couple had rejoined their cuddling and moved away. Erik appeared positively relaxed.

"Sure is sweet to see such a romantic couple these days," Erik finally offered.

Not all indigenous peoples shared common ground in the Sierra Madre, of course. When the first Spanish friar entered the Sierra Madre in the 1600s, he sought to play the role of mediator between the warring Rarámuri and Tepehuane tribes. The extent of the Apache connection to the Rarámuri and the Sierra Madre remains one of the great mysteries today. Barney Burns has spent a couple of decades in this arena, roaming the canyons as an archaeological sleuth. For another researcher, Neil Goodwin, this pursuit paralleled his own quest for his father.

On a rainy November day in New York in 1962, Neil Goodwin was handed an old leather-bound diary from a box of field notes collected by his father, an eminent ethnographer of the Western Apaches. Goodwin's father had died from a brain tumor when Neil was an infant. The diary chronicled Grenville Goodwin's extraordinary journey, three decades earlier, in the Sierra Madre in search of an elusive band of Chiricahua Apaches that was still raiding Mexican ranches. Riveted by the diary, which included an incredible collection of photos, drawings, newspaper clippings, and the first important writings on the material culture of the renegade Apaches, Neil Goodwin, a trained architect and filmmaker, launched a lifelong dream and headed to the Sierra Madre in his father's footsteps in 1976.

For the next twenty-five years, making a number of short and longer forays into some of the most inaccessible canyons, Goodwin traced his father's footsteps, using the diary as his road map to both the Sierra Madre Apaches and the life journey of a father he never knew. The parallel journeys of the two men resulted in *The Apache Diaries: A Father-Son Journey*, a northern Sierra Madre chronicle that spanned over half a century.

Goodwin's main guide and companion was Barney Burns. The two of them, joined by members of Goodwin's family and various other friends, combed the northern tier of the Sierra Madre like historical missionaries. They dealt with hostile narcotraficantes who were active in the region, traipsed into steep canyons, turned over rocks and brush for the slightest clues, and interviewed relatives of Mexican victims and bounty hunters in the same villages where Neil's father had trod years before. The ruins Grenville Goodwin found in the 1930s, which Neil and Barney rediscovered in the 1980s, were not merely the fleeting scraps of a few rebels. As the material culture and settlement patterns of the last truly autarkic Apaches, they possessed the remains of the final unmitigated attempt by Native Americans to remain free. In that sense, the ruins—and the fresh leads noted by Grenville in the 1930s—stored centuries of history.

When we departed from Tucson for our journey to the Sierra Madre, crossing the border through Agua Prieta and skirting the Mormon settlements around Casas Grandes, our road paralleled a western corridor that bands of the Apaches had used for centuries. A slight murmuring lingers even today among some historians that offspring of the elusive Athapaskan-speaking groups still reside in the Mother Range.

No other tribe in the States has been so romanticized and maligned as the Apaches. However, few tribes have consisted of such a disparate and varying array of small bands. While the official "Apache Wars" took place in the American West from 1861 to 1886, the first recorded skirmishes with the designated "Apaches" date back to Spanish reports in the early seventeenth century. Related linguistically to the Navajo and other Athapaskan tribes in Canada and around the Arctic, the Apaches were generally considered to have drifted south in waves of immigration, only to splinter into three main branches in the American West. The Western Apache branch, according to anthropologist Edward Spicer, author of *Cycles of Conquest*, still one of the paramount textbooks on indigenous groups in the Southwest today, is divided into several subgroups, as well. These smaller groups have divided into even more variegated bands, which experienced extremely different histories with other indigenous tribes in the regions, along with the Spanish, Mexican, and then American immigrants and soldiers.

Several bands of two Western subgroups, the Chiricahua and Mimbreno Apaches, maintained vigorous raiding patterns for over two hundred years. Most likely wedged between the hostilities of the Comanches on the Great Plains and the encroaching but still sparse Spanish frontier mining and ranching settlements scattered around Sonora and Chihuahua, these Apaches did not seek to conquer a shifting swath of territory, but dedicated themselves to plundering the settlements of others. They shared the Bedouin's mantra: "Raids are our agriculture." They assumed with stunning acumen one of the most precious gifts from the Europeans: horses. The Spanish finally recognized the roving demands of the Apaches and initiated a settlement of sorts; by 1800, doling out rations and goods, the Spanish nearly brought an end to the raids in the region.

Two decades later, however, the independence of Mexico fractured any stability and source of funds in the north, unleashing a renewal of bloody conflicts and counterattacks between the Apaches and the Mexican settlers and other indigenous tribes. Within years, the Mexicans declared a war of extermination in Sonora and Chihuahua. Novelist Cormac McCarthy put his imagination to the test in his novel *Blood Meridian*, painting a horrific portrait of the scalp hunters and their clashes with the Apaches in the 1850s. The scalp hunters, paid as much as a whopping $100 per head, were eventually banished after the trade turned into an indiscriminate slaughter of anyone (including other Mexicans) with "Indian" hair. Lumholtz noted: "But this law (which put a price on the head of every Apache) had soon to be repealed, as the Mexicans, eager to get the reward, took to killing the peaceful Tarahumares, whose scalps, of course, could not be distinguished from those of the Apaches."

Even so, R. F. Grigsby, an American mining prospector who first seized on the California gold rush, wrote in his Sierra Madre diary in 1864, "The Apache Indians in this country hold the Mexicans in perfect terror." In the late 1880s, Frederick Schwatka noted the graves of a Mexican couple killed by Apaches deep in the Sierra Madre at Guigochic.

The American experience was not faring much better. While the Apache originally distinguished the Americans as allies against their common enemy in Mexico, disputes over dubious treaties or land settlements spiraled into a pattern of warfare. In 1861, the same year the Civil War ignited on the South Carolina coast, a blunder by a cavalry lieutenant unleashed a twenty-five-year battle in the American West. Seeking to rescue a Mexican captive by taking Cochise, the legendary Chiricahua leader, and a few Apaches hostage, the soldier murdered them all, except for Cochise, who later launched his own revenge. During the Confederacy's short tenure of control over a part of Arizona territory in 1862, the appointed Confederate governor of Arizona, John Baylor, even made the proposal of exterminating all Apache men and enslaving the women and children. The Confederates fled back to Texas several months later.

The Apaches used the Sierra Madre as both a refuge and a launching pad for raids. By 1875, however, efforts gained toward establishing reservations in Arizona and New Mexico. Victorio, one of the leaders of the Mimbreno bands, signed a peace treaty in 1877, vowing to settle in New Mexico. The boundaries of the land, however, shifted within a couple of years, as American settlers and mining prospectors funneled into the territory. Refusing to relocate to the arid lands at the San Carlos Reservation in Arizona, Victorio led members of the Mimbrenos on another flight across the border.

One of the leaders in the pursuit of Victorio was Lieutenant Henry Flipper, the future Sierra Madre mining engineer and the only black officer to ever lead the Buffalo Soldiers. Seeking to alert the cavalry of Victorio's whereabouts, Flipper made a daring ride of ninety-eight miles in twenty-two nonstop hours, which led to a critical showdown at Eagle Springs on the New Mexico border in 1880. Joining the Mexican forces of Colonel Joaquin Terrazas, the Buffalo Soldiers and other cavalry troops pursued the Apaches to the foothills of the Sierra Madre. A few months later, injured by two Rarámuri scouts (recorded as "Mauricio" and "Rogue"), Victorio and most of his band were gunned down by Terrazas' forces at Tres Castillos, in another area of Chihuahua.

They all didn't die. One Apache survivor, an alleged septuagenarian named Nana, eluded the Mexicans and eventually rejoined Geronimo and his band of Chiricahua Apaches. By the early 1880s, life on the San Carlos Reservation in Arizona had become untenable for most Apaches. Mormon settlers had diverted part of the Gila River, affecting irrigation; mining and ranching interests encroached uninhibitedly into the region; corruption among Indian agents had become so blatant and ruthless that several commissioners were removed by the federal government in Washington. The Apaches were also not allowed to ferment and make their own homemade beer.

Geronimo, one of several important Apache military and spiritual leaders, fled in 1881 from the San Carlos Reservation after another cavalry blunder and massacre at Cibecue, in Arizona. The American soldiers murdered an Apache medicine man during a gathering, setting off a succession of rebellions and raids. According to historian Dan Thrapp, over five hundred Apaches departed and took refuge in various Sierra Madre canyons.

Geronimo's fate, and that of his followers, has been documented by scores of books and films. Thousands of American troops, including the Buffalo Soldiers, hounded Geronimo and his small band, which most likely dwindled to no more than thirty-five armed soldiers and a hundred women and children, for the next five years. General George Crook, who was somewhat more sympathetic to the Apaches, led the first campaign and raised the effective "Apache scout" brigades to chase their own tribesmen. After failing to keep Geronimo to his word, Crook resigned and was followed by a more unsavory character, General Nelson Miles, who demanded the surrender of the Apaches at any cost.

The path of the cavalry through the Sierra matched any of the feats and daring of the first Jesuits or mining prospectors. Detailing a trip in 1883, cavalry captain John Bourke wrote, "The trail from this on was, if anything, more dreadful that it had been yesterday . . . To look at this country is grand; to travel in it, is Hell."

Geronimo surrendered in 1884, fled again, and then finally surrendered in 1886 to a small brigade of soldiers and Apache scouts under the command of Lieutenant Charles Gatewood, who had served with the Confederates during the Civil War. The Chiricahua leader never returned to the West or even to the San Carlos Reservation in Arizona. Shipped off to a Florida prison with his followers, along with some of the Apache scouts who had hunted him down, Geronimo died at Fort Sill, Oklahoma, in 1909.

This was the aching question for Grenville Goodwin in 1930: What Apaches remained in the Sierra Madre? In 1902, Lumholtz claimed that Apaches were constantly breaking away from the reservation in Arizona. Once, he noted, "we came upon fresh tracks near one of our camps, and also upon small bunches of yucca leaves tied together in a peculiar way known to the Mexicans as signs intelligible only to the Apaches."

Nino Cochise, the self-proclaimed grandson of Cochise, wrote in his lively memoir, *The First Hundred Years of Nino Cochise: The Untold Story of an Apache Chief,* that as many as three hundred Apache, Opata, and Rarámuri renegades were maintaining a rather stable life at Pa-Gotzin-Kay (translated as "Stronghold Mountain in Paradise") in the early twentieth century. Few historians gave any credence to Nino's tale. But the memoir provided an imaginative view into what life could have been like for the renegades.

Grenville, who came from an affluent Connecticut family, was born in 1907 and had been sent to Arizona as a young man to recover from tuberculosis. The spell was cast; deeply in love with the Southwest, he returned after completing his studies in the East in 1927. He took various jobs and rambled among the Navajo and Apache reservations, until he decided to pursue a degree in archaeology at the University of Arizona in Tucson. Among the White Mountain Apaches in Arizona, where he did some of the most important ethnological work in the region, he was eventually known as Indaa yalti'i, "the talking white man." Still in his freshman year in 1930, Grenville couldn't be contained in the class-room. He had followed the blistering headlines, like Americans around the country, of the infamous case of the Fimbres Expedition.

In 1927, Francisco Fimbres and his family were ambushed during their journey from Nacori Chico to Pinos Altos, in the Sierra Madre. The attackers were mostly Apache women. They slit the throat of Fimbres' wife and then absconded with Geraldo, the three-year-old son, before Fimbres managed to react. According to some historians, the ambush was in retaliation for an attack and kidnapping by the Mexicans on an Apache band, which had been rustling cattle. A twelve-year-old Apache girl, who was given the name of Lupe, had been captured and brought back to live with a family related to the Fimbres.

Kidnapping had been an established mode of cultural exchange among the Apaches and the Mexicans. A fair-haired Charlie McComas, kidnapped by the Apaches at the age of six in 1883, generated a popular legend of a blond Apache war leader among the Sierra Madre Apaches. The Americans also participated in this brutal policy; in 1871, a posse of Tucsonans and allied tribes, misled over the origins of a band of raiders, attacked and massacred a peaceful settlement of Apaches at Camp Grant, killing more than seventy-seven women and children—most of the men were away—and then reportedly sold twenty-nine of the children into slavery. From 1927 to 1929, Fimbres mounted a local posse to hunt down his child and the Apaches in the Sierra Madre, who were reported to number no more than forty adults and children. The Fimbres case headlined newspapers around the world. Many of those stories were reprints from a several-month-long campaign of sensational stories by the *Douglas Daily Dispatch*, the main newspaper in the borderlands, in an attempt to draw attention to the region.

No other group was more mindful of the Fimbres incident than the Chamber of Commerce in Douglas, Arizona. Reeling from the stock market crash in 1929, which had waylaid the copper smelting industry in the border town, a cadre of local entrepreneurs saw Fimbres and his Apache expeditions as a potential source of creative tourist revenue for the ailing town. They formed the Fimbres Apache Expedition, printed stationery, elected a board of directors among themselves, and sent out letters to "Gentlemen Clubs" and newspapers around the States, inviting them to participate in the manhunt. They even announced the formation of an "Aviation Division." According to their stationery, the posse was to be a volunteer militia under the Mexican Army. The cost of the trip for volunteers was not cheap. Every applicant had to send in a $50 deposit, and then pay a fee of $7 for equipment and supplies.

Not everyone was amused by the expedition. Hearst's *New York Journal* mocked the plan: "Anybody with a good moral character, a taste for adventure and more than $200 in cash can join the Expeditionary forces. It's an idea that does credit to the business sense of its promoters. Getting shot for $200 is a bargain that ought to appeal to many who spend more than that now getting half shot."

The tenor of the Fimbres Apache Expedition was nothing less than a ditty to seduce wealthy adventurers, "hungry for excitement," for a big-game hunt. One applicant wrote, "I have hunted big game in many parts of America, but I am sure shooting at an Apache Indian would give me a greater thrill than any I have heretofore shot at." By the spring of 1930, over 160 applicants had reportedly sent in their deposits.

The governments on both sides of the border finally stepped into the fray. The recently arrived American consul in Agua Prieta, which bordered Douglas, wrote a stinging memo to the Secretary of State in March 1930. He excoriated the expedition for having nothing to do with the rescue of the Fimbres child: "The purposes of the expedition are to secure publicity for the City of Douglas and vicinity, to interest persons of wealth in the mining claims of Moroni Finn [sic] and probably, to secure an excellent financial return to the promoters of the project." Within a month, federal government officials in Mexico City also called the expedition into question, formally denying the armed group an entry permit into Mexico. Though the expedition leaders tried to scramble and organize an alternative "hunting and fishing party" into the Sierra Madre, all plans were eventually called off. The deposits were returned to the applicants.

Despite all of the international publicity about the expedition, Fimbres never gave up his pursuit of the Apaches. In fact, in less than a month after the cancellation of the infamous expedition, he tracked down and killed three Apaches, including "Apache Juan," one of the most wanted Apache renegades in the region. A photo of Fimbres and his posse holding the scalps of the Apaches appeared in newspapers around the world. It also brought an end to the search for Fimbres' son. As reported by Neil Goodwin, two other Mexicans came across the three Apaches' bodies that Fimbres had gunned down and left to rot. The Apaches were now buried in three tidy graves. Goodwin wrote, "They also find the lifeless body of young Geraldo dressed like an Apache: leather moccasins, a little knife, leather clothing. It is alleged in various reports that, in an orgy of Apache bestiality, Geraldo has been hung, crushed with stones, crucified, starved, mutilated, nearly beheaded, and then buried alive."

Obsessed with the last Apaches, Fimbres continued to haunt the Sierra Madre for years. He didn't hunt all of the Apaches down, though.

In 1932, a rancher near Nacori Chico stumbled onto a small Apache settlement, killed one woman, and captured a small child. That girl, given the name Carmela, was eventually handed over to an American couple, raised in Los Angeles, and became a nurse. In 1972, she and her American husband moved to the medieval Umbrian city of Perugia, Italy, only a few miles away from Carla's ancestral home of Spoleto, where she died in an accident in her mid-forties.

Part III

A Devilish Sort of Thing

Alfonzo was standing by the cemetery rock wall, weeping with a crowd of men who had been drinking and grieving for the past forty-eight hours. They carried their sombreros or ball caps in their hands; their hair had been molded into capricious shapes.

"Pancho," he said, motioning at the banjo strapped on my shoulder. His hand raised in a vaguely Italian gesture of pronouncement. "We need to talk." Alfonzo's face unhinged. He couldn't finish his sentence. He began weeping.

"*Country*, Pancho, *country*," demanded Cornelio, a stocky older man who lived near our cabin. He was clearly the person most affected by country music in the Sierra Madre. He once heard a song by Johnny Cash during a rare visit to Chihuahua City. The English word "country" had remained with him ever since. After a long drinking bout, he would often pound on our door at dawn and call out, "Country, country, Pancho, get out here and play some country." I would see him the following day; he would nod, I would nod, but neither of us would utter a word, as if we hardly knew each other.

A young village woman had died in Chihuahua City giving birth. She was working as a maid to a Mexican family, a common job for young Rarámuri women. Her husband had found day jobs making adobe bricks. They lived in one of the shantytowns, or *colonias*, on the outskirts of the dusty city, which was now only a four-hour bus ride from Creel, a nearby mountain town in the Sierra Madre.

Without a priest, the locals had prodded a visiting Mexican carpenter into service, who changed into his good pants and clean shirt, and then offered some verses of solace and led the chants of the rosary at the mission. After two days of viewing in the home of the mother-in-law, the burial took place in the graveyard, referred to as the pantheon.

Following a narrow trail along the cornfields, I cut behind the mission walls and slowly made for the log cabin on the other side of the hollow. Sweeps of pines and towering canyon walls served as borders for fields of corn.

I had never been to a round-the-clock home viewing before. A brigade of kids and ragged dogs met my entrance at the dirt clearing around the cabin. A collection of corncobs littered the grounds, like the corncobs and mounds found at twelfth-century Anasazi sites. Several older men, including Alfonzo, El Chapareke, and Bernabé, were chatting outside. A few others sat quietly on benches made of split logs. I was greeted with the Rarámuri handshake and waved inside.

Despite the blaring um-pah-pah of norteño music on a boom box in the corner, an air of regret hovered inside the sparse mourning room. Women huddled around the coffin in the emptied chamber. The variance in their dresses struck me; on one side sat those in home-stitched colorful skirts and matching tops and scarves, wearing huaraches, and on the other side sat women in polyester skirts, blouses, and plastic shoes. All the women were portly figures.

I spent a few minutes staring at the young woman. Her death was a horrible reminder of modernity's price for this community. Many Rarámuri women made up one of the last indigenous groups in the world that still delivered their babies on their own, sometimes in the forests. One friend once saw a woman cut the umbilical cord of her child with a piece of broken glass. The girl in the coffin had actually gone to the hospital in Chihuahua City for her delivery. I made my peace and departed.

The funeral, Bernabé told me outside the cabin, would also be a festive occasion. They were celebrating with the dead, inviting them to escort the departed soul away with them. Due to the fact that it took at least a week to prepare tesguino, tequila had broken through the dike of tradition and poured forth.

"After the funeral, the dead can leave us in peace," Bernabé said. "Go away and not bother us."

The Rarámuri concept of immortality was so strong, Lumholtz wrote, "that death means to them only a change of form." According to William Merrill, an anthropologist who spent three years in a remote village for his groundbreaking study, *Rarámuri Souls,* "People must overcome their feelings of sadness as soon as possible after the death of a loved one because if one's souls are sad, they will want to leave the body to be with the deceased."

The service at the mission lingered for hours. It appeared as if the village couldn't bear to part with the young woman. When it started to drizzle, everyone hovered by the towering wood doors, as if they had received a slight reprieve.

About halfway through the service, I entered the mission, took off my hat, and chose a spot on the men's side of the sanctuary. I spotted Carla sitting in a quilt of women on the right. The Mexican carpenter was finishing the rosary. Haggard and long faces rejoined in groans. The fiddler and guitar players slumped in the one pew to the side of the altar, barely able to pull themselves together to play a pascol song at the carpenter's urging. The young woman's husband, a close cousin of the guitar player, wept by his side.

Then I caught Cornelio's eye. Or rather, he picked up on my appearance in the mission. A grin rippled across his crooked face and propelled him from his kneeling stance.

"Pancho," he screamed. "Country, country, we need some country."

I tried to flee, but it was too late. Cornelio snagged my arm, chiding me for leaving my banjo at the cabin.

"Get it," he shouted.

I felt like running away. Instead I saw the guitar player who waved me on.

By the time I returned, the distraught villagers flanked the procession led by the carpenter, the desperate young husband clutching a blaring boom box. A band of guitar players, a fiddler, and soon my banjo straggled along, attempting to play a ranchera love song. Splashing through puddles, we swept the mission plaza with our shuffle and marched around the cornfields and then slowly made it across the arroyo. The procession reached the cemetery rock walls, with the carpenter and sober adults and children in front, fracturing into multiple ceremonies.

We marched up and down the graveyard, which had more tequila bottles than headstones. Some of the bereaved stumbled onto graves and even fell atop the coffin when we arrived at the young woman's burial ground. We received our cue to crank up the tunes. Martin, the lead guitar player, nodded for me to follow. We didn't manage to play more than a couple of cumbias, all out of tune, the dazed husband singing verses from other songs, still clutching at his boom box.

There was more than one burial ritual taking place. An elder called out orders in Rarámuri while the coffin was being prepared. The Mexican carpenter and several others continued to recite prayers and the rosary in Spanish. The fiesta for the dead spirits bantered around the edge of the crowd in laughter and song.

While the elder intoned a speech, family members opened the coffin one more time. Two women wailed and clutched the body, while a younger cousin stuffed in additional clothes, a bottle of Coke, and a package of cookies. The coffin had already been stockpiled with specific portions of corn, beans, and tortillas.

An aunt suddenly collapsed, overcome by the booze, a sleepless night on a bus from Ciudad Juárez, and the tragedy of the death. A few turned and watched her crumple onto the ground. Within a short time, a couple of teachers from the local boarding school were fanning her, holding her legs in the air.

The elder then led family members in a circular ritual procession, sprinkling drops of *esquiate*, a roasted corn mixture, Coke, and bottled fruit juices on the coffin and themselves, in order to satisfy death and ward off evil spirits. As the coffin was finally lowered, children pitched four handfuls of mud onto the grave.

After a moment of silence, people veered off to the rock walls, supporting each other's stumbles. I wandered toward Alfonzo and Cornelio and a couple of other men. They all possessed weary looks of sorrow and deprivation. They passed around an unmarked bottle.

"I'm happy you are with us in these moments," Alfonzo said.

"One more song," Cornelio bellowed.

I smiled and kept the banjo slung on my back. Alfonzo raised his hand again as if to make a pronouncement. "We Rarámuri," he said, "have a hard life." He couldn't hold back the tears. His voice had long since broken, his lower lip quivering. "I have been on the other side," he said, "but we Rarámuri . . ." He unraveled, weeping, as another man comforted him, offering him the bottle.

I stood quietly, watching him, trying to understand what he wanted to say. His allusion to "the other side," I assumed, referred to the United States. Within a couple of minutes, Alfonzo tried again to speak, but he was too upset, and shook his head and walked away.

Cornelio staggered over and leaned against my shoulder for support, grinning his riddled grin, and quietly said, "Pancho, we're all leaving for the other side one day."

The funeral was a telling example of the syncretic nature of religious worshipping in Mawichi. Many rituals and acts of "traditional" culture, in fact, were adaptations of seventeenth- and eighteenth-century Jesuit policies, from the plows, axes, livestock, and citrus to the Christian missions, icons, and celebrations. The Rarámuri, of course, hadn't received these imports from Europe in their wholesale versions. They had transfigured European beliefs and protocol into their own soil and liturgy, especially during the "period of the forgotten," when the Jesuits were expelled from Mexico for over 130 years (1767–1900). This was especially evident during Semana Santa, Holy Week.

After living in the village for a few months, I came to view today's Jesuits as the righteous bulwark against a recent onslaught of religious crusaders. My first experience with them occurred in the town of Creel. Padre Luis Verplancken, the septuagenarian head of the Jesuit missions in the Sierra Madre, took me up on an offer once, after I had casually mentioned my willingness to volunteer on his projects.

After forty years of service, the central-Mexico-born Verplancken was a legend in the Sierra Madre. Facing an astounding eighty percent infant mortality rate among the Rarámuri, Verplancken had established the first clinic in the 1960s. He followed with the construction of the Santa Teresita Hospital (also known as the Tarahumara Children's Hospital) in the town of Creel, which provided virtually free services to any indigenous person in need. Over the past decades, the Jesuit priest had founded schools, village revitalization projects, and well digging campaigns; provided and distributed corn and aid during drought and famine; and served as one of the main defenders of Rarámuri land rights. His mission shop, which sold Rarámuri-made goods, had fostered the birth of a handicraft industry among the villages. As a fluent speaker of Rarámuri, Verplancken also led or participated in religious rituals and masses. A noted photographer, he exhibited and published his photos around the world.

Carla and I admired Padre Verplancken. He was a self-effacing, warm figure who exuded a matter-of-fact awareness about the realities facing indigenous people in the Sierra Madre. He had served as a conduit and mentor for more than one generation of researchers, educators, doctors, and service providers in the region. His office was a revolving door of action, whether it was on behalf of the Jesuits or not; his archives were not hoarded with suspicion, as we had found in other academic and religious centers.

I noticed most that the Jesuit priest never appeared daunted or romantic about his work. As a defender of indigenous land and cultural rights, his work over the decades had ruffled the intentions of unscrupulous mestizo land developers. This, in turn, had generated its own mill of gossip about the Jesuit's motives and lifestyles. These rumors hadn't been confined to the canyons of the Sierra Madre; a prominent American journalist, for example, feeling snubbed that Verplancken had failed to find time for an interview, floated a few of these rumors—a supposed fleet of brand new SUVs for personal use—in his own dispatches from the region.

Padre Verplancken was not a radical activist in the mode of Central American Jesuits like former Sandinista Foreign Minister Miguel D'Escoto and Cultural Minister Ernesto Cardenal in Nicaragua. He was a humble workhorse in the trenches. He seemed driven by a compelling spirit of service and accomplishment that had turned him into an expert on indigenous cultures, respiratory diseases, and water pump repair, bushwhacking trails into the most remote areas to deliver aid to famine-stricken populations and restoring lime-based adobe walls or religious works of art.

"For us it is difficult to understand this culture because we need definitions and concepts," he told me during our first meeting. "For a Tarahumara, or Rarámuri, as they call themselves, myth is life and doesn't need any explanation. It is a daily way of life which recreates the world. We need to respect them, not preserve their culture as a museum piece."

The padre came knocking on our door one night. I ended up spending the next day, until 3 A.M., editing and narrating his video in English in his Jesuit office in Creel, which he planned to use on a charity tour through the States. He said the first video had been narrated years ago by the voice of "The Lone Ranger." I don't know if he was referring to the actor Clayton Moore, but I soon found myself reading into the microphone with a deeper baritone, "The first Jesuit missionaries came to the Tarahumara lands four hundred years ago. The Rarámuri adopted certain expressions of this new culture, such as the dance of the Matachines. With the expulsion of the Jesuits from the lands of the Spanish Crown, the Rarámuri had 133 years to mesh their culture with that which they had learned from the missionaries. They Christianized their rituals, filling our expressions with symbols; now they are the ones who evangelize us."

Since Jesuit Padre Juan Fonte's first penetration of the Rarámuri lands in 1607, evangelicals of numerous persuasions had haunted the Sierra Madre with the fervency of gold miners. An extraordinary amalgam of Jesuits and Franciscans had served in the Mother Range, including Germans, Austrians, Hungarians, Bohemians, Moravians, Croats, Sicilians, Sardinians and Neapolitans, Lombards, Irish, Flems, and Catalans; one of the last Jesuit priests expelled from the Sierra in 1767 was a Pole.

The difference now, of course, was that the soul seekers were not only Catholics. The Jesuits, representing the intelligentsia and more enlightened branch of the modern Catholic church, stood far apart from the myriad Protestant evangelical sects that had flooded into the Sierra Madre over the past couple of decades. Unlike all other missionaries, they had become the defenders of the Rarámuri's more controversial traditions, including the drinking of tesguino.

The Jesuits' religious rapport with the Rarámuri, however, was being challenged. No matter where we ventured into the Mother Range, including some of the most inaccessible canyons on earth, Carla and I stumbled onto more missionaries than we had met in our entire lives. And every single one of them was on a mission to cull the living treasures of the Sierra Madre: Rarámuri souls.

The remote stretches of the Sierra Madre and its dark unknown conjured an element of the macabre about Rarámuri for many outsiders. Padre Andrés Pérez de Ribas wrote in his travel memoir in 1644, "As I traveled their limitless cordilleras, and descended into their deep gorges I marveled that even savages could penetrate here . . . I reflected that the Devil must have deliberately led these people into such hiding places, think to thus possess them securely."

Over 350 years later, that same view endured with a new wave of missionaries. The Rarámuri were the very souls that needed to be saved from their devilish worshiping.

The view was never-ending from the ridge, cascading in dark hues of gorges and kelly-trimmed clusters of pines. I had hiked to a couple of ranchos on the rim of a side canyon that drained into the Copper Canyon. A solitary hut sat on the edge of the plateau, surrounded by the remains of a cornfield. As usual, a brilliant blue capped the sky, a reminder of the long months of drought. There was this feeling, like in so many places in the Sierra Madre, that I had reached the ends of the earth.

When I returned to the top of the bluff near the village, where a trail had been carved into the stone face of the cliff like a ladder, I hesitated for a few minutes. In the village below, which was tucked into a rock canyon basin like so many other settlements, a couple of Americans were chasing the village mutts. The dogs were having the time of their lives; I imagined they had never been granted so much attention. When one of the Americans caught up with a little puppy, jamming a needle into its neck, you could hear the cries from three side canyons away. The rest of the dogs vanished, followed by head-scratching Americans, as if they had been betrayed by the Philistines.

Wary of those needles, I made my way down the trail and into the village. Carla had been interviewing teachers at the local school. I found her inside the school lunchroom, along with a gaggle of more Americans. The mess hall was a simple structure, lined with a few tables and benches. There was no screaming this time; a child sat in a wobbly chair in complete silence as an American missionary dentist in a bloody frock towered above her, tugging at one of her molars with his dental pliers. He ripped out the tooth with a final grunt. Blood abounded. The doctor looked confident but agitated. He stroked the girl's hair and back to calm her, unaware that he was initiating the first touch from a man in this conservative culture, however sincere and tame, in her entire life. Carla sat to the side, patting the young girl's hand. "Ask her if she's got any other teeth that hurt," the doctor commanded to Carla. The young girl held her hand to her mouth. Her round eyes widened in horror.

The missionaries had arrived in the village, armed with Bibles and their volunteer doctors and veterinarians. No one in their group spoke Spanish or Rarámuri fluently; none of the doctors or nurses knew either of the languages. The man I saw from the plateau, a lanky veterinarian from Texas, swaggered into the lunchroom carrying his needle as if it were a pistol. "Got two more," he said. "Mangy looking things." The young girl rose and quietly brushed by him, leaving the building.

These missionaries from a Protestant sect in Texas and Oklahoma had set up their own encampment in a nearby Mexican town, where they hosted summer camps for American volunteers who wanted to spread the Word and serve in Mexico.

The list of evangelicals, both Mexican and foreign, was endless in the Sierra Madre. The Rarámuri ranked at the top of a Faustian nightmare list composed by one international organization intent on converting every non-Christian in the new millennium. As one missionary told me, "You know, these Indians don't have any God of their own, so it's up to us to save their lives. Otherwise, we'll leave them behind to the devil's work."

The new missionaries were an agitated lot. So many of those we met, outside of the Jesuits, possessed a nervous dissatisfaction and highly charged stress levels that were absent among the Rarámuri. In comparison to the calm, sanguine, and spiritually assured indigenous folks, the evangelicals were almost comical in their gung-ho approach.

Yet I felt a queasy sense of intimacy among evangelicals in the Sierra Madre. First, there was the family question; along with my ancestor Stephen Stilley's legacy as the first Baptist missionary among the indigenous populations in southern Illinois, my father and my uncle had been Methodist ministers in the Midwest. One of my father's closest friends died on a mission in the Congo. I even had one dear cousin in the Methodist seminary, contemplating a summer mission into Mexico.

The Sierra Madre was also a small world. The handful of long-term foreigners and gringos crossed paths often enough that Carla and I had befriended many Protestant missionaries. There were the usual exigencies of favors and exchange. We attended a Christmas celebration at the home of one missionary, swigging punch and singing carols. I didn't find these evangelicals to be insincere. In fact, it was their unquestionable fervency to spread what they considered to be the truth that concerned me.

I have one other religious confession to make, which I was reminded of every evening: the solar panel. When I first shopped around for solar panels in Tucson, prior to our departure, I had been shocked by the costs; the panel, battery, and cables went far over our budget. We debated throwing our laptops to the wind. I eyed my old Royal typewriter for a long time. Then I spoke with a Sierra Madre–based missionary who also resided in Tucson. He gave me the name of a nonprofit religious organization in Tucson that provided solar panels to missionaries around the world. They had a catchy motto: *Using God's sun, for God's son.* I called their office.

"I'm en route to the Sierra Madre," I said, "and I'd like to discuss the possibility of purchasing a solar panel from your group."

"Do you take Jesus Christ as your Lord and Savior?" the man responded.

There was a rather long pause on my end.

"Excuse me?" I said, trying to buy time.

"Do you take Jesus Christ as your Lord and Savior?" the man responded.

"Is that a requirement?" I asked.

"Sure is," he said.

I didn't know how to respond. My religious tendencies had fractured over the years. But I wanted that cheap solar panel. Another awkward moment of silence.

"Well?" he said.

"Sure," I mumbled.

"Good, you can come by and pick up your equipment in the morning."

Every time I flicked on the power switch or encountered a missionary, I expected some sort of reckoning.

One Protestant Texan doctor in Creel, who roamed alone to the most remote locations in his truck, once told me, "First I heal their bodies, and then I heal their souls." In the town of Samichique, we encountered a group of born-again Amish from Ohio. Despite their traditional homemade dresses and cultural mores and German dialect, they no longer considered themselves Amish, who they categorized as morally corrupt and sexual deviants. "They're into cocaine, having premarital sex, and making money," one young born-again told me, as he and his friends played cards and listened to a cassette of an animated evangelical preacher. They were building a Protestant-funded hospital to serve the Rarámuri in the canyons that had no Mexican clinics or access to health care.

While the missionaries now were often the prime providers of health care services, especially the Jesuits and their well-established Tarahumara Children's Hospital in Creel, their early history and contact marked a troubling reality of disease and death for indigenous peoples.

Numerous diseases related to contact with people from Spain and Europe devastated indigenous people. Lacking both the immunity and the knowledge to combat such new diseases, entire communities in the Sierra were wiped out over a three-hundred-year period. Many of the diseases preceded the physical invasion of the Spanish. Padre Juan Fonte, a Catalan and the first Jesuit to enter the Rarámuri lowlands in 1607, recorded baptizing a child dying from smallpox. "How wonderful are these chances God provides for the salvation of souls," Fonte wrote in his report. He baptized the infected child "with great pleasure, for the child was on the point of expiring."

The disease lingered for decades. Thirty years later, in his report on missionaries among the Rarámuri, Padre Andrés Pérez de Ribas noted that "smallpox carries off countless children and adults." After the hanging of an indigenous leader in 1652, Padre Jose Pascual wrote, "Meanwhile, those who surrendered suffered the punishment from heaven; such a severe plague (most likely smallpox) fell upon them that in many rancherias not a single living person remained."

The plagues returned with every encroachment of the Spanish settlers or where the Rarámuri had the most contact with the evangelizing priests. In 1723, Jesuit Joseph Neumann, a Brussels-born Austrian priest who served at missions in the Sierra Madre for over fifty years, wrote a historical memoir of the region. He found that

> in the year 1695, a pestilence attacked this nation, and ravaged most of the villages which had been won to the Christian faith. A great many deaths ensued, and in particular it was the younger men and girls and the children who succumbed to the disease. That is to say, those who perished were the very flower of these new Christian settlements . . . Indeed, we were warranted in believing that from among this nation many souls were transported to Heaven through the agency of the pestilence, and that God ordained it thus in order to save these souls from the evils which were to follow.

Around that same period, Jesuit Padre Juan Fernández de Abee recorded that "here at Carichic all such aids are lacking and 259 died in the great epidemic. It looked as though the whole pueblo, left in its natural state, would be decimated for lack of medicines."

One of the most devastating outbreaks related to the "Spanish Flu" epidemic in 1918. When anthropologists Wendell Bennett and Robert Zingg ventured into the Sierra Madre in 1930 and started their fieldwork among the Rarámuri, the era of the epidemic "was still remembered vividly. The Indians died like flies, and whole families were exterminated."

Known as "the grip," borrowed from the Spanish *la gripe*, the 1918 epidemic was also heralded as the "Spanish Lady" for its supposed origins in Spain. (These origins were never conclusively demonstrated.) Speculation resulted from the first reported cases at army barracks among soldiers returning from service in Europe during the war. The impact of the flu, nonetheless, swept like fire across the Americas and the rest of the world. On an international level, according to Gina Kolata, author of *Flu: The Story of the Great Influenza Pandemic of 1918 and the Search for the Virus That Caused It*, it was the worst infectious disease epidemic in recorded history. As many as forty million people may have died; the epidemic nearly annihilated the Eskimos in Alaska.

According to one report in 1918, the best way to avoid the disease was to "stay away from crowds, outsiders and unknown foreigners." This made me think of the Rarámuri, who have been relentlessly described by missionaries, travelers, and even contemporary tour guides as inordinately shy and aloof of chabochis. After learning their history with European and American diseases, I realized they were wise to heed the admonition of the report.

For the Rarámuri, however, the cavalcade of evangelicals functioned as an assembly line for goods and services. One younger man in Mawichi told me, "When the Jehovah Witness come, I say I'm a Witness so I can get their clothes. There is a group called 'The Family,' from the other side, who bring good basketball shoes. I joined them, too. The best groups bring food, but they make you go to a lot of meetings first."

Bernabé surprised me one evening when he strolled by our cabin, sporting a large pair of fashionable women's glasses. Going from village to village in a truck, a Protestant sect had been distributing used and donated eyeglasses throughout the region.

"I think I can see better," Bernabé said, blinking his eyes. "But they're a little strong."

I never saw him wear the glasses again.

A young Jesuit padre, assigned to deliver the Sunday mass at Mawichi for a short period, seemed amused by the other religious groups.

"I know what's happening," he told me one Sunday. "One man once insisted on having the mass later that day, so they could collect some donations from a Protestant group. And then, with their gifts in hand, they came back to the mission for mass."

The little kids found me by the woodpile. I was resting on some logs, next to the pen for the fighting cock, a lean, muscular fowl that had no headdress. I had just returned from chopping trees on the mesa.

"They're making Judas now," Noreida shouted, followed by her younger brother and another tiny friend. The girls were dressed in homemade skirts. The boy was clad in a cast-off T-shirt.

"They're making Judas," she repeated, "and he looks like you."

The drums had been sounding since *candelaria*; high-pitched tenor beats on goatskins had bounced off the canyon walls of our village every night for two months in preparation for Holy Week. Over the past three centuries, Semana Santa has functioned as one of the most elaborate ceremonies. Lumholtz claimed that "such ceremonies were a clever device of the Jesuits and Franciscan missionaries to wean the Indians from their native feasts." For me, this was a rare misstatement by the great ethnographer. I wondered if the ceremonies, especially the role of Judas, had become a clever device to wean the missionaries from their Christian charge.

My first interaction with the Holy Week activities came during my narration of the Jesuit video. In the words of the priest, I read this script, watching the images of a film roll through a ceremony: "During the Holy Week, the Rarámuri form two groups, the Soldiers who represent Good, and the Pharisees, who represent Evil. The Pharisees paint their bodies in representation of the white man, in whose history he has always tried to impose himself on the Rarámuri way of living. The Pharisees and the Soldiers dance throughout the holy days making circles, coming and going, representing the Rarámuri life, waiting for the triumph of Good, knowing that one day it will come because they are the children of God."

I was anxious to see the transfiguration of those concepts around the mission plaza. There was excitement in the air. Little boys scurried around with their wooden swords and tiny drums. The cooking, corn beer making, and preparing of arches and other rituals had taken place over the week. A slight drizzle broke free and chilled the morning air. The roosters had lost their time clocks, dogs barked at the hairy pigs; the road to the mission filled with women and children wrapped in rebozos and men clutching sombreros in their hands as if they were sacred.

Around the mission grounds stood twelve huge *arcos*, or arches, constructed from pine saplings and decorated with sotol wreaths. Three crosses rested at the base of each arch.

An elder launched the procession in the morning, cleaning the evil spirits from the premises with his rattle. Over twenty-five drummers on each side followed the elder. There were fathers and sons, trailed by stumbling little children and then the village dogs, who were always excited to join any affair. The procession moved swiftly, hurrying from the mission steps, back through the arcos, and around the mission plaza.

The marchers then split into two groups, the Soldiers and Pharisees. A man in shades and a long white trench coat directed their movements. Four of their leaders sported turkey-feathered headdresses. Four men with bows, one man carrying a staff, led the Soldiers, with two lines of drummers, and a gaggle of young boys dragging wooden swords.

At one stopping point, the elders addressed the gathering and gave sermons in Rarámuri, holding the staff as they spoke in an extemporaneous fashion that resonated more like a chant, a fury of words in a single, enduring breath.

And then they were off again, the Pharisees carrying white flags, the Soldiers carrying red flags. A handful of Mexican tourists darted to the sides, looking on with longing cameras, as if to capture the same rituals that had been handed over and replanted in the conquest.

Padre Verplancken was upbeat at the morning mass. He had only requested that the community refrain from drinking until after the festivities. After years of service, he realized that huge ollas of tesguino corn beer were simmering back at the cabins and caves. This ceremony stirred its own mixed brew of the spring planting rituals, the resurrection of the corn and the Christian God's son.

The padre worked the packed mission. It was a simple temple of adobe and plaster, the trim of the walls lined with cubic designs, with a painting of the Virgin of Guadalupe above the altar. There were no pews; women plopped to the right in mounds on the floor of wood beams, while men stood on the left. A severe-looking man with a cane smashed dogs huddled among the women and children. The Soldiers stood erect with their wooden swords in the front as a woman knelt with the incense, and a solitary reed flute player sounded a haunting scat in a hidden corner. On cue, the scratching violins and guitar creaked into a song.

The priest nodded at the crowd and their modern dress; ball caps had replaced sombreros, which replaced headbands; boots and high-tops had replaced tire-soled and leather-hide huaraches; pants had erased the traditional breechcloth. Even the dress of Semana Santa had changed. The Pharisees had put only a smudge of white paint on their cheeks, instead of painting their entire bodies as in the past. "The dress may change," the padre said, "but the rhythm and the ritual stay the same."

I made notes. What we will never lose:

- babies crying in the most sacred moments in the church
- the power of the lame to inspire humanity
- the severity of men with sticks and guns
- the proximity of children to women
- dogs trying to enter churches or homes, despite knowing they will be beaten
- the hunger for faith in a higher authority
- the smell of sickness
- the need of boys to bam, bam

- the desire to drink and get drunk
- deformities and injuries, the village dwarf and mute
- the will of little girls to take care of smaller siblings
- the giddiness of standing in front of your peers in a confused
  silence
- those who will watch others from afar in bewilderment and
  envy
- the need to kill and resurrect

The procession continued all day. The Pharisees and Soldiers took turns leading the marchers through the arches, reciting the rosary. The Rarámuri dropped to their knees in the mud, while the Mexican and foreign tourists pretended to crouch in order to remain clean. The drums never stopped.

By nightfall, fires riddled the canyon walls like fallen remnants of Mars. These were the cliff dwellings of neighboring visitors who had walked for miles to the village. The solitary flute player stayed in the mission all night, playing notes more than songs, playing to a different history, while two Pharisees, faces painted white, remained on guard at the mission entrance. Two bayonet-wielding Soldiers guarded the altar.

The drumming never ceased during the night, sending the rain across the sky in waves of stars. The drums were not exuberant, nor did they goad fear or war or brawn, but pounded in a monotonous reminder of the heart, the continuation of Rarámuri life, with the endurance of long-distance runners. Along the mission plaza walls, women and children slept around bonfires.

On Friday morning, the blue sky of the Sierra Madre returned. The wind still howled, whipping caps from men, who ran after their sombreros.

Soldiers suddenly descended from the canyon walls. Their large drum skins cascaded like boulders to the village, merging back into the procession of a growing crowd of locals and tourists. The presence of so many outsiders made me feel awkward for the first time in ages. Despite my chats and greetings with friends and marchers, I realized I had no role to play, other than that of any foreign observer; I was simply a chabochi now. I stood and watched like the rest of the tourists.

We walked the stations of the cross in the afternoon, taking the via crucis up the canyon trail, led by two lines of drummers. The elders headed the march, clad in modern wraps and old stares, occasionally calling out and teaching the ritual steps to the young. At each stage in

the cross, the priest read in Rarámuri, retelling the story of the crucifixion. The drummers marched everyone up the canyon trail and then fell
silent for a moment at the final station on the forest mesa overlooking
the village. Everyone bowed their heads. Suddenly the drummers hammered a rhythm as the leaders reenacted the crucifixion with a haunting
fatalism and ease. People watched as the drums pounded, as if this final
act will always happen and the people will always watch in accord. After
the crucifixion, the wooden Jesus was removed from the cross, lowered
to the ground, and people lined up and prayed and kissed the statue's
feet as the drummers circled with a mourning tempo.

Even more bonfires blazed around the canyons that night. We
watched the waterless shell of a moon. The drizzle had been only a teasing reminder of the severe drought that year. The procession continued
all night without a nod of sleep, as marchers hustled to keep warm. Little boys dragged their wooden swords and drums to keep up the pace.

By dawn on Saturday, the Pharisees were already parading a hoisted
Judas and his wife. The tesguino drinking had been launched. Soldiers
and Pharisees made pit stops at designated cabins hosting plastic barrels
of the brew. Judas, with huge genitalia, was dressed like a mestizo, with
a beard, sombrero, and modern clothes; his wife and baby also wore
Mexican clothes. Noreida was right: he looked like me.

The drumming intensified as the Soldiers continued to make peri-
odic stops for tesguino. Altering an old tradition, the Soldiers and Pharisees agreed not to engage in the usual wrestling match among their
cadres. With little fanfare, the Pharisees peacefully surrendered Judas
and his wife at one of the arcos. The Soldiers seized the stuffed figures
and paraded victoriously, celebrating the procession through the arcos,
as an air of excitement grew. The drums increased in tempo. The volume rose. The pace quickened. The drummers started to run.

The Soldiers dragged Judas and his wife below to the arroyo, where
they beat and mocked them, entertaining the large crowd of villagers
and tourists, which now covered the hills. The Soldiers then raced the
stuffed figures to a nearby cabin for one last drink. When they returned
to the arroyo, the leaders stood up the Judas figure and his wife. Across
the arroyo, Soldiers raised their bows and prepared for the execution.
The stuffed figures fell down, as if drunk themselves. With great exaggeration, the Soldiers attempted to shoot their bows, which were symbolic relics, the arrows falling only a few feet away. The crowd chastised
the Soldiers, who tried again and fell even shorter, bringing on more
laughter.

The Soldiers then erupted, attacking Judas and his wife, performing for the crowd. The drums pounded as others ripped the straw stuffing, tore the clothes, broke off the wooden heads and arms, and tossed the shoes and clothes to the ground. The crowd roared as the Soldiers hauled remnants of the figures up the hill and across the cornfields, where the remains of Judas and his wife were set on fire.

An air of triumph riveted the village like never before. The dehumanizing captions of indigenous survival, such as the murals of the noble savages on hotel walls in the tourist strip of nearby Creel or the daily dismissals of the Rarámuri by the mestizos, faded amid that exuberance. The Rarámuri moved as if they had been resurrected by the act of execution.

For the first time since our arrival, I felt like my presence was at odds with the Rarámuri. I hadn't been offered any tesguino, nor did I believe my place was at the drinking clusters. I hadn't been asked to play my banjo. Whether or not I wanted to accept it, I represented the culture of Judas. I scattered to the side with the tourists.

Everyone returned to the mission, where the padre admonished the wobbling parishioners to go the way of Jesus. "Do not become a Judas to the community." Later he explained to us: "Judas is the symbol of Evil and symbolizes the oppressor, the exploiter, and the greedy. During Holy Week, Judas dies, symbolically discharging the Tarahumara of all the animosity they feel against the Mexican mestizos who have been exploiting and oppressing them for centuries. With the death of Judas, the harmony in the community is reestablished symbolically with the triumph of Good over Evil."

The drums pounded in accord. The Pharisees, the partisans of Judas, were driven from the church and chased like dogs into the plaza. They laughed and tore down all of the arcos.

Families descended from the mission and drifted into the hollows and cliff dwellings for tesguino parties. The tourists packed up their vans and trucks and left. Carla and I quietly returned to our cabin.

There was an eerie silence the next morning without the drums. Down by the carcass of the abandoned truck, as I ambled to the wood pile, I saw Noreida and her friends. She was playing with the smashed doll that was used as Judas' daughter.

The first non-Catholic group of religious stalwarts to penetrate the Sierra Madre did not actually come as evangelicals, but as refugees. The status of the Mormons, though, had changed remarkably since then.

During a visit to Nuevas Casas Grandes on our journey from Arizona to the Sierra Madre, we had spotted numerous Mormon families shopping on the side streets, dressed in their overalls and straw hats. Their recent history in Chihuahua, however, was not without conflicts of Biblical dimensions. This included the Great Exodus, three times.

Fleeing the fallout from the federal Edmunds-Tucker Act of 1882, which not only prohibited polygamy but mandated a stiff penalty for any infraction, Mormon settlers came into northern Mexico in droves in 1884. Considered one of the "twin relics of barbarism" (slavery was the other), polygamy drew the wrath of an American Congress that wanted to break up the theocratic stronghold and vast land holdings of the Mormons in the West. Forty years before, Mormon founder Joseph Smith had been killed in Carthage, Illinois, which served as the impetus for the great migration to the West in 1846, the same year the Americans invaded Mexico. Brigham Young himself made a tour of Mexico in the 1870s. By 1893, an estimated one thousand Mormons were convicted for unlawful cohabitation or polygamy.

Forever inspired by foreign investors and colonists, Porfirio Diáz embraced the Mormon cause. He announced, "It makes no difference to Mexico whether you drive your horse tandem or four abreast." Much of the land eventually sold to the Mormons—and to many other foreign ventures—was expropriated from smaller ranchers and communities and auctioned off by Diáz and his northern counterparts. The Mormons ended up paying for this noted iniquity within three decades at the hands of Pancho Villa and other northern revolutionaries.

Lumholtz stumbled onto the Mormons in the Sierra Made in 1890. He found that "their life is hard, but they live up to their convictions, though these, in some points, date from a by-gone stage in the development of the human race." As he journeyed around the nearby ancient cliff dwellings, many of which incurred destruction by "some Mormon relic-hunter, who had carried off almost everything removable; he had taken away many of the door lintels and hand-grips, in fact, most of the woodwork, from the houses," Lumholtz heard the Mormons retell their own legends about the arrival of three races in the Americas. "The first landing was made at Guaymas in Sonora, the people being fugitives from the divine wrath that destroyed the Tower of Babel. They were killed."

The Mexico-bound Mormons fared somewhat better than these wandering Nelphites in the Mormon Genesis. They built numerous colonies, two of them aptly named after opposing Mexican leaders Diáz and Juárez, and even founded settlements high into the Sierra Madre.

One upland colony, Chuchuichupa, according to the Mormons, had been taken from the Rarámuri term for "Valley of the Mist." Lumholtz came to a different conclusion. Visiting the Mormon settlement in the lush valley tucked into the wooded canyons of the sierra, noting the plethora of ancient burial caves in the vicinity, he assumed that "the name signifies the place of the dead."

The Mormons didn't die out. They thrived. They were the beneficiaries of the changing land laws under Díaz and the oligarchic governorships of Enrique Creel and Luis Terrazas. (Once, when asked if he came from Chihuahua, Terrazas reportedly answered, "No, Chihuahua comes from me.") According to historian Friedrich Katz, the Mormons controlled most of the important businesses in Casas Grandes, one of the largest towns in the region, around the turn of the century. Along with dominating the lumber and food-processing enterprises, four of the seven flour mills belonged to Mormon entrepreneurs.

With the outbreak of the Mexican Revolution in 1910, the Mormon settlers became alarmed at the rebellions brewing in northern Mexico. Besides Pancho Villa, the vast ranges of Chihuahua and Sonora were the hazing grounds of several rebel and bandit forces, mustered with angry soldiers and volunteers who had been displaced by the devastating land policies over the past thirty years. The Mormons were well armed; they secretly engineered shipments of rifles and ammunition across the border. Numbering as many as four thousand, some members of the colonies even wanted to offer themselves as soldiers on behalf of Díaz's faltering government.

By 1912, isolated and vulnerable in Chihuahua and Sonora, they surrendered to the increasing raids on their ranches, farms, mills, and markets. In exchange for their weapons, over thirteen hundred Mormons boarded the trains or their wagons for the first exodus out of Mexico. They sought refuge in El Paso and smaller towns in New Mexico. Many bade farewell to Mexico and returned to Mormon settlements in Arizona and Utah.

Damage to their communities varied. While Colonia Díaz was sacked and burned to the ground, Colonia Juárez was largely protected by the Mormons' Mexican neighbors. Rebels looted and occupied many of the smaller settlements in the sierra, including Chuchuichupa. Some Mormons trickled back to their farms and ranches over the next two years. The landing of the American Marines off the coast of Veracruz in 1914, reliving the invasion from over a half-century before, along with the chaos of the Mexican Revolution, resulted in the next Mormon exodus.

With Pancho Villa and Emiliano Zapata marching on Mexico City and embroiled in a power struggle with Carranza and Obregon, Chihuahua fell back into the warring fiefdoms of numerous rebel bands.

Once again, increasingly smaller waves of hardy Mormons drifted back to their colonies. Their ranks, however, had diminished. The third exodus, written down in the Mormon chronicles as the "flight of the modern Israelites from Egypt," occurred in 1917, when "Black Jack" Pershing and his American cavalry crossed the border on his fruitless search to capture Villa. The Mormons fled Mexico with Pershing's armed protection.

It didn't spell much of a reprieve for the Rarámuri. The Mormons eventually parted the Rio Grande on the border and came back to the Mother Range, just like the other missionaries, intent on rebuilding their Mexican Zion.

Disaster struck Mawichi's religious center in 1967. The bell tower of "The Five Holy Men" mission collapsed, bringing down over 220 years of history with it. In the rubble of the mission's nave, Padre Verplancken scurried to rescue a collection of dark paintings that had clung on the church walls like forgotten relics of another age.

"The paintings were so dirty, I had no idea what they represented," the Jesuit priest told me one day, during a visit. Even Lumholtz, forever the meticulous chronicler, had overlooked the paintings on his visit to the village in the 1890s. In all probability, they were already too filthy to have been recognized.

Verplancken left the paintings in Creel for safekeeping. He didn't consider investing in their restoration at the time. They didn't seem worth it. But in the early 1970s, the Mawichi community and the priest came together to rebuild the mission and stone bell tower. Impressed by the effort, an American tourist bankrolled the materials. The priest then took the chance to clean the paintings damaged by rain, dust, and bird droppings. It revealed a great mystery, and an incredible discovery, about their origins.

"One report in the 1790s," Verplancken said, "only noted two paintings. I knew Padre Merino rebuilt the mission in 1826. During the reconstruction of the bell tower, we found lime plaster and parts of the original mission."

Inside the mission, he pointed at the name of Padre Felix Merino and the date 1826 engraved in the beams from the towering choir loft.

This particular beam provided the first clue in unraveling the mystery of the paintings.

Verplancken started to research the old archives. He read letters and reports from the eighteenth- and nineteenth-century Jesuits and Franciscans who served in the area. He finally stumbled onto a faint letter from a priest in 1900, who noted "several good oil paintings" hanging on the walls in the mission; an earlier report by a Franciscan in the 1790s only referred to the mission as a small barn.

"They must have been procured in the time of Padre Merino," Verplancken declared.

The Jesuit narrowed their arrival to Merino's tenure at the mission in the 1820s and 30s. Still, he lacked definitive evidence of their origins or even authorship. Verplancken also became absorbed by the puzzle of the paintings and what they represented. Due to limited funds, he eventually hired a traveling artist, who offered to clean the canvases. Unskilled in restoration techniques, the artist painted over several of the portraits, nearly destroying some of the works in the process. But his stumbling techniques paid off; the itinerant painter revealed the signature of the original artist on two paintings. The discovery was startling.

"Miguel Correa in 1713," Verplancken told me, with a large smile. "A well-known Mexican artist, who was the teacher of great colonial painter Miguel Cabrera."

Verplancken withdrew a piece of paper with a matching signature copied from the national archives in Mexico City. He also discovered the untold story of the paintings.

The twelve panels chronicled episodes in the life of the Virgin Mary, from her birth and a visit to her cousin Elizabeth, to Jesus in the temple at the age of twelve. The intense tones and sorrel colors demonstrated an understanding of the Venetian school in the sixteenth century. They reminded me of Artaud's declaration that "it was not in Italy but in Mexico that the pre-Renaissance painters found the blue of their landscapes."

The priest returned the paintings to the walls of the mission in Mawichi in 1973. Two of the paintings were immediately stolen, then left days later on the church doorsteps after an appeal was made to the village. The rescue of the paintings had just begun. Still lacking funds, Verplancken searched for professional restorers. He spread the word to his contacts in Creel, the Sierra Madre, and around Mexico.

At the same time, the classical pianist Romayne Wheeler, an American who lives part of the year in a Rarámuri village, encountered two Czech restorers during one of his concert tours in Prague. Wheeler had heard about Verplancken's dilemma. He beseeched the Czechs for assistance. In 1992, the Czech restorers finally agreed to come to the Sierra Madre. They couldn't believe they had stumbled on this artistic treasure.

"The paintings are jewels of Mexican art from the Baroque period," Professors Jan Coufal and Hubert Cepissak wrote in their first report. "They are master works of extraordinary grace."

Working full-time for three months, the restorers rescued seven of the paintings. Verplancken had to collect the proper chemicals and materials from around Chihuahua. Then, in 1994, the restorers returned to finish the project.

As part of the Correa family, Miguel Correa's paintings did not win the same acclaim as those of his brother or father. But the historical reviews of his work also failed to include the twelve paintings in Mawichi. Their procurement and formidable delivery to the remote Sierra Madre in that epoch remained a secret.

"Here in the Sierra Madre, they must have been forgotten," Verplancken said. "These paintings constitute a truly spectacular series of incomparable historical and artistic value," wrote William Merrill, curator of anthropology at the Smithsonian's National Museum of Natural History, after viewing the collection in 1993.

Concerned with the uncontrollable environmental conditions of the mission and fearing another robbery, Verplancken launched another collaborative effort with villagers of Mawichi during our sojourn. The Museum of Mawichi had been proposed as a showcase for the Correa masterpieces, alongside traditional Rarámuri art and artifacts.

With designs donated by an architect from Ann Bella Associates in Boston, the museum became the first of its kind in northern Mexico. Eschewing cheaper cement, the plans called for using lime and sand plaster, adobe, and stone in order to maintain the historical surroundings of the eighteenth-century mission. The project also provided paid work to community members, such as adobe makers, during a period of drought and economic depression. In the end, the villagers also viewed the museum as a permanent place in the preservation of their own customs.

I watched with interest at the fine line Verplancken and the villagers walked between creating a museum for the paintings, the church history, and the Rarámuri past, and their desire to keep this indigenous culture viable. The concept of a museum was a tricky matter for the villagers and the priest; no one wanted to encapsulate contemporary indigenous ways, as if to freeze the process of transformation. Verplancken's earlier admonition resounded in my mind: we must respect their culture, he had said, not preserve it as a museum piece. At times, this made for a contestable discourse on what artifacts, such as forms of pottery, made up Rarámuri antiquity, and what ancient traditions still lingered as part of a living heritage. Would a vat of tesguino someday end up in the museum as a relic, instead of being a vital component of village life? Would the last chapareke become a museum piece instead of an indispensable instrument?

Mexican author Octavio Paz addressed this paradox in his Nobel Laureate address in 1990: "In Mexico, Spaniards encountered history as well as geography. That history is still alive: it is a present rather than a past. The temples and gods of pre-Columbian Mexico are a pile of ruins, but the spirit that breathed life into that world has not disappeared: it speaks to the hermetic language of myth, legend, forms of social coexistence, popular art, customs."

I wondered: Did the museum paradoxically represent the ancient spirits breathing life into Spanish ruins?

Down by the creek in this windswept canyon, a cluster of Rarámuri men stirred a pool of mud and pine needles with splintered fence posts. Others poured buckets of the mixture into wood frames spread across a field. A pyramid of adobe blocks sat to the side. Up at the mission plaza, a massive pile of rocks had been dumped in anticipation of laying the foundation. The rocks had been obtained from the same quarry that had supplied the original stones for the mission.

The scene didn't vary much from the photos of the 1967 disaster. This time, however, the endowment of their reconstruction would not be about the mission's devilish past, but the village's unpredictable future.

Part IV

The Treasure We Long For

The irrepressible old prospector, Howard, in *The Treasure of the Sierra Madre*, recounts a wicked story of deceit toward the latter part of the novel, after the American desperadoes have successfully culled their gold dust from the land. Desperate to heal his blind son, a chieftain of the Chiricahua Indians in the Sierra Madre approaches a monk for help. In need of ready cash, the monk agrees to assist the chieftain for a fee, sending the indigenous leader off on an excruciating pilgrimage to Nuestra Señora de Guadalupe in central Mexico. Angered by the lack of a miracle, explained to him by priests as most likely a result of an Ave Maria technicality, the chieftain turns to a famous Spanish doctor for help. His response is honest: "The main question is what you can pay me." Offering to lead him to an ancient gold mine, which had been covered and cursed by his tribe, the chieftain convinces the doctor to operate on his son. The Spanish doctor miraculously brings back the son's sight; the chieftain, then, escorts the doctor to the mine, which indeed holds a fortune of silver and gold. The chieftain, pleased to have brought back his son from darkness, leaves the astonished doctor with the proclamation that "gold makes no one happy." Falling into the same chain of events that had led to the first demise of the mine, the Spanish doctor eventually loses his life to an Indian rebellion after he ruthlessly treats his laborers as slaves. His wife, undaunted by the task, takes up the mantle and dreams of wealth and fights off mutinies and bandits to haul an extraordinary fortune to the capital of Mexico. Her triumphant arrival marks the promise of her golden dreams of castles and kings. Finally retiring to a soft bed in the most luxurious hotel in the city, she mysteriously vanishes in the night, never to be seen again, her treasure left behind in the coffers of nobility.

Humphrey Bogart's character, Dobbs, was unimpressed by the prophecy: "We don't want any of your good stories."

Gold, like good stories, came in many forms in the Sierra Madre. While the pursuit of that magic dust or bullion nuggets continues to draw prospectors—rumors abounded during our sojourn that the largest gold mine in the world had been located in the bottom of a canyon near Batopilas—bandits, revolutionaries, soldiers, loggers, narcos, and even travelers such as ourselves had come to the Mother Range in search of other treasures. Their stories, as Traven's Chiricahua chieftain had predicted, were rarely happy.

I left my cabin one morning with an edition of poems published in Philadelphia in 1849. The air was cool and spiced with puffs from woodstoves and distant sawmills that operated in one of the biggest logging industries in the hemisphere. I also carried a cup of coffee, vapors steaming. I had already heard Bernabé's departure from his house, the scattering of chickens, the bang of a gate hinging on strips of tire rubber nailed into bottle caps, as he ambled down the fields toward the corral to free the cows and goats. On his return to the edge of the cornfields, Bernabé loitered nearby and casually asked about what I was reading. He treated the book like a shadowy place of doubt and fascination.

I reckoned my book that day would interest him. In defense of his own lack of education, the poet had written, "Homer and Ossian, for anything I have heard, could neither write nor read." The collection included poems for the old farmer and his New Year salutation to his old mare, not unlike the rankled creatures that lugged Bernabé's plow, "on giving her the accustomed ripp of corn to hansel."

I told Bernabé that Robert Burns, a common farmer and Scottish bard, wrote numerous poems at work in the meager clay fields of his father. He thrashed barley as a child and labored on failed parcels of rented land until he finally gave over to a job as an exciseman.

It was more difficult than I had imagined to explain a poem dedicated to a mouse, "on turning her up in her nest with the plough." *The best laid schemes o' mice and men gang aft a-gley.* Our conversation on Burns and farm mice was soon derailed. While we chatted, a convoy of logging trucks rumbled around the bend of the Mawichi dirt road, having descended from the higher plateau. Bernabé glared.

"Look at the logging trucks that pass," he told me every time a flatbed chugged down the road, trees stacked ten feet high. They reminded me of the fat trunks I didn't attempt to cut. "Those trees are nothing compared to the virgin forests we used to have," he finished.

With two-thirds of the standing timber in Mexico, the Sierra Madre was in the midst of a clear-cutting disaster. The first loggers had penetrated the high mountain region at the turn of the last century. With the completion of the train routes in 1961 and the Gran Vision highway three decades later, full-scale logging operations based out of train depots like Creel and San Juanito had decimated the virgin forests that Bernabé noted, which once included numerous species of pines. Chico, the young *leñador* I often accompanied on wood-chopping expeditions, could only name a handful of trees.

Logging flatbeds were by far the most common vehicle on the Gran Vision. While a lot of the clear-cutting still took place by illegal wildcatters who bribed their way through updated Mexican laws and past Rarámuri land rights, often operating at night, the strong logging interests in the state of Chihuahua, and the nation, had sanctioned most of the unchecked destruction of the forests. Even the World Bank had encouraged Mexico to exploit the Sierra Madre to combat one of the worst foreign debts in the world. Never ones to miss out on quick profits, the narcotraficantes had also bought into the logging industry, as well as the tourist hotels, as a way to both launder money and maintain the access roads carved into the canyon. Both types of commerce shared the same destination: Mexican pulp and wood products, including the paper for the books I read, along with untold shipments of marijuana eventually made it across the border.

By the 1990s, the tragic situation of overexploitation by the loggers and narcos had been so well documented that a contemporary Nancy Drew–Hardy Boys mystery for young readers, *The Copper Canyon Conspiracy*, was published about the plight of the Rarámuri and the Mother Range.

The situation was not uniquely contemporary, of course. "Such a Parcel o' Rogues in a Nation," would be an apt Robert Burns poem from the eighteenth century for the economic forces in the Sierra Madre today. In fact, it could be applied to virtually every opportunistic economic venture and player in the Mother Range over the last four centuries, from the early soldiers, missionaries, miners, and revolutionary figures to the recent stalwarts of tourism, logging, and drug trafficking.

History, once again, even the annals of those on the other side of the world, could play the role of a prologue to our modern story. In disgust of Scotland's historic union with England in 1707, Burns wrote, "We're bought and sold for English gold." The poem referred to compensation for a parcel of Scottish aristocrats, some of whom had bankrupted the country on a get-rich-quick (mostly logging) scheme to establish a colony in the forests of Panama. The catalyst behind the Scottish wiles was none other than a late seventeenth-century travel writer and his memoir.

The Darien Disaster, as it was later called, revolved in large part around the written narrative of a romantic buccaneer who had lived among the indigenous Kuna tribe in the tropical forests of present-day Panama. Lionel Wafer, a mysterious Gaelic-speaking adventurer from the British Isles, took refuge for a few months in 1681 among the Kuna with an accidental injury after fleeing from a pirate attack on the Spanish. Enamored with the ways of the forest dwellers and their valleys "generally water'd with Rivers, Brooks and Perennial Springs," Wafer returned to Europe and filled a manuscript with descriptions of Eden. The book rivaled the heroic tales in Sir Walter Raleigh's 1596 travelogue, *The Discoverie of the Large, Rich and Beautiful Empyre of Guiana.*

Wafer's memoir, *A New Voyage and Description of the Isthmus of America,* was also written like a catalogue for future investors. He found fruit, including pineapples the size of a human head, along with tobacco, jams, tapioca, and sugar cane. "'Tis a very noble delightful Bay; and as it affords good anchoring and shelter, so the islands also yield plenty of Wood, Water, Fruits, Fowls and Hoggs, for the accommodation of Shipping." He described fertile valleys with black soil and vast stretches of forests that could be felled, both of which could finance an expedition to the New World in months.

"As this Country is very Woody, so it contains great variety of Trees, of several Kinds unknown to us in Europe, as well Fruit-Trees as others." An American-based logging industry was born. Besides, the storyteller wrote, the Kuna were a simple and friendly people who hated the Spaniards.

His manuscript fell into the hands of a miserable and demoralized Scotland languishing in their bitterly cold poverty. Any hopes of becoming an independent mercantile power in Europe had been dashed on the high seas. Under the Navigation Acts of 1660 and 1663, England forbade Scotland from taking part in the growing trade and plantations in America, Africa, and Asia, except through contracts with English ships. Finally, in 1693, the Scottish Parliament passed "An Act for Encouraging Foreign Trade," with nations at peace with the King of England. Still without the permission of England, a Scottish company formed and raised investments among incorrigibly hopeful Scots across the nation. The nation's private treasuries were drained in the process.

With Wafer's text in hand—he was paid an extra one thousand pounds to not publish it before the ships departed—five ships were equipped and staffed with a "caste" of characters, from councilors to planters to servants, that unraveled in class, clan, and personal conflicts before they arrived on the beaches in Darien. By New Year's 1699, though, the sick colonists established the Colony of the Company of Scotland, drew up an accord of friendship with the Kuna, and began to build a New Edinburgh.

Wafer's journal didn't dwell on the untold months of torrential rain, malarial dreams in the torrid zone, or the Darien land claims already made by the Spanish. Suddenly aware of Scotland's plans for a colony, England withdrew any support, including supplies desperately needed from Jamaica. Within six months, relying largely on turtle meat, all but six dying men abandoned the forts. It was too late. Unaware of the demise of the colony, the Scots had already plundered their personal savings again and stocked and shipped off another expedition that would skirmish with the English and the Spanish. By the spring of 1700, the colony was abandoned a second time and the ships surrendered to the Spanish; three vessels escaped to Jamaica. Two of the ships fell into the hands of pirates. New Edinburgh dissolved back into the tropical forests.

When the news of the colony's demise reached Edinburgh, the nation dissolved into horrific riots. With an economy in ruins, Scotland capitulated and signed the Union of the Two Kingdoms seven years later.

Burns nearly ended up in the Americas himself. At his wit's end with the failure of his crops, farming on fallow and rocky land, he relinquished his part of the fields to his brother and sought out passage to a plantation in Jamaica. The instant success of his first book of poems, just before his departure, launched him as the darling of the literary circles in Edinburgh and saved him from the ranks of indentured Scottish servants in the Caribbean, many of whom had been rounded up in chains and ripped away from the Highlands and debtor's prisons.

The Darien colonists weren't the first Scots in Central America or Mexico. Scottish adventurer Thomas "Tom" Blake, known as Tomas

Blaque, served with Coronado's forces that skirted the edges of the lower valleys of the Rarámuri in 1540 in pursuit of the Seven Cities of Cibola and its apparent gold. After venturing as far as Kansas they returned to Mexico in defeat.

Despite the folly of the Scots, the Kuna experience was not dissimilar to that of the Rarámuri. In 1980, Panama established the Darien National Park to protect the deforestation of one of the richest and most dense forests in Central America outside of the Sierra Madre. The Kuna themselves, like the Rarámuri, are still defending their traditional forest culture.

Little did Lionel Wafer realize that his great Central American paradise, as far as the Sierra Madre, was about to be plundered.

In need of a sugar fix one afternoon, I headed to the village cooperative shop to pick up some *galletas*, those wondrous packaged Mexican cookies. Scrappy, one of Bernabé's smaller mutts, or *kochi*, tagged along at my heels. I had fed him our table scraps one morning, which he devoured in a scramble among the chickens and pigs; he looked at me from then on as if we were connected for life. This worried me slightly. It was a merciless world outside our family compound for dogs. More than one bloated carcass had littered the road and fields that week.

Leaving Scrappy outside the shop door to fend off two other bony and miserable-looking mongrels, I stepped into the dark confines of *la tienda*. It resembles a lot of country stores in the hinterlands. The place was open as long as the sun shined. Dark and dusty, it functioned more like a trading post or meeting hall, stocked with the essentials for those who had walked for miles, their few pesos tucked inside a folded piece of paper or cardboard.

The ceiling hovered in a web of activity across the beams, entangling leather cord, rebozos, fabric, and dangling shoes; the shelves sloped with tins of tuna, sardines, packages of cookies, instant coffee, instant Maruchan soups, instant everything. A few sacks of bulk grains and legumes and crates of scanty vegetables sat on the floor.

"Give me four cigarettes," a man said at the counter. "And two batteries." He paused, making his order in increments. "And a Coca," the man added.

The soft drink industry, like the village dogs and smallpox, had reached the most remote canyons in the Sierra Madre. Filmmaker John Sayles pegged this phenomenon in his brilliant movie *Men With Guns*, set in an unnamed Mexico and Guatemala: a Coca-Cola truck navigated roads and ruts that even the health care workers and rebels had abandoned.

I poked my head into a side room, which was packed like a warehouse with Rarámuri material culture. It served as the display room of a cottage industry of handicrafts for tourists that had surged in the last five years in Mawichi. The loaded shelves reminded me of Barney Burns. Assisted by the efforts of Jesuit priest Luis Verplancken, Barney, Mahina, and a handful of other traders, including Canadian J. B. Edmund Faubert, handicrafts from around the Sierra Madre had reached an international audience since the 1960s. Brought by the local villagers in exchange for hard cash and food, the selection was vast: ollas, vases, and cups made from local clay, baskets woven from sotol and pine, plates and bowls carved from madroño wood, frames made from pine and *tascate* wood, scores of Virgin of Guadalupe carvings, masks chipped from *alamillo* wood, kick balls, bows and arrows shaped from ash trees, violins, rattles, reed flutes, and even chaparekes. Women had carted in necklaces strung with *chilicote* seeds, drums assembled with sheep or goat skins, and blankets woven from wool. Key chains, in this largely car-less society, had been added as a contemporary touch.

I wandered back into the main shop room. A Mexican deliveryman wearing a company shirt, jeans, and cowboy boots stood at the counter, drinking a bottle of Coke, chatting with a young shop clerk, who stared to the side of the counter. The deliveryman's van sat outside, packed to the gills with packaged foodstuffs he would cart to remote villages throughout the canyons. Both men wore ball caps; the Rarámuri clerk had a brand new Chicago Bulls cap. The Mexican sported the common mustache of the *serranos* (mountaineers), while the clerk, like most indigenous men, had little facial hair. They lounged around a counter that called for loitering, planed and engraved by sweaty hands, sacks of goods, tins of sardines, and soiled coins. A small calculator rested on the edge. Every transaction was pounded out, regardless of the quantity, as if following the protocol for cashiers.

The tinny sound and slow rhythm of a pascol tune creaked from a radio in the background. After an announcement in an indigenous language interrupted the music, I recognized the radio station. Established by the National Institute for Indigenous People, the Xetar radio station in Guachochi transmits indigenous tunes and local announcements—"Pedro in Choguita says to tell his brother to bring the baskets to the river crossing"—in various languages, including Rarámuri, Pima, Tepehuane, and even Spanish, throughout the remote canyons.

The Mexican stood aside as two little kids, fugitives from the boarding school, bustled to the counter, stood on their tip-toes, and surrendered their single pesos for a sack of *cueros*, or crisps. The clerk totaled up the amount on the calculator. The kids, wearing cast-off American T-shirts, long pants, and huaraches, grabbed their crisps and ran off.

I sensed the stare of the Mexican deliveryman as I stepped up to the counter, greeting the clerk.

"Kwira," I said, reaching out my hand.

"Kwira," the clerk said, grinning, sanding the pads of his fingers across mine.

I asked about a couple packages of cookies. He reached back and then plopped them onto the counter.

"Are you visiting from Creel?" the deliveryman asked me, in Spanish, as I reached into my pocket for some pesos.

The clerk widened his grin.

"No," I said, shifting toward him, my cookies in hand, "my wife and I are actually staying in the village for a while."

"In this village," the deliveryman exclaimed. "Why? What are you doing in this god-forsaken place? Are you missionaries?"

"My wife's a teacher," I said, to simplify matters.

"What do you do?"

"Various things," I said, but I quickly invented a title, as if not to appear too cryptic. "I teach, too."

For all of its magnitude, the Sierra Madre was a small world; the tentacles of the narcotraficantes were long. I didn't want to appear mysterious or too cheeky about my long-term residence. Barney had warned me, especially if I chose to roam extensively through the canyons, about being confused for an American DEA agent.

The yelp of Scrappy lured us to the door. Near a mound of garbage, the dog had been cornered by a gang of malformed mutts, all of them baring their teeth and growling. The Sierra Madre dogs were hardly brave or *bravo* ("mean," in Spanish). They vanished the second we pretended to throw something in their direction. Scrappy bounded to me as if we were bonded for life now. The Mexican deliveryman had remained by my side, still carrying his bottle of Coke.

"Hijole, so you're living in this pueblito," he said. He gazed at the nearby cornfields, which had been razed. The dirt road in every direction was deserted. The few cabins looked dumpy and forlorn. The pack of dogs had scattered the remains of the garbage. The Mexican probably saw the obvious: while a few of the families in the central valley had a spigot with running water, the majority of the people in the ejido obtained their water from a small well or an untreated water source and had no outhouse. Beyond the school mess hall and the clinic, and one mestizo who had a generator, we were the sole residents with a solar panel or any source of electricity.

"These people have nothing here, nothing," he said. "They lack ambition." He turned back at me, and laughed. "They don't want to work for others. They want to drink their tesguino. No wonder people are moving in on their land."

His concept of work intrigued me, this reference to a salaried job and a creed in wages in a society that was only a generation away from tilling the soil or scraping an existence off the land. His question to me—What do you do?—was telling, too. Neither Bernabé nor any other man I had met in the village had ever broached the subject. Instead, they put the same question to me, as they did to any other man in their culture: "What does your father grow?"

The labor conventions for the villagers were simple: a man tilled his plot of corn, beans, and squash, and if he ran out of corn before the next harvest or needed hard cash, he either sold a goat or a cow—the banking assets of the canyon—or sought precarious day-work in the ejido sawmill, temporary construction sites, or as a migrant farmworker.

This situation had been evolving for years. I met one young man in the village who worked three months of the year in Chihuahua City, fabricating adobe bricks, and then returned to the Sierra for several months to tend to his one-room cabin, assist his mother with her cornfields, and play his guitar. He returned to Chihuahua whenever the money ran out.

The shop represented a step in the direction toward more consumption of commercial goods and its accompanying need for wages. It supplied desired goods and foods beyond the staple diet of corn and beans. Even more items, such as boom boxes and fabric for women's dresses, could be found in Creel. These products required a lot more cash than corn. They were part of a new treadmill for the Rarámuri, no less wicked than the fateful chase for gold by outside prospectors.

The villagers in Mawichi first encountered wages in the 1930s, when a mestizo set up a sawmill in the area. The work was sporadic and poorly paid; the local people gained little, and eventually retreated. The sawmill didn't pervade the area until the 1950s, when the National Institute for Indigenous People chose Mawichi to be the first indigenous lumber venture in the Sierra Madre. It provided the first start-up loans and ad-

ministrative assistance. Despite years of corruption by mestizo adminis-
trators, who skimmed from the profits, the sawmill provided a source of
income for the entire village and engineered the first dramatic change
in the traditional ways of labor. The sawmill didn't supplant farming,
though; all ejido members were eligible to work at the plant, reducing
the number of positions and shifts to a part-time availability. However,
it paved the way for young men to seek seasonal work on the railroad or
the construction of the Gran Vision highway and in agricultural sectors
in the lowlands.

The sawmill was dormant during our stay. Recent administrative
problems and delays in forest permits had kept it closed for months.
Carla noted that most of the children's parents listed their occupations
as *agricultor*, or farmers.

The Mexican deliveryman ducked back inside to return his empty
bottle and then scurried back out the door.

"So, what are you going to do now?" he asked me.

I shrugged my shoulders and smiled.

"Time to chop some wood," I said.

He grinned, making for his truck.

"Back to Creel for me," he laughed.

No one had any running water in Creel on several visits during our
sojourn. The reservoirs had been drained. Only the private tanks at
some of the hotels afforded the tourists, not the locals, with enough water to wash their hands and flush their modern toilets. The demands of
the drought spared no one; some living in the remote Rarámuri villages
hauled their water from a creek or spring for over a mile. Without permission, quiet convoys of trucks appeared in Mawichi in the evenings,
pumping water from the creek into twenty-gallon containers. In this
plumbing-dependent tourist boomtown, delivery trucks from private
water companies became as common as the tourist buses and trains.

Established in 1906 as an experimental colony for the "betterment
and cultivation" of the Rarámuri, Creel had changed drastically over the
last century. Governor Enrique Creel founded the town as part of his
campaign to "civilize" the Rarámuri. Creel's father had been the U.S.
consul to Chihuahua; Enrique remained in Mexico, married into the
Juan Terrazas family, which owned properties in northern Mexico the
size of some eastern states in the United States, and became the governor of Chihuahua, and at one point, the secretary of foreign relations.
The town, like the rest of the Sierra Madre, rapidly shifted from the

designated seventy-five percent Rarámuri allotment to an overwhelming majority of mestizos. With the advent of the railroad, it grew from a muddy frontier outpost to a muddy, largely Mexican lumber town.

Creel was a booming tourist and train depot on the periphery of the famed Copper Canyon, equipped with luxury hotels, cafes, clothing boutiques, an optician's shop, and even an upscale KOA Kampground on paved roads. The sawmill still belched out pulp and a pall above the town. The rest of the locals, estimated at 3,500 souls, made their living off two products: Copper Canyon and the Rarámuri.

We headed into Creel every week or so for supplies we couldn't find in Mawichi and to send e-mails from a pay phone. Less than a few miles away from the nearest ejido, less than a hundred yards from those who still lived in caves, Creel followed the two-level road of development that had fascinated me in my journeys in India: people reached town on horse and buggy, many on foot (having walked for hours out of the canyons), wearing homemade traditional dresses, babes hanging from the backs of women in folded blankets. Others in designer clothes from Europe and Mexican urban centers arrived in the latest-model Blazers, Troopers, and Suburbans, on luxury trains, and in air-conditioned buses full of tourists who were deposited into hotels with satellite dishes, faxes, and Internet access. A private helicopter pad lay just off the main avenue.

In many respects, Creel sat apart as its own biosphere in the Sierra Madre. Some of the transplanted locals fancied it as a Mexican Moab or a throwback to Taos in the days of D. H. and Frieda Lawrence, Adolph and Fannie Bandelier, and Georgia O'Keefe. These were the urban ecotourist enthusiasts, creative mavericks from Mexico City, Chihuahua, and San Miguel de Allende and abroad, in search of a quieter life and a closer communion with nature and indigenous communities. Ecotourism had emerged as the best way for them to accomplish this pursuit in the Sierra Madre.

The usual cadre of international backpackers dotted the streets and one or two spots for nightlife, where alternative Mexican and international artisans competed with Rarámuri mothers and children for the handicraft trade. A group of senior citizens from the States generally huddled on the train platform and along the main street, which featured wood arcades and a small plaza; Creel itself didn't possess anything other than the blitz of souvenir shops filled with indigenous artisan work. The tourist town was simply the place to sleep in a hotel, catch the train or wilderness tour, and dine in restaurants that featured an international cuisine. Even the Rarámuri families roamed the streets like visitors themselves, generally en route to buy food and supplies.

The gentle walkers and bikers of ecotourism were only a small portion of the tourist plans of the state and federal government. Their Gran Vision, so to speak, had been made possible by the newly paved road that now arrived on the breathtaking edge of the Copper Canyon in Divisadero, a cluster site of expensive hotels literally perched on top of Rarámuri cliff dwellings with families living inside them. During our journey, Mexico's national tourism development agency, FONATUR, announced plans to increase tourism in the Copper Canyon sixfold, to over four hundred thousand visitors a year by 2010.

Thus the frenzy of hotel raising, restaurant building, and the clutter of mass tourism shops to accompany them. We saw a change in the landscape each time we visited Creel: foundations poured for multilevel hotels or apartments, the renovation of an older shop into a boutique or "Swiss Alpine" restaurant, Spanish and English billboards at the entrance of the town advertising new hotels and discotheques.

Still, there was no water in the town.

This tourist boom had exploded only in the last decade. Its existence in such a breathtaking landscape was inevitable and reasonable. Carla and I were tourists, of course, albeit long-term ones. Creel, as its epicenter, was incredibly symbolic. Just as Enrique Creel had established the colony in his own name to determine the future of the Rarámuri, with or without their consent or participation in the decision making, the new town had based its fate on the marketing of the Rarámuri and the barrancas, with or without their consent or participation in the process.

In this respect, I saw Creel as our reality check in the Sierra Madre. It served as our link to the mestizos.

According to one hotel operator, Creel was also the portal into another world. He had left behind the life of a businessman in Chihuahua City to be closer to the source of his dreams: UFOs. Sitting at the restaurant of one hotel, he showed me photos of spaceships that had passed over the area, a reported landing zone.

"There's a man up the road, apparently from Switzerland," he went on, "but he isn't from this world." He winked knowingly. "He's an alien, I know it. He's watching what we're doing."

The rapid change, even chaos, in the Sierra Madre and Mexico bothered this hotelier. He understood the paradox of his industry. He had fled the stress and grime of the city for the mountain air and easy life. He recognized the lack of infrastructure for the burgeoning town. He was outraged one day over the introduction of screaming three-wheeler motorcycles, the latest items for rent. He mumbled quietly in disillusion at the increasing role of the narcotraficantes in tourism; everyone recognized the forbidding presence of the drug traffickers, who had laundered some of their fortunes through the purchase and development of luxury hotels.

Back to the bright, twinkling lights of the UFOs, the hotelier pointed out their placement in the photo's night sky. Indeed, there were red, yellow, and blue lights swirling in that picture. Then he shifted toward a huge mural of the Rarámuri on the hotel wall, the stern-looking natives dressed in traditional breechcloths and red bandannas, peering up at the sky as if searching for UFOs.

"The problem is that when the indios change into Mexicans, no tourists will want to see them," he said. "And then Creel and tourism will disappear, as if we were abducted by the aliens."

Tourism entered Mawichi thanks to two men with the same surname. One might have achieved immortality; the other only dreamed about it, but that dream eventually came true for another generation and left its irremediable imprint on the Rarámuri. The first imprint was at the village shop.

The Muki Sekara shop in our village was a cooperative founded on the Rochdale principles. A young Jesuit priest once insisted that the independent nature of the Rarámuri spelled doom for any cooperative venture. "They don't cooperate," he said. Muki Sekara, translated from Rarámuri as "a woman's hand," had defied his judgment.

The shop emerged after numerous group discussions, as in the case of Rochdale's English factory workers, among people who were tired of paying higher prices in the commercial shops in Creel. While there was a very small government-supported shop near the mission, most villagers had journeyed to Creel to buy fabric for skirts or purchase things beyond the staples.

Influenced by the earlier experiments of worker-owned cooperative stores in New Lanark, Scotland, not far from my ancestral town of Biggar, the Rochdale workers acted on the principles and examples of social reformer Robert Owen. They founded the Society of Equitable Pioneers. The Rochdale villagers established the cooperative store, launching a revolution in management and economic enterprise that would touch the lives of the indigenous people in the Sierra Madre a century later.

The rules of Muki Sekara were largely the same as those in Rochdale: goods were sold at a local price, profits were distributed to cooperative members and workers in proportion to sales, both sexes had equal rights, each member had one vote, and regular meetings were held to cavil over policies. The Rarámuri had broken one rule; credit was allowed. Nonetheless, after taking four years to repay the initial loan to launch the store, the members now received monthly profits.

Robert Owen almost became a regional neighbor in the Sierra Madre. The son of a Welsh saddle maker, he worked up the ranks of a textile industry that was exploding due to the invention of the spinning jenny and water-powered mills. In 1799, he crossed the borderlands into Scotland and bought a cotton mill in New Lanark. Appalled at the living and working conditions of the laborers, he later wrote that he found the state of Jamaican slaves to be more favorable: "They are greatly more happy than the British or Irish day-labourer."

Owen's reforms were radical for the times; he raised the minimum working age to ten, lowered daily shifts to twelve hours, provided free day care for toddlers, and set up schools for kids and musical programs for adults. He then closed down the commercial stores and developed a cooperative shop that distributed the profits back into the schools.

In 1824, Owen journeyed to the United States to "sow the seeds in that new fertile soil, new for material and mental growth, the cradle of the future liberty of the human race." He purchased a farming community from German settlers in western Indiana along the Wabash river and announced his plans to launch the agricultural utopian community of New Harmony.

Owen's success in marketing overwhelmed his talents for management. He attracted writers, scientists, reformers, and hangers-on from around the world. Within four years, the community divided and in shambles, he abandoned the social experiment to the hands of other reformers and scientists, including his five kids.

Mexico still remained an option to Owen. He was convinced that the northern regions of Texas and Coahuila were fertile for an experiment on a truly massive scale. Despite the warnings of the Mexican ambassador in London, Owen embarked on a voyage to Veracruz to win the favors of the irascible General Antonio López de Santa Anna, in the midst of another Mexican revolt. Owen declared: "The world is full ripe for a great moral change, and it may be, I think, commenced the most advantageously in the New World; the Mexican Republic presents perhaps at the moment the best point at which to begin new and mighty operations."

Owen's cooperative principles reportedly enthralled Santa Anna. He promised to support the reformer's crusade. Instead of Texas and Coahuila, he offered the Scotsman the desert buffer zone of Chihuahua, on the plains before the Sierra Madre. The promise never came to pass; the Mexican Congress failed to consider the land grant. Santa Anna eventually surrendered the same parcel of land twenty years later after the disastrous Mexican American War.

Fifty years later, in the 1880s, Albert Owen, an unrelated surveyor and entrepreneur from Pennsylvania, relaunched Owen's dream for a utopian community in Mexico. The impact of his community and another idealistic plan spawned one of the greatest intrusions on the cultural ways of the Rarámuri in the late twentieth century.

This point became clear one day when a young kid called on me to help out at the Muki Sekara. For the first and only time, the shop needed my assistance in translating for a large group of American tourists who had arrived to visit, according to their brochures, a "quaint Tarahumara village of the Indians, a shy, mysterious people. You'll meet the Tarahumara wearing bright turquoise and red headbands, their fine features chiseled under dark, black hair."

The American tourists had disembarked in Creel on the Sierra Madre Express, a luxury train of refurbished vintage rail cars from the 1940s and 1950s, replete with gourmet food and American ice; they had spent $2,700 a head (in 1998), more than the annual income of anyone in the village, for a fabulous ride from Magdalena in Sonora, through 87 tunnels, across 35 bridges, and up a climb of 8,000 feet over two days on an engineering miracle that had taken 80 years to complete.

The train traffic had dwindled significantly that winter. According to one hotel operator in Creel, over seventy percent of the reservations had been canceled. That dip in tourism, as foretold in another brochure, was caused by a headlining scandal: a Swiss tourist was fatally gunned down during a regular train robbery by bandits. After robbing the passengers, one of the bandits noticed the European filming the whole affair on video. He demanded the camera. The Swiss refused. Other passengers later postulated that the tourist might have assumed the robbery was part of a "Pancho Villa act." One tourist manual had warned: "In the unlikely event of a train robbery, be calm, quiet and cooperative. In other words, don't argue; just hand over the loot."

Inspired by the endless possibilities of community development and commerce during a surveying venture along the Pacific Coast in 1880, Albert Owen had a vision for the bay of Topolobampo in Sinaloa. He wanted to create a port authority that could link up with the mining and logging interests in the north and the seaboard communities to the south. And he planned to engineer this feat through the creation of a railroad through the Sierra Madre. After wrangling the support of Porfirio Díaz, who was polishing his forces to subject Mexico to twenty years of dictatorship, Owen decided to carry out his vision through the agency of a utopian socialist community.

In the footsteps of Robert Owen, and years later to be followed in other parts of the United States by radicals like Upton Sinclair, Owen issued the call for fellow socialists to join his new colony. Based on Owenite principles of cooperation and joint labor, Albert Owen even abolished the concept of currency, opting for a system of labor credits and shared profit. The colonists were told they would participate in the construction and wealth of a port town equipped with water, a telegraph system, and a railroad through the Sierra Madre. He failed to mention the epidemic of smallpox and malaria sweeping through the coastal lands. Over six hundred followers, largely from California, arrived in force by 1886.

Within the same four years that it took to drive Robert Owen out of New Harmony, the Topolobampo Colony disintegrated into a wreck of conflict and failure. Unable to obtain a year-round source of water, Owen moved the colony inland. The idealists fractured into rival camps over corporate or individual ownership of the land and farms. Illness and crop failure left the colony in dire straits. The first of the "deserters" began to register their experiences in the American newspapers.

The former financial director, Alvan Brock wrote, "that prison-house of horrors—Topolobampo, the natural home of malaria, measles, smallpox, where, even if plenty of good water existed, as it does not, life can never be made unendurable, except to savages."

While the last colonists straggled away in defeat from the utopian grounds over the next decade, Owen continued his pursuit of the railway, convincing other American investors to fund the scheme. Bankrupt and in despair, he finally surrendered his dream to financier Arthur Stilwell in 1900, who had formed the Kansas City, Mexico and Orient Railway Company, transferring his shares of the railroad in the process. At the height of the bloodiest period of the Mexican Revolution in 1914, the ties and irons of civilization were laid between Ojinaga and Chihuahua. By that time, the coffers of the American investors were exhausted as well.

The Sierra Madre had yet to be challenged. But the dream lived on.

In 1943 the Mexican government raised the first funds to continue the railroad through the mountains. By 1961, our Mawichi neighbor Maria, a founding member of Muki Sekara, stood on the platform in Creel as the Ferrocarril de Chihuahua al Pacifico blew its horn for the first time on the rim of the Sierra Madre.

According to historian W. Dirk Raat, "Before 1961 most tourists, foreign or Mexican, had never laid eyes on a Tarahumara." After centuries of isolation, penetrated only by the fleeting efforts of missionaries and ragged cadres of miners and loggers and ranchers, Maria knew the ramparts of her Rarámuri communities, utopian or otherwise, had been shattered.

Tourism had finally arrived in the Sierra Madre like a rainbow, and with it came the hordes in search of a pot of gold.

The traditional Rarámuri kickball race, *rarajipari*, was one of the biggest draws for the tourists. Pitting village runners against regional competitors, or even inter-ejido runs, the races usually took place in the fall. A collection of tourist vans and buses from Creel often hovered nearby at the race's proposed kickoff time, even though the promoters wouldn't begin the competition for a few more hours. Despite this outside attention, the rarajipari hadn't mutated into a crass tourist attraction; it still served as one of the most intense and anticipated events in village life.

The local boys from Mawichi and the boarding school were always chasing wooden balls carved from madroño wood with an ax they could barely lift. Playing in teams, they raced down the Mawichi dirt road like dust devils, trampled through the dried stalks of the cornfields, splashed across the creek, and managed to kick the ball in a loop toward the school. Each kid clutched one of his huaraches in his hand, preferring to scoop and fling the ball with his bare foot. A lot of them were missing toenails. A pack of dogs followed.

Lumholtz termed the kickball foot races the "national sport" of the Rarámuri. "No doubt the Tarahumares are the greatest runners in the world, not in regard to speed, but endurance," he wrote. "A Tarahumara will easily run 170 miles without stopping." According to Francisco Almada, a Mexican historian in Chihuahua, the longest recorded race covered over 340 miles. "However, this runner (the victor) became crippled and was never able to participate in a race again."

Even Humphrey Bogart's irascible Fred Dobbs couldn't help but note the running feats of the Rarámuri in *The Treasure of the Sierra*

Madre. Following the directions of an Indian in the canyons, he lamented: "They say it is one hour away, but they don't tell you if they mean an hour run by a Tarahumare."

Like Lumholtz and nearly every other chronicler for the next hundred years, Schwatka reported wild stories of the Rarámuri running abilities. "Not a great many years ago the mail from Chihuahua to Batopilas was carried by a courier on his back, who made the distance over the Sierra Madre range, a good 250 miles, and return, or a total of 500 miles, in six days."

The races in Mawichi usually began late in the evening on a Saturday, after hours of furious betting and haggling, and ended the next afternoon. This endurance compelled Lumholtz to associate their *Rarámuri* name—he wrote that *rala* meant "foot"—with their competitive sport. The word spread. The Rarámuri ability to run nonstop over vast distances drew sports and medical researchers to the Sierra Madre for years. Their unique diet of pinole mixed into water mystified most physiological formulas. The Mexican government even entered a group of Rarámuri runners in the marathon at the 1928 Olympic Games in Amsterdam. Accustomed to much longer races, the runners failed to place anywhere near the front. The marathon was simply too short. Years later another cadre of runners found themselves in the international front ranks at races in the Colorado Rockies, which ranged over one hundred miles.

Rarajipari, or "foot throw," was the name given by the Rarámuri to their game. In fact, the runner didn't actually kick the wood ball, which was the size of an orange, but flung or tossed it with his toes. Both men and women participated. Still clad in huaraches, the runners wore shorts and T-shirts in our village but maintained the tradition of wearing a good luck charm belt of bells or rattles around their waist. They also adhered to a strict regimen before the race of no sex or tesguino, and they were obliged to wager a bet on themselves (to avoid any corruption).

The Rarámuri obsession with gambling rivaled their love of sports and tesguino. (I quietly placed bets on the weekly basketball games. To not do so, according to one friend, would have been an offense.) The betting prior to the kickball race had its own ritual and protocol. Like any local event, it lingered for hours. The crowd matched a Sunday gathering. Women with babies sat wrapped in their rebozos for the entire day; kids and dogs chased each other up and down the road like the pregame entertainment. Men swaggered around the center ring of jousting promoters. A couple of women roamed with baskets of tamales;

bottles of Coke rattled through the crowd. Throughout the afternoon, the *chokeame*, or promoter of the race, sent out his assistants, or *sakeame*, to prompt the bets. Spread out in front of the shop on either side of the road, two massive blankets held the loot for each runner's promoter. A sakeame would present a particular item, such as a knife or blanket or feather, which indicated a chicken, and then would chide the crowd for a rival bet. By the time the race started, there were two huge piles topped with clothes, feathers, food, corn, money, yarn, and even a car battery.

As Lumholtz noted, "A race is never won by natural means." Shamans for both sides prepared hexes and illnesses to bewitch the runners, who had prepared their own defensive remedies.

The race began. The runners flicked their wooden balls and vanished into the forest. The crowd settled in for a long day's night.

Later the next afternoon, the winner having long since crossed the line in a race that looped through the forests and valleys guided by teammates with torches, we watched from a rancho at the top of the ridge as the loser limped up the Mawichi road. His shoulders tilted forward in pain. His feet moved in heavy thuds. He finally stopped in front of the shop amid a crowd that seemed incredibly indifferent. Many of them had already started to celebrate the other runner's victory.

"I bet you don't believe in brujería [witchcraft]," our friend, an older man on the ridge, chided me.

I smiled and shrugged my shoulders. He shook his head.

"He's a chabochi," his daughter said, looking at me, standing to the side.

"Well, that runner was definitely cursed," the older man continued.

He had lost a wager of over 150 pesos.

In my role as a freelance jack-of-all-trades in the village, I lent my bones to a local tourist cause when one of the women's cooperatives decided to launch an ambitious project. They had received a loan from the government to build a row of tourist cabins near the roadside entrance into our valley. As part of the agreement, the husbands and sons of the women members of the cooperative had to carry out the construction work, along with a hired supervisor. If a member of the cooperative could not keep up her end of the agreement, she had to hire someone to work in her place.

Despite my vague misgivings about mass tourism, I agreed with the plan. With tourism growing by the trainloads, geared largely around interaction with Copper Canyon and the Rarámuri cultural experience, it made sense for the villagers to be on the receiving—instead of giving—end of the benefits. At this point, the only nearby accommodations were in Creel or remote locations operated by mestizos or Americans.

The cabin project was ambitious. It included bathroom plumbing that none of the members of the cooperative possessed. The plans also called for the construction of brick fireplaces instead of woodstoves, far less economical and efficient but more appealing to tourists. Based on a rocky hillside, the cabins were also to be grouped around a restaurant or dining hall.

All of these grand notions required a lot of digging. And digging in mostly rocky sheets on the slope of a canyon. Armed with a shovel and a pick, I joined a cadre of a dozen men and even more women. After the initial ease in clearing a section of land and laying the concrete foundations for the cabins—another luxury many of the cooperative members didn't possess—we steeled ourselves for the digging of the sewage and water ditches. Within a week, our numbers dwindled to three men and a couple of occasional teenage boys; a few women arrived in the late morning, in order to prepare some beans and tortillas for lunch.

Part of the exodus had nothing to do with the rock-hard surface we were cracking like a prison chain gang. A series of tesguinadas had taken place for various onomastic religious rituals and saints days. For most Rarámuri, an invitation to a tesguinada was as binding as any social contract. It was often associated, as well, with work parties to assist family and friends. To refuse a party, so to speak, would risk the loss of the cooperative efforts of others when your turn in need came around. The mestizos who employed Rarámuri workers in Creel and around the Sierra Madre were always incensed by this reality. In the midst of a scheduled work week, it was not uncommon for some Rarámuri men to miss several days or even quit their jobs in order to attend a tesguinada or two. No mestizo could understand the protocol and obligations of the tesguinada work parties. The Rarámuri were simply lazy drunks to them.

In the end, however, the days of rituals evolved into a week-long and then an even longer hiatus from the cabin project. Many men then insisted that they needed to work on their fields. With the project under a time constraint with the loan and hired mestizo supervisor, I continued to join the hardy souls who persisted on working throughout the week. Not wanting to upset the traditional rituals, Bernabé had opted not to work. When he returned the next week, along with a few other men and women, the tensions between the traditionalists and the modern factions heightened.

I dug my canal and quietly watched the intrigues and arguments. There were the usual problems and accusations on any construction lot: who was working, who was lazy, who was right about the plans, who knew more about building walls, who was responsible for the broken shovel. At the root of the conflicts, however, was a fascinating clash of cultures. The more amestizado (Mexicanized) members, who spoke only Spanish, wanted to work in a certain hierarchical fashion and on a 9 to 5 schedule, versus a large cadre of traditional women and a few men who spoke only Rarámuri and insisted on maintaining their own rhythms and rituals.

I found the mountain air to be invigorating, the sun strong; the digging became easier each day. Scrappy scampered by my side on the walk to the cabin site each morning, darting for a plethora of birds. Aldo Leopold, the gallant author of the environmental classic, *A Sand County Almanac*, fell in love with the *guacamaja*, or thick-billed parrot, during his brief sojourn in the Sierra Madre. "Only the deaf and blind could fail to perceive his role in the mountain life and landscape. Indeed you have hardly finished breakfast before the chattering flocks leave their roost on the rimrocks and perform a sort of morning drill in the high reaches of the dawn."

Working with a couple of teenagers, I avoided any of the factions by digging far away from the center action, keeping down my head. I picked and shoveled without any lengthy breaks in order to keep from being sucked into one side of the conflict or the other. I sensed the same ill at ease among the teenaged boys. We grunted the first day, making eye contact only when our heads popped out of the growing canals with a shovel of dirt. Within the second day, we were exchanging words in a call and response chorus of Rarámuri, Spanish, and English, a sort of vocabulary lesson based around digging.

"Rocks," I called out in Spanish, then English, echoed by their Rarámuri.

"I hate rocks," continued the next verse, in three-part harmony.

The day after one tesguinada, Bernabé visited the site and inspected our work. As one of the elders and supposed peacemakers, he was slightly removed from the conflict. He resented, however, the hiring of the mestizo supervisor; like any building veteran, he assumed he could direct the construction of the cabins in a better way.

"Why are you working like a white man?" he suddenly bellowed to the teenage boys. They immediately halted their picks and shovels in midair, and then shot a furtive glance in my direction. I kept working. Bernabé's comment stunned me. I didn't know how to respond. After working on numerous projects together for several months, getting praised up and down the tesguinada circuit for my free hard labor, I couldn't believe the invective in his words.

"You see," he went on, crouching by the teenage boys, "Javier can only keep up this work because he sleeps in the afternoon and evenings. But you have to work all day, so slow down, unless you want to join him in his bed."

The line brought a round of laughter. I laughed. Bernabé was referring to the fact that I generally left the site in the afternoons and headed back to our cabin, where I often wrote down my notes and stories for the day and dedicated time to reading. I believed in Albert Camus' concept of *solidaire* and *solitaire* for a writer. For the Rarámuri, the cabin was for sleeping; my excuse to retire early for the day was simply a front to put my feet up. The role of a writer and reader in a largely unlettered society where books were as common as gold was so extraneous it seemed like a betrayal to the surroundings.

That night, though, in agony on the floor, trying to stretch my aching back muscles, unable to sit in my chair and write, I cursed the man as if he were the devil himself.

I decided to set up my laptop outside the next day. I'd show Bernabé, I mused; I'd write in public. My term as an outdoor writer lasted for about ten minutes. Cocks chased chickens around my legs; dogs attacked pigs in the same direction; kids swarmed in search of Carla and candy; the wind swept up dust devils around the clearing and onto my screen. I surrendered and packed up, returning to the cabin.

Around twilight that evening, I overheard Bernabé talking to Carla in front of our cabin.

"Can you tell Javier to get out of bed and help me bring in the cows?"

Splitting along family lines, the controversy surrounding the tourist cabin project entered my mind as I hammered the rocky earth in the form of a Rarámuri staging of Sophocles' *Antigone*. The women's cooperative functioned in a form of Antigone's defiance of the king. Instead of burying their brothers against the wishes of the crown (or, in the villager's case, the mestizo supervisor and his Spanish-speaking Rarámuri male cohorts), the women's cooperative had rejected their own past of timidity and sought to dig out their future in accordance with their own divine laws: they wanted to dig the ditches and build the cabins their way. The teenaged boys and I served as the chorus, musing about mortality, hard rocks, and impending disasters.

Creon (or the mestizo supervisor) then delivered a soliloquy on the rule of the king and the proper role for women. As the gods (or Mexican bureaucrats) would have informed him, this was to no avail, of course, since the loan for the tourist cabin remained in the name of the women's cooperative. From the government officials to the gossip on the tesguinada circuit, the public opinion, as in the time of the Greek myth, stayed in favor of the women.

Antigone and the women's cooperative were then banished to their caves or cliff dwellings (or remote cabins). The mestizo supervisor told them to go home and find men to dig those trenches. The chorus to Dionysus, of course, erupted into a sing-a-long at a drunken tesguinada in a Rarámuri bluegrass version of "My Main Trial is Yet to Come." In the meantime, despite Creon's change of mind, the doomed fate of Antigone and the women's cooperative and the tourism cabin project was inescapable.

Within two months from its launching, the tourism cabins dissolved into a bitter conflict between factions. All sides threw up their hands and walked away. The concrete foundations and half-dug ditches remained abandoned on our departure, as hopeless as the ruins of Signy's house, the unremitting woman hero of my mother's Norse gods. The hired mestizo supervisor returned to Chihuahua. (I never understood what transpired on the details of the loan and incurred expenses.) As a chorus ending, the lads and I could have sung a Greek melody about gaining wisdom through suffering, in tourism's get-rich-quick vision of the world.

A flatbed truck rumbled to a stop in front of our cabin one afternoon. The old truck, with a smashed front bumper and a spider-webbed windshield, was loaded down with several layers of red adobes, topped by two Rarámuri men sitting on tires. They were looking for Bernabé or Maria. The bricks had been ordered by the women's cooperative in the village.

Dropping my ax at the wood pile, where I had been engaged in my daily regimen—the Rarámuri would probably agree with the Zen proverb: *Before enlightenment, chopping wood, carrying water, after enlightenment, chopping wood, carrying water*—I greeted the Mexican driver and his companion, as well as the Rarámuri workers. No one was around, so I casually played the host, checked the delivery, signed the papers, and designated the clearing for the bricks. After living in the village for months, I no longer felt self-conscious about my chabochi appearance to other outsiders.

When I started to unload the adobe, along with the two Rarámuri men, the three of us naturally easing into an assembly line from the top of the pile to the side of the truck to the clearing, the Mexican driver swaggered over and wagged a finger at me.

"No, what are you doing? Let the indios do the work," he hissed, clutching my arm. "You don't need to do the work of indios."

I smiled, slowly freed my arm, and kept on working. I didn't say anything. In truth, I wanted to blast the mestizo driver to kingdom come.

The Mexican retreated, snickered with his companion at my effort, *stupid gringo*, and then climbed into the truck. A rainstorm suddenly thundered down half-way through the load. The mestizo waved for me to get inside the truck.

"Andale," he shouted, "you'll get drenched."

I looked at the Rarámuri men. I felt this odd sensation of having to choose sides. Squatting underneath the truck flatbed, I huddled with the two Rarámuri in the mud. They wore the traditional *tagora*, or breech-cloth, a somewhat frilly collarless blouse called the *napacaka*, vaguely reminiscent of the medieval European undergarments, and tire-soled sandals. Their haircuts had been shaped from the same bowl. Their legs rippled in muscles. Sitting side by side, I realized they were father and son. The monsoon was providential. Relieved from the burden of the mestizo driver, my roost among the Rarámuri workers revealed a new story.

"Where are you from?" I asked, in Spanish.

"Batopilas," the father said.

Then he made a gesture with his hand, as if to denote a place further away into the canyons. Several non-Christian settlements were tucked along the steep confines around the Rio Batopilas. At the basin of the river, Batopilas was a legendary mining town that had gone through a number of famous silver bonanzas. Founded in the early eighteenth century, the boomtown numbered over ten thousand inhabitants in 1810, most of whom were Rarámuri or Yaqui laborers used for hauling leather sacks of ore out of the precipitous mines on *muesca* ladder steps carved incrementally in tall pines.

After the independence of Mexico in 1821, the town dissolved into ruin. In 1880, the former territorial governor of Washington D.C., Alexander Shepherd, bought the mining district for $600,000, traveled over six months with his family to the mining town, and introduced

modern industrial methods, including leaching, steam and then gaso-
line hoists, compressed air drills, and even electric-powered hand drills.
Within a few years, Shepherd resurrected the town, built an aqueduct
and electricity plant, blasted the longest mining shaft in Mexican history—diplomatically named the Porfirio Diáz Tunnel, after the dictator—and reported annual dividends of $1 million. He extracted nearly
twenty million ounces of silver from 1880 to 1906. The ore had to be
lugged out of the Sierra Madre by mule trains, then transported nearly
three hundred miles to El Paso on wagons, where it was shipped by train
to smelters in Aurora, Illinois. Joseph Conrad even referred to Batopilas—the second town in the entire country, after Mexico City, to have
electricity—in *Nostromo*, his classic novel on greed at play in a silver
mine in South America.

Along with the indigenous workers, over five thousand Mexican and
recent immigrants streamed into the mining town before 1911. I once
met a young Mexican in the archaeological library in Chihuahua whose
great-grandfather, an immigrant from Poland, had gone straight from
the ship to the mine in 1895.

"Romeino Wheeler," the Rarámuri father suddenly said to me, after
a few minutes of silence. He repeated the name again.

"I don't know him," I said.

"We do," they both answered. They shared huge, familial smiles.

Romayne Wheeler would be a character befitting a Conrad novel,
not because of silver mining greed but for his extraordinary generosity and life as a traveler. Raised in Mexico, Santo Domingo, and the
States and trained at conservatories in Vienna and Salzburg, the American concert pianist and composer drifted into the Sierra Madre in 1980
on a spiritual pilgrimage. After playing for years in the most prestigious
concert halls around Europe and the States, as well as in Japan, Latin
America, and the Caribbean, "I came full circle and felt I was repeating
myself," Wheeler once told the *New York Times*. "I knew there had to be
more, or else I was just becoming a musical robot."

Wheeler had already journeyed among other indigenous groups in
the Americas, including the Hopi in Arizona. Among the Rarámuri he
found a spiritual (and soon a permanent) home. He wrote in his book of
poetry and essays, *Life Through the Eyes of the Tarahumara*, "When I returned for the tenth time to my adopted land in the Sierra Tarahumara,
I felt as if I could see with new eyes, and simultaneously felt an intimate
relationship with everything around me." Relocating to a remote village

on the edge of the canyons, Wheeler learned Rarámuri, incorporated himself into a community, built a stone house, and eventually was elected a member of the ejido.

Wheeler didn't leave behind the concert life. In fact, after his solar-powered electric piano faltered over the years, he loaded up a 1917 Steinway concert grand (which was allegedly the former piano at the Guadalajara Opera House) and transported it by dump truck to his isolated village. It bumped along the Gran Vision highway and logging access roads for seventeen hours. The piano was couched under a dozen or so mattresses, blankets, and sacks for corn. It arrived unharmed, and Wheeler set up in his new concert hall on the rim of Copper Canyon.

The Rarámuri were fascinated by Wheeler's work, which they referred to as "water music." In return, he listened to and interpreted indigenous chants and songs on the violin and guitar. Shocked by the high infant mortality rate among the Rarámuri, Wheeler made an annual concert tour on the international circuit each fall in order to raise funds for Jesuit Father Luis Verplancken's clinic in Creel.

Wheeler's piano, as the Rarámuri father-son duo from Batopilas knew, was not the first piano in the far reaches of the Sierra Madre. Alexander Shepherd, at the behest of his wife and family, had a piano transported to their Batopilas home at the bottom of the canyons in the 1880s. Without vehicles, transporting it through the canyons would seem impossible. But as Shepherd's son, Grant, wrote in his memoir, *The Silver Magnet: 30 Years in a Mexican Silver Mine*, "From what you have read you will realize that although a pack-mule with his arriero is capable of carrying almost unthinkable loads, you cannot see him coming along the mountain trails with an upright piano draped across his back."

He echoed the words of the mestizo truck driver. "Don't forget that we still have the Indian."

Shepherd then described how a cadre of 24 Rarámuri men carried this "great box" for 185 miles in 15 days. They were paid $1 a day. "It is really quite simple," Shepherd gushed. "They get under the poles in a squatting position; at the word 'Vamonos!' they straighten up. The piano is off the ground, and the carriers move off with the inward satisfaction of knowing that all they have to do now is carry this great box for a hundred and eighty-five miles." He concluded, "It is expensive transportation, very. Yes, but think of the pleasure you will derive from that piano."

We finished unloading the bricks in a drizzle. The mestizos watched us work from inside the truck cab. They smiled and revved up the engine when the last brick was placed on the stack. The two Rarámuri men jumped on top of the flatbed and secured their places on a couple of large tires as the truck rumbled down the muddy road. Only the mestizos waved goodbye.

The perceptions, or misconceptions, of us by the various residents in the Sierra Madre had a backside, of course. Everyone, from the urbanized Mexican vendor at the four-star hotels to the cavedwelling Rarámuri corn tiller in the most remote canyons, dressed us with their own ready-made views and assumptions about who we were as gringos and what transpired on our side of the border. A certain level of scrutiny never let up during our entire period in the mountains; no matter where I was standing or working or chatting, there was always someone gazing at me with an intense deliberation. I don't think they were simply making an inventory of my wardrobe. For the boys at the basketball court, or with the men at the tesguinadas, or among the mestizo shopkeepers in Creel, I served as an ambassador by default from the other side.

Toward the end of our sojourn, Carla came home one evening toting some of the textbooks from the school. A Rarámuri and Mexican panel for the state of Chihuahua, as part of a special program for indigenous education, had prepared the texts. In the third-grade book, there was a script for a play that the kids were to perform in Spanish. The play had three characters: two indigenous children and a gringo. The gringo, dressed in a rich fashion, enters the scene with a camera, struggling to speak Spanish. He tells the children, who are in their native dress, that they are pretty and he would like to take their photo. The children ask the gringo why he wants to take their photo, to which he responds, "I am going to sell them and make money," and then he takes their photos without letting the kids respond. He tosses them some pesos. Then the excited gringo asks the boy what he is making. Grinding the corn for pinole, the boy informs the gringo, who immediately takes the pinole and gives the boy a couple more pesos. (One note on this scene: oddly enough, grinding pinole is traditionally a female duty, which might suggest that an urban mestizo composed this play, adding another dimension to the intercultural dynamic.) Then the gringo turns to the girl, who is making a basket for Holy Week. The gringo grabs the basket, gives her some pesos, and walks away.

The play ends with the boy and girl chatting about their encounter with the gringo, how they have been treated, and what they have left.

Boy: He took away my corn.
Girl: And my basket as well.
Boy: But he left us this money.
Girl: And why do we want this money? It doesn't help me
    dress for Holy Week.
Boy: It doesn't help to solve our hunger in the mountains.

"Javier is different," I once heard Bernabé say to another man at a tesguinada. "He's not like other chabochis or gringos. He wants to work with us and drink our tesguino. He's learning the chapareke."

Bernabé spoke within earshot; I wasn't sure if he was speaking from his heart or merely flattering me in a soft moment of tesguino. The other man looked at me, scanned my figure, and then spewed out some laughter, as if Bernabé had told a great joke.

I once heard two little girls chatting about me around the cabin. They were trying to decide if they should call me a chabochi or a gringo. One insisted that since I was from the other side of the border, I was a gringo. The other girl was a generalist; all non-Rarámuri were chabochis, and besides, I had a beard, which was the true definition of chabochi.

I grew up a gringo in southern Arizona. My backyard had been part of Mexico until the war in 1846–1848; the actual demarcation of the present border was set under the Gadsen Purchase. During the same decade that the Americans gained the new territory and "sides" were drawn in the Chihuahua and Sonoran sands, the term "gringo" became a common sobriquet for those on *el otro lado*. Its origins, like the name of "Arizona," were unclear, but the possibilities were endless.

One possibility: While I was more familiar with Robert Burns' anthem to the lassies, "Green Go the Rashes, O," some historians claimed the hordes of American volunteers marching to the Battle of Monterey sang the tune (taken from an old Scottish ballad, "Green Grows the Laurel") of an American soldier in love with a Mexican *linda*, "Green Grow the Lilacs," which ended its refrain, "But by our next meeting I'll hope to prove true, and change the green lilacs to the Red, White and Blue." "Green grow," or Burns' "Green Go," in the ears of the offended and defending Mexicans evolved into "gringo." Another theory documented the green uniforms of some of the American soldiers in Texas, to which the Mexicans responded, "Green, go," as in "Yanqui go home." The less romantic adhered to the alteration of the linguistic origins of *griego,* or "Greek" in Spanish, which was occasionally attributed to foreigners by Mexicans.

The Irish had old ties with Mexico. Hugh O'Conor had been the Spanish governor of Texas and laid the foundations for the presidio of Tucson, where I was raised; Juan O'Donoju (O'Donahue) served as the last Spanish viceroy in Mexico; Michael Wading, who changed his name to Miguel Godinez in order to serve in the New World, was one of the earliest Jesuits in the northern provinces. The family of Alvaro Obregón, president of Mexico from 1920 to 1924, changed their name from O'Brien. Vicente Fox (like the great Chihuahua-born actor Anthony Quinn), who won the presidency in 2000 and toppled the seventy-year one-party political system, came from Irish origins.

Raised in the borderlands between Arizona and Mexico, I stumbled onto the infamous tale of the San Patricio Battalion, the Irish heroes of the Mexican American War, by accident. My history teachers in school had never mentioned the war. Even today, despite being the first war on foreign territory for the United States, the War of 1846–48 remains an enigma for most Americans and a forgotten chapter of our history.

The wound from the continental invasion still festered in the lingering tension between Mexico and the United States during the era of Pancho Villa and the Mexican Revolutions from 1910 to 1920. During both periods, Mexicans, including the governor of Chihuahua, fled into the Sierra Madre and hid out among the Rarámuri and mestizo settlers. Some would argue today that the territorial laceration from the war, driven by our manifest destiny to create a country from sea to shining sea, still spirals along the Mexico-U.S. border.

This fact is hard to imagine: the land Mexico lost to the United States was greater than the area of France, Italy, and Switzerland combined.

The origins of the Mexican War dated back to the declaration of independence of the Republic of Texas in 1836. Never accepted by Mexico, the stakes were raised when the States declared its intention to annex Texas as a slave state in 1844 and placed American soldiers on the Rio Grande. In Mexico's eyes, the Americans had invaded their declared border on the Nueces River. Skirmishes broke out, and war was declared. Within a year and a half, American soldiers occupied the Valley of Mexico.

In many respects, the war in Mexico was a precursor to the conflicts of slavery, expansionism, and territorial rights that spawned the American Civil War. Along with General Zachary Taylor, an ingenious war hero on the northern Mexico front and a prominent slave owner who used his fame to ensure his short-lived presidency in 1848, and Jefferson Davis, who had married Taylor's daughter and later became president of the Confederacy, the rolls of officers serving in the war in Mexico included Robert E. Lee, Ulysses Grant, "Stonewall" Jackson, James Longstreet, Joseph Johnston, Pierre Beauregard, George Pickett, and numerous other leaders on both sides of the Civil War. Thousands of volunteers poured into the war effort from Nebraska to Maine. Their military training, including the first American amphibious assault on foreign soil, did not go unused fifteen years later.

Many of these volunteers and mustered soldiers came directly from the steerage boat chambers of Irish immigrants fleeing the famine that was ravaging Ireland and parts of Scotland. (The rise and fall of potato-based agriculture was another recent acquisition from indigenous people in Mexico and the Americas.) Their ranks among the immigrant slums in the States had already provoked the wrath of the Know-Nothings and other American Protestant "nativists," who carried out frequent assaults on the Irish Catholic communities. The treatment of the Irish soldiers didn't fare much better, resulting in a high desertion rate.

Over five hundred American soldiers, at least two hundred of them Irish, deserted the American side and took up the cause of the Mexicans on behalf of gold and glory, to form the San Patricio Battalion, or "St. Patrick's Company." For chauvinistic Americans, especially among those in the slaveholding South, their act was nothing less than treason. For those who viewed America's land grab with outrage, later called "unnecessary and unconstitutional" by Abraham Lincoln, the San Patricios' defiance might have been considered understandable. Henry Thoreau wrote his historic treatise *Civil Disobedience* while in jail for refusing to pay his taxes in support of the war.

Amazingly, both patriotic Irish immigrants, fearful of reprisals, and revisionist American historians, outraged by the act, kept the mercurial story of the Irish brigade and deserters quiet for years. The Mexicans, on the other hand, turned them into folk legends.

"They're heroes in Mexico," an Irish artisan in the plaza of Creel once told me. He had spent the last twenty years living in the Sierra Madre, Baja California, and Chiapas, selling leather bracelets and bags. He said his Dubliner status always carried a hallowed place among the Mexicans. "There are even San Patricio stamps."

On September 12, 1997, President Ernesto Zedillo of Mexico gathered with Sean O'Huighinn, the Irish Ambassador to Mexico, at the village of San Angel to celebrate the 150–year anniversary and salute "the San Patricios, who were executed for having obeyed their consciences."

Led by John Riley, a native of Galway, who had also deserted the British Army in Canada, the San Patricios (who included plenty of other immigrants and Anglo deserters) became one of the most dependable artillery divisions in the Mexican Army. Their salaries were raised from $7 to $57 a month. The Mexican brass promised them land grants (320 acres) for their services; others applauded their sympathy with the Catholic Church. One handbill of recruitment, circulated by Riley and the deserters among the Americans, declared: "Come over to us. You will be received under the laws of that truly Christian hospitality and good faith which Irish guests are entitled to expect and obtain from a Catholic nation. May Mexicans and Irishmen, united by the sacred tie of religion and benevolence, form only one people."

In the end, they proclaimed themselves the San Patricio Battalion and flew the Mexican flag with an emblem of St. Patrick and the harp of Erin. The Mexicans originally referred to them as the *colorados*—the red-heads.

Vanquished at the battle of Churubusco, sixteen Patricios were hanged in the village of San Angel after a staged military trial. General Winfield Scott, the bristly commander of the U.S. invasion on the shores of Veracruz and who had also led the brutal Trail of Tears relocation of Native Americans, enforced the orders. The seething American soldiers eventually executed over fifty men; they imprisoned and branded several others, including Riley, on the cheek with the letter "D" for desertion. (Riley was branded twice, so the legend goes, because the first "D" had been branded upside down.) Many in the battalion escaped and remained in Mexico as mercenaries, only to be disbanded out of distrust by the various factions at odds in Mexico City.

Like any Ossian saga, the story of Irish Lord Delaval James de la Poer Beresford in the Sierra Madre was one of intrigue over scandalous love and betrayal. As the world headlines announced in the days following his death in a mysterious train collision in North Dakota in 1906, the lord had a lady, a "negress" known commonly as "Lady Flo." In contesting Beresford's will, Lady Flo claimed to have "lived with Beresford on his ranches in Mexico for more than twenty years." She added that she was "the common law wife of the decedent, and as such is entitled to a share of his estate."

Lady Flo was actually Florida Wolfe, an African American woman from southern Illinois. She grew up within sixty miles of my family cluster in Salem, the gateway to Little Egypt. (The town was also the birthplace of another legend of that epoch, William Jennings Bryan.) Wolfe served as a maid and nurse for various white families, including the consul in Chihuahua City, where she met Beresford and "formed a mutual liking for one another." Within a short time, Wolfe joined the lord on his ranches, including a 160,000–acre spread at Los Ojitos, in the shadows of the Sierra Madre.

Such an interracial commingling was not only scandalous to the Americans but illegal (Alabama became the last state to repeal its anti-miscegenation laws in 2000). Texas law at the time mandated a sentence of prison for not less than two or more than five years for any intermarriage among whites and blacks. Historian Eugene Porter found that when the lord and lady visited nearby El Paso, "Lord Delaval would cross from Juárez alone in a cab and she would follow in another." Beresford was arrested once for meeting Wolfe on an El Paso street.

This didn't prevent the Irishman and his lady from celebrating their love affair, legal or otherwise, in Mexico. One visitor to their ranch remembered "when this tall and stately colored woman entered and Lord Beresford introduced her with all the English royalty flourishes as 'Lady Flo Beresford,' and after the hifalutin' introduction was over she came over and sat on his lap while the conversation continued. I don't think at that time I had ever seen a colored person and I remember not being able to keep my eyes off her in wonderment."

Beresford's brother, Lord Charles, the one-time admiral of the British Navy and a socialite among the royal families in Europe, felt otherwise. Arriving to sensational headlines in El Paso and then Mexico City and Chihuahua, in order to settle the dispute of the will (in potentially four countries), he refused to budge beyond the terms of Beresford's own orders. "Florida Woolf, of Salem, Illinois," according to the will, was only to receive 2,000 English pounds (equivalent to $10,000 at the time). Charles referred to Wolfe as his brother's housekeeper.

Lady Flo had maintained her own brand, apart from Beresford's brand, on a large part of the herd in Mexico. One neighboring rancher told the British lord, "When she [Lady Flo] took over Los Ojitos, your brother was close to bankruptcy. He was drinking so much that he was incapable of handling the ranch. Flo put it on a business basis. She paid the debts, helped him accumulate land and guided his investments. In consequence, the property, not including cattle, is worth $250,000. Half or more of them [the cattle] are in her brand."

Along with Lady Flo's ranching feats, Lord Beresford's drinking was infamous in the region. Lieutenant Britton Davis, who passed through the ranch during General George Crook's campaign in the 1880s to capture Geronimo in the Sierra Madre, noted that "I had never met an Irishman who was a prohibitionist and Beresford proved no exception."

With the legal and racial odds against her—even Porfirio Diáz deferred to the famed British admiral—Lady Flo had no choice but to surrender to Charles' terms. She signed a statement that declared their twenty-odd years together resulted in nothing more than the rapport of master and servant. In return, she was given $15,000, along with a few hundred head of cattle.

Lord Beresford's body, per his request, was transported across the sea and then buried in Curraghmore, Ireland. Florida Wolfe took up residence in El Paso, where she lived until her death in 1913. Despite the legal settlement and the fallout over the racial scandal, she never relinquished her title. At the curb in front of her home in El Paso, chiseled in concrete, was a block with her name, Lady Flo.

We planted corn by hand that late spring, row by row, following a gaggle of women in sweeping skirts, all of us clasping digging sticks. Carved from an oak trunk and branch, the plow was dragged by a horse, pockmarked and mangy, stumbling down clods of gray soil that the blade had churned into mahogany ruts. With the reins draped across his neck, Bernabé struggled with a crooked back, hissing at the horse.

Corn was not just the staple in this rugged range of the Sierra Madre. Corn was at the root of the Rarámuri existence. They ate it, roasted it, fried it, fermented and drank it, mixed it with water, milk, and now Coca-Cola, and traded and sold it.

A bag of potatoes sat unclaimed at the edge of the fields. "I only grow corn, some beans," a neighbor told me. He looked at me as if I had missed the punch line. "That's how we've always done it." I felt as if I had taken a step closer to the cliffs of Genesis; the Rarámuri earn their daily bread by the sweat of their brows and corn fields.

The women had their own rhythm, most barefoot, some in huaraches; up one pace, stab the hand-carved stick into the rut, twist it, drop three kernels of corn at the base of the stick, and then, as you twist and remove the stick in the same movement, the seeds trickle into the hole, no more than a few inches deep, followed by a layer of topsoil rolled across by your foot. One young woman, carrying a baby on her back in a rebozo for hours, two tiny feet hanging to the side like holsters, disregarded the stick, moving her foot like a ballet dancer.

The work crew was quiet for the most part. We worked all day until sunset smeared across the canyon walls and topped the sentries of pines. Our host offered a meal of soup made from ground seeds of pumpkins served with blue corn tortillas. After we finished the last field, everyone celebrated with tesguino, getting drunk on mush, and then headed to the neighbor's fields the next day.

The week was cloudy, but still no rain, though now everyone was convinced, as if willing it into existence, that the rains would come.

I often spent the twilight in this period with Bernabé, both of us silent, staring at the fields. Scrappy dug his mug into the dirt, then circled and sat. In times of drought the first corn blades poked through clods of unrequited furrows like limp gravestones. Only the clumps of cow pies and some goat pellets tampered the color of exsiccation. Bernabé's crooked back told me this: seasons come with the fields despite the rainless clouds. The winds cut and levy shades of topsoil on rows that have turned to lees. He held up the weathered hands of faith that still believed in cycles and existence.

We looked around. The chickens still had chicks, stoic in their pecking order of fluff, and dogs still bayed at the moon and attacked intruders, and cows yielded calves that hobbled onto the empty arroyos on their third day of existence. The vampire bats still sucked blood from the same wound on the same cow. The black birds perched in the weeping willows, mocking the brown hues below, echoing the cries of burros and rib-poked horses scratching for roots.

In times of drought men crumbled onto the roads carved from stone and dust and evasion, picking up their belongings in handfuls. The Rarámuri men in this village knew that if the rains didn't come, they would go in search of day labor. They were brittle and mobile as kindling in search of fire, leaving all, even their lives, behind for fear of hunger.

The newspaper in Chihuahua spoke the unspeakable the next week; northern Mexico was going through the worst drought in the country's history. This generated a considerable amount of debate at the village shop. Some say it was a ploy by Chihuahuan politicians to attract more aid and emergency funds to line their corrupt pockets. Then, everyone fell silent and looked out at the grey fields.

"The key," Bernabé told me, "is to plant at the right time, so that when the rains come, the corn will be about a foot high. If it is too small, then the rains will wash it away. If it grows over a foot, two feet, then it will crumble and die."

I stared at the fields. I realized that a family's entire future was predicated on the roll of the seeds. We stood outside each night for days, gauging the lunar expanse. Bernabé planted according to the position of the moon and the stars.

One night we assembled at a neighbor's cabin at twilight for a propitiatory *yumari* dance of thanks. I saw Alfonzo, Bernabé and Maria, Tomas and Jorgina, Cornelio, Chico and Anna, and many others I knew well. According to their teachings, the deer taught the yumari dance to the Rarámuri as a celebration of the land. In truth, no one called it a rain dance, though that was clearly the buzz in the village. The elder who had been summoned to chant was wearing a cast-off Dallas Cowboys rain breaker.

The chanter's gourd rattled the bones of drought before three crosses pounded into the hard earth while the guts and blood of a sacrificed goat boiled for the *tonari* stew. The old man hobbled in his rain jacket and prayed, hobbled back eight tiny steps, shaking those rhythmic sighs from his lungs in thanks to Onoruame, the mother-father god, chanting to the clouds that hinged off the Pacific Coast like hoary doors to the future. For the first time, fear of the future was voiced in this village, as if the faith behind the yumari dance had not only been fermented in corn, but despair.

The chanter held his gourd like a white flag, a signal of endurance, hobbling in his rain jacket. Pieces of the goat boiled in hops on a fire fed by *ocote* and other pine and attended by the children who slept outside. Inside the cabin everyone else danced to cassettes from a Veracruz band on a boom box, celebrating the gift of tesguino, while babies purred in piles in the corners like hearthstones of family life. The yumari man came inside in intervals, taking a break, passing around the single gourd of tesguino.

"We drink this tesguino in thanks to God," the chanter told me, as we huddled in a corner.

He went back out and danced alone. The gourd rattled the bones of drought until dawn, the tonari goat stew webbed and blanched, the morning canyon walls scudded by smudges of red. The goat meat was devoured when the light flooded the fields. The chanter quietly hobbled away on a path into the forest.

The first rain of the season arrived by ten in the morning. I heard frogs later in the next evening.

It was not long before Bernabé and I began weeding the cornfields, yanking crabgrass from the furrows. The parcels of land carved from this pine-rimmed hollow were confined by rock walls and arroyos. When Bernabé headed for *la junta*, the weekly Sunday village meeting that hovered around the mission walls, I left the fields and returned to our log cabin. I was incredibly depressed. I had been carrying a tragic letter from my mother and uncle in my back pocket all morning.

My mother's family homestead, down in Eagle Creek in the forest highlands of southern Illinois, was gone. The old pond, the four plum trees, the two-hundred-year-old family log cabin, and the cornfields were buried in a crater two hundred feet deep. That old log cabin, where my grandfather had carved out the first window, had finally surrendered to the coal mine; another mine had taken my grandfather's lungs and left nuggets from a cave-in in his head. The man was buried with part of the mine. Another company bought the rest of the land that spring and blasted away our family memories without a funeral. The process was called mountaintop removal. They numbered the logs of the cabin, disassembled it, and now planned to reassemble the cabin at a state park as part of an exhibit.

"A part of our lives that only exists in our minds now," Uncle Richard wrote my mother, "will be completely erased when we die, as if it never existed."

Looking out at Bernabé's hopeful fields, I realized I knew very little about my Eagle Creek, the geography, the people, our family. I possessed snippets of history, like lines from a bluegrass gospel, but I didn't understand the hidden meanings and cadences of my grandparents' lives. I had recently learned that Uncle Henry and cousins Elmer and Dallas often packed up a small cardboard suitcase in the off-season of their dirt farms and hit the road in search of work. Dallas strapped on his peg leg, hobbling behind the others, in order to be considered fit for a job. All of the men sent back what few dollars they earned.

My mom told me this after I had written about the drought in Mawichi. The men here, if the rains did not coax blades from the dark soil, were preparing to pack up their lives and amble down the road in search of work in the Mennonite orchards or vast farms in Sinaloa or Chihuahua.

In the end, I probably knew more about the Rarámuri than about my own family in southern Illinois, because I had taken notes, listened to interviews, read their history, played my banjo at their corn beer fiestas, and worked by their sides in the cornfields and forests. This was something I had never managed to do with my own kin.

As part of the late 1960s burst of prosperity, we repeated our migratory family history and left Illinois, settling in the borderlands of Arizona and Mexico. Arizona became my generation's frontier, transient and fickle, not quite California, not quite Mexico, more western than southern, more invented than understood.

The world of Eagle Creek remained a part of our lives, but a distant one; perhaps it functioned as a mythological homeland in the way a Sicilian American in Chicago might view his native Mediterranean island, cut off from the daily news but privy to the local language and nuances. And the old songs; my banjo playing had begun as a homage to the hollows.

I recalled one summer, huddling on the porch on a rare visit back home, while Uncle Richard pointed out where one of his cousins had accidentally hanged himself, but survived, during a particularly intense game of cowboys and Indians. Once the women had prepared the lunch, the men entered the cabin and ate first. Then the kids were summoned, and I remember picking at a plate of chicken hearts and gizzards, fried catfish, cornbread, fried okra, stacks of fresh vegetables, watermelon, custard and rhubarb pies, and all of the rest of the trimmings of southern cooking that had crossed the Ohio River. The women chatted in the kitchen and waited for the final round of the meal. This was probably in the mid-1970s; I had not been back to our family hollow in over twenty years. Like an outside visitor, I had been fascinated by this gender division of labor and eating habits, of sorghum-making and hog-killing time, and the stories of my cousin's grandmother spitting tobacco into a spittoon with incredible accuracy. I felt estranged and at home at the same time; still, for the first time in years, I felt like I was among my kin.

An old Rarámuri woman hobbled down the Mawichi dirt road, dressed in her skirling traditional dress, while I read the letter. She was followed by little boys racing up and down and then the accompanying band of disinherited dogs. I looked out from our cabin and saw goats and cows corralled in the pantheon, the cemetery of tequila bottle headstones and disheveled graves. I could hear a young woman slapping her wash on the rocks at the nearby creek. Chickens pecked in front of our cabin, as if searching for land mines.

There was a hodgepodge of cultures here, a can of processed coffee aside a pile of corn that had been ground by an ancient stone mano on the metate. There seemed to be so many paradoxes in our definitions of progress, our longings.

How odd it was that we had come to this remote indigenous village to examine the stories and changes in a struggling indigenous culture and language, when I was losing mine at the same time. My own family treasure had been stolen without my ever knowing its value. Our family had been well known as traditional sorghum makers; they had lived off the rugged forests and hill country for over two hundred years. That heritage had disappeared now; I had let it fade from my life for years.

I went outside the cabin and scurried around the wood pile. I pretended to chop some wood. The constant stream of people on the dirt road, especially the slow-moving elders, calmed me slightly and reminded me of their own struggle for viability in an age of mountaintop removal. Indeed, the Rarámuri were dealing with more than prospectors for gold or coal; beyond the treasure, the outsiders were removing their very cultural existence.

A little kid finally summoned me. The village meeting was over. The *conjunto* band in the village, the three-string fiddler and his guitar-playing brother, had called for my banjo at a tesguinada that evening. Scrappy rose to accompany me on my walk to the neighboring cabin. I picked a three-finger rhythm on their pascol dances and strummed along on the Mexican rancheras. After midnight it didn't really matter, everyone passing the gourd of tesguino and laughing.

We would even play some bluegrass standards, "Rank Strangers" or "Molly and Tenbrooks," as if we were down in my own Eagle Creek.

When we headed back to the tourist hub of Creel one weekend, I met a fascinating chef at one of the luxury hotels. He was from Morocco. He was an incessant talker. He recited love poems in Spanish to Carla, then shifted on his elbows and discussed the first chapters of a book he was writing on Mexico (and the world), aptly titled, "Indifference," which he pronounced with a devastating French accent.

"Look at the crudos," he charged, dismissing the barflies crowding the halls of the luxury hotel where he worked. "What do they know about me, or Morocco? What do they know about the world?" He clicked his tongue and shook his head at a fellow hotel operator, who nodded in a bewildered acquiescence.

"Indifference."

The chef was raised by a Muslim father from Yemen who had multiple wives and numerous kids. The turmoil in the family was daunting. By the time he reached his teens, the chef had fled to Europe to attend a cooking school and soon found work in Germany, San Marino, Italy, and Spain. He spoke all of the romance languages fluently.

"What language do the crudos think I speak in my dreams?" he continued. "They don't even know." He paused and then spat out, "In-difference."

An investment opportunity in his own restaurant led him to Mexico. The endeavor failed, so he sought work in Chihuahua, entering another partnership. This partner escaped in the middle of the night, taking their bank account and possessions with him.

"Indifference."

With no other options, he took the job at this luxury hotel in Creel. We watched as an international clientele of tourists funneled into the restaurant. The adjacent discotheque was already thumping with action. I had poked my head inside and noted the presence of a few locals in jeans, polished boots, and crisp sombreros, a couple of Mennonite men, and a hodgepodge of Americans, urban Mexicans, and Europeans.

The Moroccan chef finally turned to me, having spoken in a collage of Spanish, Italian, and English, and asked where I came from.

"Arizona," I said.

"Do you know anything about Morocco?" he scoffed.

I felt myself slipping into the category of the *crudos*, the indifferent.

Moorish culture arrived in the Sierra Madre long before the Moroccan philosopher-chef. I didn't tell him that, though, not wanting to upset his theories of singular discovery. According to linguist Don Burgess, the Rarámuri word for their violins, *raveli*, first noted by Jesuit Matthaus Sheffel in his report in German on the Sierra Madre in 1767, possibly dated back to the Arabic spiked fiddle, the *rebab*. An early model of the violin, the rebab was a dronal string instrument in the classical Andalusian orchestras that had performed in Spain for centuries. Another connection with Morocco might have occurred in the early sixteenth century.

When I was growing up in southern Arizona, we celebrated Rodeo Week, not Black History Month, in February. In fourth grade, I was paraded into a local TV studio in Tucson with two other kids for one of those predawn talk shows. Our roles were to speak about our respective races in Arizona history; first came the Indians, then came the Spanish and Mexicans, then came the Anglos, I mumbled.

On our way home, we passed Estevan Park. "The park has something to do with blacks," my folks told me. At the time I didn't know that it had been renamed during the Second World War after the first African explorer in the Americas. Estevan was a black slave from Morocco who had served as a guide for the Spanish expeditions. During the war, with the Buffalo Soldiers in town, the park served as the first swimming pool available to African Americans; they could use the regular city pool only once a week. The city drained the water after "Negro day" at the regular city pool.

The neglect of Africans in American and Mexican history has become an old story. Estevan would be no exception. His role as the first nonnative explorer in the American Southwest, whose expeditions from Florida to Mexico, and then in Arizona and New Mexico, surpassed those of Lewis and Clark, has been overlooked by the plethora of stories about the Spanish conquistadors. No contemporary scholar has undertaken a full academic treatment of his life or the possibility of his background as a Muslim. (For example, on his final trip north to the Pueblos of New Mexico, Estevan brought along two greyhounds, or salukis, the only dogs considered clean or sacred and in possession of *baraka*, or blessed power for Muslims in northern Africa.) In fact, the most accurate portraits of his life exist on the shelves of children's literature.

According to Cabeza de Vaca, one of Estevan's fellow travelers, whose account of their journey was the first travel memoir on North America, the African served as interpreter and scout, determined the routes, learned the languages, and dealt with the native tribes. American historians in the late nineteenth century couldn't accept the Spanish documents or this implicit leading role; they either ignored Estevan's part or lowered his status to "the swaggering negro slave." Modern portraits in popular texts, films, and fiction, influenced by these historians from a period of inquisition or racial deception, followed by conjuring a fascinating "black legend" mired in sexual and savage intrigue. From a sex fiend "lusty Arab" to a gigantic "emperor of the African slaves," Estevan became one of the oldest literary caricatures in North American history.

Unlike his peer Don Quixote, Estevan's story was not only true, but a fascinating odyssey in the exploration of America. As part of a failed expedition to conquer Florida in 1527, he was one of five survivors, out of six hundred, who sludged through malarial swamps in search of gold and then reboarded rafts that wrecked along the eastern coast of Texas. For nearly a decade, the survivors endured slavery, hunger, torture, and deprivation among tribes in Texas. They were the first men from the Old World to see buffalo skins.

In 1535, four of the five men escaped and headed west, intent on walking back to Mexico. Gathering a legion of followers, they played the role of America's first snake oil sellers—they even claimed to have raised the dead—until they stumbled onto Spanish slave-raiders over a year later in northern Mexico. Their trail skirted the periphery of the Sierra Madre plains; the Rarámuri did not flee the lowlands for another 150 years.

Estevan's slave master, amazingly, was also one of the survivors. The men had journeyed a decade together under extreme circumstances, including cannibalism among the Spaniards, traveling over six thousand miles by boat, barge, and foot.

With Mexico City abuzz with the rumors of gold in the north when the survivors finally returned, Estevan's owner then sold (or, in one document, he loaned) the African back into slavery in order to serve as a guide for future expeditions.

Clad in the feathers and rattles of local tribes, traveling days ahead of a Franciscan friar from Nice, who was given historical credit for the journey, Estevan became the first nonnative to enter Arizona and New Mexico. He passed through the outside boundaries of the Rarámuri for a second time.

The friar and the slave made an agreement; Estevan was to send back a cross the size of a hand if he made any discoveries. He sent back a cross the size of a man. The symbolism was providential. Entering the Zuni pueblos, Estevan was finally killed. The friar fled back to Mexico City and proceeded to describe the pueblos in grandeur, launching Francisco Coronado's infamous expedition, which put the last nail in the Spanish conquistadors' North American traveling coffin.

The park in Tucson was one of only two places attributed to Estevan in the States. We spotted him in the Mexican borderlands, though; he appeared in murals of the roaming travelers from the Old World on municipal buildings in Chihuahua and Ciudad Juárez.

While I was chopping wood one morning, Bernabé walked up from the stalls, where he had been dealing with a pregnant cow. He lingered around the woodpile, wordless, without making eye contact, in that wary way of the elder inspecting the progress of a protégé. I went through a few squat logs, shattering all of them into approved pieces of firewood, before Bernabé nodded in that aloof way of his, as if I had passed the test.

"Pues," he began, bending down to roll a couple of logs toward me, "I heard you tell El Chapareke about Africans." He was referring to my comment that the banjo originated in African communities, among slaves. I asked El Chapareke the same about his instrument. A few musicologists openly questioned whether the chapareke was indeed indigenous to the Sierra or had been introduced by African slaves or miners.

Bernabé rarely asked a direct question. The conversation skirted around his quandary or observation for a few lines, interspersed with plenty of physical labor or gaps of silence, a couple of jokes, until he turned and smiled and quietly nudged the question out of his mouth.

"Are Africans from the other side?" he said, and then he backed up. "You know, they're not from here."

The African presence in Mexico occurred long before Estevan made his trek across Texas and Mexico. In fact, while Estevan was residing in Mexico City in 1537, a revolt of African miners occurred in Amatepeque and around the country. During the uprising, the Africans elected a king and sought to coordinate the rebellion with African slaves in other mining settlements. In his first act in the New World, Francisco Coronado, the conquistador who ultimately followed Estevan's road to the Zuni pueblos and then to Kansas in his failed search for the Seven Cities of Gold, took charge of suppressing the African uprising with Spanish soldiers and indigenous allies. Twenty-four of the African leaders were captured, hanged, and then quartered; the rebellion fizzled. In the process, however, it so terrified the viceroy that he wrote an urgent letter to the Spanish king to end the importation of African slaves.

However, with the passing of (poorly heeded) Spanish laws against the enslavement of indigenous people within a few years, even more African slaves were brought into Mexico to work the mines and agricultural plantations.

The mix between the Africans and the Rarámuri occurred with the first Spanish inroads into the Sierra Madre. Ambrosio, one of the leaders in the Rarámuri rebellions in the late seventeenth century, was often referred to as a mulatto in colonial records. By 1730, Africans appeared regularly in Jesuit records on the Sierra Madre. In his review of the Sierra Madre missions, Jesuit Padre Juan de Oviedo decried: "All this land is full of Spaniards, mestizos, blacks, mulattos, coyotes and Indians from the outside."

Over 150 years later, mining prospector J. R. Flippin wrote in *Sketches from the Mountains of Mexico*, a book about his Sierra Madre experiences in 1877, "There are a few negroes living here also; but 'they are strangers in a stranger land.' They learn the language, strange to say, with a noticeable facility . . . The negro is courted by this class of the Mexican population (the peon class)." Flippin was unaware that the abolishment of slavery in Mexico, including blacks and mulattos, occurred in 1829, over thirty years before Lincoln's Emancipation Proclamation.

Henry Flipper, the first black cadet to graduate from West Point, would have laughed at Flippin's racial asides and failure in the mines. Having been railroaded out of the army on a dubious charge of embezzlement in 1882, Flipper found work as a mining engineer and land surveyor in the Sierra Madre on behalf of several American mining companies for the next few decades. (More than likely, Flipper was the victim of a plot to discredit him, after the black officer had begun a social relationship with a white woman.) He went on to survey most of the mines in northern Mexico for Bill Greene, the "Cananea Copper King" and business partner of William Randolph Hearst, who even sent Flipper to Spain to research ancient Spanish documents on lost silver mines.

Flipper was an extraordinary traveler; he could have been a character in Traven's novel. He was born a slave in Georgia right before the Civil War. After attending school, he received an appointment to West Point and then published a memoir. He eventually became one of the leading experts on Spanish and Mexican land laws in the country, served as the first black editor of a white-owned newspaper in Nogales in 1885, worked as a special agent for the Department of Justice, and then followed his friend Albert Fall, one of the first senators from New Mexico, to Washington, D.C., as the assistant to the Secretary of the Interior. Fall, who also launched the Sierra Mining Company in Mexico, publicly heralded Flipper as "my right hand man and advisor."

One rumor, spread by American newspapers during the Mexican Revolution, headlined erroneously that Flipper was the "brains" behind Pancho Villa. After Fall's demise in the Teapot Dome scandal in the 1920s, Flipper journeyed to Venezuela and there became the first black petroleum engineer.

Flipper brought the African journey of Estevan full circle; in 1896, the American authored the first monograph on Estevan's pioneering travels, *Did a Negro Discover Arizona and Mexico?* Not only did Flipper make some of the first translations of Spanish documents about Estevan, but he provided a brief analysis challenging the unsubstantiated calumnies, accepted by most historians, concerning the African's sexual deviation and interaction with the indigenous tribes. Flipper's work and defense of Estevan, largely ignored by chroniclers and historians over the next hundred years, was cited in W. E. B. Du Bois's classic text, *The Gift of Black Folk.*

Hard times didn't leave Flipper alone. The stock market crash ruined him economically, sending him back from South America to his native Georgia as a penniless wayfarer. Flipper was seventy-five. He relied on the charity of his brother and extended family. He spent the rest of his life in the disconsolate pursuit of clearing his name on the rolls of the court-martialed.

Bernabé's question was providential. During our sojourn in the Sierra Madre, President Bill Clinton finally granted Henry Ossian Flipper a full pardon, nearly sixty years after the black soldier's death.

Flipper reemerged in Sierra Madre history, ironically, in the strange story of the Confederate exiles who had fled into Mexico after the American Civil War. His life, in fact, served as a vinculum along a changing frontier that had seen a procession of foreign military victors and vanquished, from the mid-nineteenth century until the American cavalry's denouement in their calamitous search for Pancho Villa in 1917. It reminded me that northern Mexico, and the Sierra Madre, had served as a scorched battleground for a continual series of wars and armed conflicts over the last several centuries, dating from the aboriginal conflicts between the Rarámuri, Tepehuane, and Apache incursions to the assault and conquest of the Spanish conquistadors and military presidios, the Mexican wars with the Apache and Yaqui, the War of 1846 and invasion by the United States, the filibusters and fallout of the American Civil War, the invasion of the French and the reign of the Austrian emperor, the American and Mexican hunt for the Apache renegades, the various outbreaks and branches of the Mexican Revolution, and the last shots of the American cavalry under the leadership of General John Pershing in 1917.

Not that this armed conflict had ended. Any trip through the Sierra Madre during our sojourn ensured an encounter with an armed roadblock by the Mexican military and federal police. Huge truckloads of young Mexican soldiers, gripping their automatic weapons, became common sights on the Gran Vision. The soldiers were en route to the burning fields of selected marijuana and poppy cultivation.

We were once flagged down on a very remote road, which had probably seen only a handful of passing vehicles that week, by a group of young men in undershirts, all waving their automatic rifles. I assumed they were bandits or narco gunmen. I knew our Bronco was a precious commodity in the Sierra Madre. After hesitating for a moment, I slowed the truck to a stop. The armed men approached the vehicle. I turned to Carla.

"Do your Italian thing."

The young men were Mexican soldiers, assigned to this isolated post. They had washed their uniforms in the nearby creek and left them out to dry. We chatted as if we were old friends. They hadn't seen anyone all day and were starved for communication. They huddled around Carla's side with big eyes.

"Italiana," they laughed. "Somos primos. We're cousins."

I purposely maintained a distant and indifferent attitude about the narcotraficantes in the Sierra Madre. My indifference was more calculated than casual. I was not interested in the banalities of the narco true crime lifestyles and legends; I was not indifferent to their unremitting scourge or the suffering of defenseless Rarámuri or mestizos who had been displaced by narco violence and cultivation. The world of the Mexican narcos was as entrenched, complex, and maddeningly violent as their counterparts in Colombia. There had been plenty of ominous reports by human rights groups and muckraking journalists about the growing narco influence and violent control as masters of the region. Mexican author Carlos Mario Alvarado's *La Tarahumara: Una tierra herida* was a passionate exposé on the region's drug violence and a plea for intervention in what he termed "a zone of death and marijuana." As a longer-term resident, I didn't take this lightly.

Given Mawichi's importance in the tourist market and its proximity to Creel, the immediate area surrounding us was relatively free from any narco incursions or cultivation. The presence of weapons throughout the Mother Range, though, was evident. The fatal train robbery in the fall had been attributed to a gang of former narco gunmen. This reality of banditry was nothing new or unique to Mexico. If anything, it underscored a brutal undercurrent that had ebbed and flowed throughout the Sierra Madre history with the habitual shift of nature.

In the mid-1950s, Pat Jenks happened onto the village of Guadalupe de la Concepción, on the western side of the Sierra Madre. He wasn't that far from the highlands where Yaqui guerrillas had earlier taken refuge. The number of blond and blue-eyed villagers peeking behind their doors astonished him.

Jenks had a fine eye for historical details. He was one of the last people to interact with the young artist Everett Ruess, the legendary "atavistic wanderer for beauty" who disappeared into the northern Arizona canyonlands in 1934 in a swarm of intrigue and mythos. The collapse of the stock market in 1929 and the subsequent looting of his family's mine claim by Doña Poinciana, one of the only female bandit leaders in the Sierra Madre's history, derailed Jenks' own dream to complete his PhD studies in ornithology. Jenks once explained to one of his co-riders:

"She's a remarkable woman. She's a bandit who rules with an iron hand over a gang of Tarahumara Indians. John [the manager of the mine] tells me they're terrified of her and will do anything she says."

Jenks spent the better part of twenty years scouring the canyons of the Sierra Madre on horseback and in jeeps for a mule trail to transport gold bars from his family's mine in Monteverde. He wandered into Guadalupe de la Concepción, then a smattering of adobe huts, in search of a haunting orphan boy he had encountered years before.

The fair-haired children playing among the cottonwood trees, according to the orphan, were the descendants of a German prospector who had arrived in the Sierra Madre in the early 1800s, along with three American soldiers who appeared in the 1850s.

Those three soldiers, whose surnames of Clarke, DeMoss, and Moore rippled among families in the valley, later founded their own village of Bermudes, named after the British colony and archipelago that lies 570 miles off the North Carolina coast. Jenks assumed the soldiers had been from the muster rolls of the Mexican American War. According to the orphan, the soldiers arrived after the United States had invaded Mexico, in a wounded and ailing condition. Nursed by the villagers, they recovered and departed for the States, only to return later as settlers. "Soon the valley was full of blond and red-haired children," Jenks was told.

The real story, however, might be tied to a different war. Almost sixty years before Jenks stumbled into the village, Henry Flipper arrived in the village of Bermudes in 1888 at the invitation of Clark (minus the final "e"), whom he had met in a nearby town.

In Bermudes, Flipper stayed with the legendary three soldiers, but their accounts, according to his memoir, had nothing to do with the Mexican American War. Raised in North Carolina, the three "brothers," as Flipper referred to the men, had joined the gold rush in California in 1849, where they struck it rich. When the Civil War ignited at Fort Sumter in 1861, the three men gathered up their gold and boarded a boat for North Carolina, via Panama, where they planned to join the Confederate Army. They never made it past Mexico. Their ship wrecked along the west coast, and the men lost their entire fortunes. Compelled to scramble for a living through the Mexican countryside, the three men veered into the Sierra Madre for safety. It was a volatile time in the country: the French, British, and Spanish were landing troops at Veracruz to force President Benito Juárez to repay Mexico's debts, and a lingering hostility still simmered over the American invasion in 1846–48 and the continual American filibuster attacks in the northern states in the 1850s. The men eventually cleared some land in an unoccupied valley, took Mexican wives, and founded the village of Bermudes (after Bermuda, where they most likely had passed en route from their native North Carolina).

Their agricultural prowess astonished Flipper. "They farmed, raised hogs, made ham and bacon, tobacco, potatoes, milk, butter, etc. and when I left, they loaded me down with hams, bacon, tobacco and many other good things to eat. They raised the finest Irish potatoes I ever saw and fine onions." Flipper noted that the three men had built "old-fashioned" log houses with puncheon floors.

Despite the color of Flipper's skin and his slave heritage and their Confederate orientation, the men enjoyed each other's company so much that Flipper stayed an extra day. "The old men fiddled and the young folks danced all day and all night." Flipper remained in touch with the men for several years.

Flipper later encountered another American in the Sierra Madre, in the village of Bacadehauchi. This former soldier, Smith, had actually deserted the Confederate Navy on the west coast of Mexico and fled inland. His fate was more pacific; he told Flipper he was serving as the teacher in the town's one-room school.

The appearance of a Johnny Reb in the Sierra Madre was not as outrageous as it may sound. As many as five thousand soldiers from the Confederacy fled south of the border after Robert E. Lee's surrender at Appomattox in 1865. (In 1969, Rock Hudson starred as a fleeing Southern colonel in *The Undefeated,* a movie with John Wayne about the Confederate exodus to Mexico.) Thousands of others founded communities in Brazil, Venezuela, Honduras, and Jamaica; some took refuge in England, France, and Cuba; and the most adventurous served as mercenaries in the Egyptian Army. Their ranks in Mexico included Confederate generals, Southern governors, and Matthew Maury, the internationally celebrated oceanographer and astronomer who eventually became the imperial commissioner of immigration for Mexico.

The Confederates' timing was disastrous. Mexico was embroiled in its own internal war. Seeking a reprieve for his bankrupt nation, President Benito Juárez, a Zapotec Indian and the only fully indigenous person to serve as president of Mexico, had declared a two-year moratorium on paying foreign debts in 1861. The arm-twisting policies of the IMF and World Bank didn't exist in those days; Spain, England, and France simply invaded the country to collect payment. Aware of the turmoil of the Civil War in the United States, and clearly wary of the American policy of manifest destiny, Napoleon III sent his French troops deep into the Valley of Mexico, while Spain and England retreated to Europe. The nephew of the first Napoleon had visions of his own empire. Despite the Mexican victory in the Battle of Puebla in 1863 on May 5—the origins of the Cinco de Mayo celebrations—the French pushed on, taking the infamous Chapultepec Castle that the Americans had occupied less than twenty years before.

The first Confederate refugees began arriving on the heels of the new "emperor," the thirty-two-year-old sandy-haired Austrian Archduke Maximilian, who entered Mexico City in 1864 in a ceremonial charade guarded by French soldiers and anti-Juárist monarchists. Propped up by the ambitions of Napoleon III, who had sold armed ships to the Confederates, Maximilian's folly soon fell victim to the overwhelming Juárist forces.

While the French marched Maximilian around Mexico City, General William Tecumseh Sherman was laying waste to the Confederacy in Georgia.

The Confederates played their own role in the French debacle. According to the diary of Brigadier General Alexander Terrell, the original idea of the fleeing Confederate rebels was to "take the country up to the Sierra Madre mountains." Indecision on the part of the Confederate leadership in the west, however, fractured the allegiance of the regiments, leaving only small cadres of the battalions in place. The plans for a Confederate buffer zone in northern Mexico were abandoned. When Lee surrendered in 1865, the reckless scramble across the Rio Grande and along the Gulf of Mexico took place in indiscriminate waves.

One of the most dubious characters was the Honorable William Gwin, a former senator from California. Claiming that Napoleon III had appointed him as the "Duke of Sonora," Gwin convinced legions of

Southerners that the French Army would liberate and then hand over the northern states of Durango, Sinaloa, Sonora, and Chihuahua—including the Sierra Madre—to the Confederates as their own colony. In June 1865, the *New Orleans Times* declared, "There is no doubt Dr. Gwin will get his project through. It only awaits the signature of Maximilian to become a law." Alas, Maximilian refused to sign off on the chimerical dream. Gwin returned to the States and was arrested.

Later that year, however, the embattled emperor set aside land grants around the tropical areas of Veracruz for the Confederate refugees. The rebels named the town in honor of the new empress of Mexico, Carlotta. Other smaller colonies were scattered around the country. Within months, more Confederate settlers and their families arrived (some even with slaves), intent on rebuilding their agricultural plantations of coffee, cotton, and sugar in the Mexican jungles.

At one tesguinada in our village, a Rarámuri man joked with Carla about her name and European origins. The young Carlotta, a hapless Belgian princess, still resonated in the country's collective memory.

The world was small, even in the 1860s. While Maximilian, the latest incarnation of the Hapsburg archdukes—the oldest reigning monarchy in Europe—and Carlotta paraded around Mexico City under the canopy of emperor and empress, Carlotta's brother, King Leopold II of Belgium, took the throne. Under the guise of bringing civilization to the natives, he launched his plunder of the jungles in the Congo for ivory and rubber, carving out Joseph Conrad's heart of darkness. By the time of his death in 1909, nearly ten million Africans, according to author Adam Hothschild, had died due to murder, torture, starvation, and deprivation.

In the tropics of Carlotta, however, the Confederates, not the natives, fell victim to their own greed and warring tendencies. In little over a year, the colonists in the newly named township of Carlotta, as well as most of the other Confederate colonies, suffering from illness, violence, and internal disputes, were sacked by Juárist-supporting mestizo and indigenous guerrillas. The *New York Tribune* mocked the Confederate settlers: "The far-famed city of Carlotta . . . consisting of a house, a barn and a stable, has been destroyed."

They weren't the only foreigners expelled from the country. Already routed out of Mexico City, the fleeing emperor made a last-minute attempt to rally the Confederate forces to his rescue. It was too late. Most had fled the country via ships in Veracruz.

Committed to his empire to the end, eschewing any chance of escape,

Maximilian was executed on June, 19, 1867. He had presented each one of his seven executioners with a gold coin, beseeching their accuracy at his heart. One of the Mexican soldiers missed and struck Maximilian's eye, which was replaced with a glass eye during the embalming of the body.

Carlotta herself, the namesake and patron saint of the Confederates, was abroad at the time of the fall of her fugitive empire, seeking support from Napoleon III, who had turned his back on their exploits, as well as from the Pope. Informed of Maximilian's death, the twenty-seven-year-old collapsed and was eventually isolated in a Belgian castle, where she was declared insane.

A demented and tortured soul, Carlotta died in 1927, the same year that the Fimbres Apache incident brought Mexico's bloody times back into the international headlines.

Sizing up their enemies, the Sierra Madre Apaches realized that it didn't take a bogus international expedition to round up a foreign legion of bounty hunters. This included the Mexican Rurales, a fierce paramilitary police force based in Sonora, which sometimes joined the Americans in pursuit of the Apaches in the Mother Range. Their commander, Colonel Emilio Kosterlitzsky, even made the dubious claim of having captured Geronimo.

Kosterlitzsky's journey to the Sierra Madre ran in the opposite direction of Alfonzo's travels away from Mawichi. The woolly-mustached traveler, the son of a Russian father and a German mother, emerged onto the international stage like a character from Nobel Prize–winning author Mikhail Sholokhov's classic novel on the Cossack wars, *And Quiet Flows the Don*. Kosterlitzsky's father had lost a leg in the Crimean Wars in service to the army of Czar Nicholas I. Raised in Moscow and then Germany, Kosterlitzsky returned to St. Petersburg to attend a military academy, and then transferred to the Royal Naval College in Moscow.

Training to become a seaman, the cadet boarded a ship for a worldwide cruising exercise in 1872. The world at sea, however, didn't appeal to the future landlubber cavalry leader. He jumped ship in Puerto Cabello, Venezuela. After working on freighters from New York to San Francisco, Kosterlitzsky finally disembarked in the port of Guaymas, Sonora, just before Albert Owen's train venture at Topolobampo. Within two days, Kosterlitzsky enlisted in the Mexican cavalry.

The Russian allegedly spoke, read, and wrote eight languages, including Chinese. He once spent a night in the Sierra Madre chatting in

German with Adolph Bandelier. He crossed paths with Henry Flipper numerous times. He also assumed the Mexican ways within months. Quickly climbing the ranks of the Mexican military, Kosterlitzsky participated in the attacks on the various revolts by the Yaqui and Mayo, including the capture of the Yaqui leader Cajeme at Alfredo Vea's ancestral village near Cocorit, and then served in the Mexican wars on the Apache. As a colonel of the Rurales, Kosterlitzsky gained an international reputation for his task of clearing out all desperadoes, renegades, and bandits in the region.

By 1886, just as Geronimo was readying to surrender again, Kosterlitzsky found himself Porfirio Díaz's hand-picked chief of military intelligence and the eventual commander of the military forces in the "third zone" in northern states. While the dictator consolidated his power, Kosterlitzsky's own stature as the "mailed fist of Díaz" remained intact in Sonora, Chihuahua, and the American borderlands. Kosterlitzsky and his Rurales gained American notoriety when they helped quell a strike by Mexican miners at an American-owned mine in Cananea in 1906.

After forty years in the service of the Mexican army, the Russian colonel finally saw his career succumb to the upheaval of the Mexican Revolution. When Francisco Madero and a bevy of revolutionary leaders ousted Díaz in 1911, the commander watched as revolts and counterrevolts fractured the country. In March 1913, Kosterlitzsky and his Rurales fled across the border and surrendered to the Americans in Nogales. In the end, overrun by General Alvaro Obregon's revolutionary forces in Sonora, the foreign commander chose exile over a presumed execution in his adopted country.

Relocating to Los Angeles, Kosterlitzsky found a position in the U.S. Department of Justice as an undercover special agent in 1917 and was used in the infiltration of pro-Kaiser German groups and other immigrant organizations. His American tenure lasted until his death in 1927, at which point the Russian expired with "a faint attempt at a battle yell that had terrorized the Yaquis in the dim long ago."

While Kosterlitzsky was entering the underworld in Los Angeles, another international military leader resided in the Sierra Madre, writing his memoirs and short stories for the *Los Angeles Times*. Suffering from asthma and other illnesses, General Ben Viljoen, a one-time notorious guerrilla leader of the Boers (settlers of Dutch origin in South Africa), had sided with Kosterlitzsky's foes in the Mexican Revolution. Viljoen's guerrilla exploits in his own country rivaled those of Pancho Villa in Chihuahua. His daring acts against the British forces even won the attention of Winston Churchill, who chronicled the war in the late 1890s as a correspondent. Churchill gushed: "A Maxim-Vickers gun abandoned by the Boers in a donga was about to fall into British hands, when that notorious ruffian, the fearless Viljoen himself, brought back a team of horses and escaped with the gun, threading his way between the red flames and black clouds of lyddite shells which the British artillery concentrated on him—a feat that, were it done by a British officer, he would assuredly be covered with decorations."

Viljoen's feats aside, he was finally captured and imprisoned by the British forces in 1901. He didn't waste any time: the Boer wrote a memoir of his travails while in the prison camp. Along with thousands of other Boers at the end of the war, Viljoen refused to sign an oath to the British Empire and sailed for the Americas. Some set off to found settlements in Argentina, Chile, East Africa, and the States. Thanks to Teddy Roosevelt, also of Dutch ancestry, no Boers were ever detained at Ellis Island.

Viljoen and other Boers headed for Mexico and then the American Southwest. Riding the lecture circuit to Mexico City, where he riveted the crowds with stories of the guerrilla outback in South Africa, Viljoen attempted to win the favors of the Diáz government. The dictator wasn't entirely impressed with the South African rebels; he encouraged them to settle among the revolting Yaqui in Sonora. Another Boer leader, W. D. Snyman, fared better, negotiating for the permission to settle along the Conchos River on the plains before the Sierra Madre in Santa Rosalia, Chihuahua.

Despite the settlement of numerous families in the area, the Boers struggled to sustain their newfound colony. Within a few years, devastated by the flooding waters of the river, which swept away their orchards and crops and buried their fields in silt, most of the Boers packed up their belongings and straggled across the American border. The rest of the settlers followed after the outbreak of the revolution in 1910.

Viljoen wouldn't accept defeat. Boer farms and communities sprouted along the Rio Grande. Settling in the Mesilla Valley, in New Mexico, he became the first Boer refugee to be granted American citizenship in 1909. A writer from *Collier's Weekly* reported the New Mexican community's shared sentiments and success: "The Boers have come to be recognized as among the most successful farmers of irrigated land in the Southwest. They have reclaimed thousands of acres of desert and have been the direct agents in causing the cultivated lands of the Mesilla valley to double in value."

The tug of old Mexico still lingered in Viljoen's military heart. When the revolution exploded in various parts of the country, the Boer general jumped into action as an adviser to Francisco Madero in Ciudad Juárez, across the border from El Paso. Brought into Madero's war cabinet, Viljoen formed *kommandos* to launch attacks in Chihuahua. Not all the Mexicans and foreign mercenaries approved of the Boer's involvement. Guiseppi Garibaldi, a roving international mercenary and grandson of the famed Italian revolutionary, referred to Viljoen as a "military adviser to the President, but we regarded him as a harmless crank." Even so, in 1911, on the orders of Madero, Viljoen led a command of two hundred volunteers into battle in Baja California.

Guaymas, Sonora, the port on the other side of the Sierra Madre where Kosterlitzsky first landed, drew Viljoen deeper into Mexican affairs. Newly elected President Madero assigned the Boer the task of negotiating a settlement with the Yaqui and various Mexican and American settlers at odds over the rights to the land. Ironically, Anthony Ivins, the head of the Mormon settlements in Mexico, compared the brutal experience of the Yaqui to that of Viljoen's and Kosterlitzsky's own homelands: "For unless history shall reverse itself, there can be but one result, the scenes of Finland in Russia, and the Transvaal of South Africa, will be re-enacted on the Yaqui River."

The Boer's relationship with Madero, a liberal reformer from a wealthy family in Coahuila who was overthrown and executed in 1913, remained close. After taking a rest for his ailing health at one of Madero's San Lorenzo baths in Tehuacan, the Boer was sent off to Germany as the appointed Mexican consul.

Viljoen's health prevented him from serving Mexico more than a few months. After treatment in Bavaria and Austria, he returned to the States and sought relief in the Sierra Madre. The precious mountain air could not save the Boer's ailing lungs. He died at his New Mexico farm in 1917, the year the Russian commander joined the Department of Justice as an American spy against the Germans.

The Mexican Revolution and the lore of Pancho Villa captivated more than a few adventurers from Russia, Italy, and South Africa. A foreign brigade emerged and served under his command. His exploits, as well as the incredibly complex web of intrigue and players in the revolution, headlined the newspapers and magazines around the world for years. Launched in 1910–11, the violence of the revolution became one of the most discussed global warnings in a world that was inching closer to that disastrous fault line of the First World War and the Russian Revolution.

One of the most curious aspects about Villa was his use of airplanes, which even appeared in this Sierra Madre. These planes intrigued Tomas, the police commissioner. During his service in the military—Tomas was the only Rarámuri I ever met who had donned a uniform—he briefly took the reins of a helicopter that scouted the side canyons.

"You could say I was the first Rarámuri pilot," he laughed once, on a trip to his nearby homeland of Tejaban. We returned on several occasions for the less than twenty-hair-raising-mile drive on the edge of Copper Canyon. The trip took a few hours. Tomas was proud of the narrow dirt road that zigzagged like shelves down the steep valleys. He laughed at the crumbling edges, which cascaded into the abyss. Years before, he had carved the first access route with a bulldozer, hired by the owner of a luxury hotel. The hotel sat perched on a breathtaking overlook on the rim of this grand canyon.

"You drive too slow," he scoffed at my driving. "I drove a bulldozer along this ridge faster than you, and I was knocking down trees and rocks. I could even turn it around."

"How long did it take you?" I asked, diverting attention from my white-knuckled grip on the steering wheel.

"Seven months," Tomas said. "I slept on the bulldozer at night when I got tired, or I walked to my mother's rancho."

Usually attired in dark jeans, a vest, boots, a sombrero, sunglasses, and a slight swagger, Tomas was a crafty autodidact who had earned the respect of the ejido for his judgment and verdicts of justice as the village constable. Having skipped school as a child, he had taught himself how to read and write in Spanish. He possessed the skills of an electrician and a mechanic. As the police commissioner, interacting with the village governor, he dealt with the local disputes, petty crimes, and even the adulteries. He ensured the peace at the tesguinadas and rituals. More importantly, he enforced the laws that kept outside mestizos and corrupt ejido members from pillaging the forests. Without a weapon, this sometimes called for creative community measures. Years before, awaiting the assistance of the federal police to halt the illegal sales by an ejido administrator and truckloads of illegal loggers, Tomas had helped to organize a human blockade of the main dirt road through the village. Cadres of villagers, including aged women and men, weathered an untimely brutal snowstorm in their all-night barrier. They faced down acts of violence from the mestizos and threats of death for days. In the end, thanks to a military officer contacted through Tomas, the federal police and a federal investigator finally intervened. The corrupt mestizos were expelled from the ejido.

Tomas's family rancho was located in a bucolic valley in a nearby side canyon. We slept under a rock overhang whenever we visited, which Tomas recalled fondly from his childhood. The kids from the nearby ranchos had slept in this cave when their parents attended the tesguinadas. Other members of Tomas' extended family lived on the neighboring plateau, which jutted off into Copper Canyon like a sky peninsula.

Tomas took us on a tour of the area. A rugged stone church fascinated me, laid out in the design of a cross, hugging the rim of one plateau like a launching pad. The church possessed nothing other than a huge stone in the center that had been carved into an altar. The temple's Catholicism seemed to have melded back into the geology of the canyon, reclaimed by indigenous customs. Mounds of melted candles stained the stone altar and floor like living prayers. It reminded me of the sixteenth-century Church of St. Thomas in Chichicastenango, Guatemala, where Mayan worshippers had continued to leave their prayer offerings and candles on the floor, as they had for their pre-Columbian deities.

"The priest who built this church," Tomas said, "was an extraordinary man." He whirled around and pointed at a narrow field that ran along the plateau. "The priest learned to fly his own airplane and arrived every Sunday from the sky."

His fate was tragic. Tomas joined the search party for the priest and his crashed plane in the 1960s. He helped to carry the priest's body out of the canyons.

The first airplanes in the Sierra Madre dated back to Villa and the American invasion during the final years of the upheaval from the Revolution. I learned this at a tesguinada. Giving me a hard time about my "Pancho" nickname, one young Rarámuri man once sang a verse of this *corrido*, or ballad, at the corn beer fiesta:

> Nuestro Mexico, febrero veintitres,
> dejo' Carranza pasar Americanos,
> diez mil soldados, seiscientos aeroplanos,
> buscando a Villa, queriendolo matar.

> (Our Mexico, on February 23rd,
> Carranza let Americans cross the border,
> 10,000 soldiers, 600 airplanes,
> looking for Villa, wanting to kill him.)

While fewer than two dozen—not six hundred—American airplanes dogged General Francisco Pancho Villa (born Doroteo Arango) and a small band of his rebels through the lower slopes of the Sierra Madre and northern Chihuahua for eleven months in 1916–17, the invasion and eventual retreat remained fresh in the minds of the Mexicans and the Rarámuri. Springboarding his revolt out of Chihuahua, often using the canyons of the Mother Range as a hideout, Pancho Villa sightings and his legends still abounded.

The history of Villa has been chronicled by historians, novelists, and Hollywood on a par with Geronimo. Historian Friedrich Katz's nearly one-thousand-page opus, *The Life and Times of Pancho Villa*, remains a definitive work. A raucous Hollywood production in 1934, *Viva Villa!*, starring Wallace Beery and Fay Wray, is the most amusing. In the end, thousands of American soldiers chased both revolutionaries in the same region; unlike his Apache counterpart, Villa eluded surrender.

After navigating the mind-boggling entanglement of revolutions and counterrevolutions in Mexico for several years, and having marched on Mexico City and served briefly as governor of Chihuahua, Villa found himself in dire straits in the spring of 1916. Until 1914, he had courted and won the admiration of the Americans. President Woodrow Wilson's Secretary of State, William Jennings Bryan, considered Villa the preferable alternative among the early revolutionary contenders to the throne. John Reed's dispatches and eventual *Insurgent Mexico* travelogue, a dramatic portrait of Villa's forces, endeared the rough-edged revolutionary to a large American audience, including Wilson. At first, the American Left was enamored with the revolutionary. As governor and commander of the northern forces, Villa even wrote Wilson in 1914 and offered to make a prisoner exchange for Mother Jones, who had addressed miners in Chihuahua when she was in her eighties, after she was arrested and imprisoned by Rockefeller's private forces in the Colorado mining camps.

In the early years of the revolution, a foreign legion of mercenaries and observers, including Sam "the Fighting Jew" Dreben, Oscar "the Dynamite Devil" Creighton, and the celebrated writer Ambrose Bierce, joined Villa on the battlefield. The foreign legion had been lured by Villa's offer, in the words of an announcement posted along the border of Juárez, of "weekly payments in gold and glory." Reed was less than impressed with this international brigade. He termed them "hard, cold misfits in a passionate country, despising the cause for which they were fighting, sneering at the gaiety of the irrepressible Mexicans." In his novel *The Old Gringo*, Carlos Fuentes depicted the spirited abandon of the septuagenarian Bierce, who had covered the American Civil War half a century before as a journalist: "Crossing the mountains and the desert, he felt that he could hear and smell and taste and see as never before." Bierce later wrote to a friend, "To be a gringo in Mexico. Ah, that is euthanasia." Most historians assume the white-haired author of *The Devil's Dictionary* was killed on the battlefield or murdered by bandits. His demise remains a mystery.

When the Americans landed the Marines in Veracruz and Wilson eventually endorsed former Coahuila governor Venustiano Carranza's presidency after the volatile national political machinations in 1914, Villa didn't only feel betrayed. He lost the very source of his weapon and ammunition imports. Within two years, the commander who had once conquered cities and the imagination of the world and led thousands of troops across the country found himself a defeated rebel on the run, scurrying to raise a ragtag army of forcibly enlisted recruits.

In his memoir, one Texan pilot claimed Villa purchased planes from the United States and hired American barnstorming pilots. These airplane legends even inspired a corny American film in 1968, *Villa Rides*, starring Yul Brynner as Villa and Robert Mitchum as his American pilot.

In 1916, Villa's band of 485 men (Villa was not present) made the first attack on American soil by a foreign army since the British assaults in the War of 1812, at the border town of Columbus, New Mexico. Seventeen Americans were killed. Much to Villa's plans, the attack provoked the Americans into a full-scale invasion, which the revolutionary leader hoped would spark a national uprising.

Within ten days, Wilson empowered Pershing to lead the Punitive Expedition in search of Villa and his men. While never signing any agreement, Carranza had no choice but to quietly acquiesce to the American invasion into Mexico. Departing with over five thousand troops of American cavalry, along with eight Curtiss JN-3 airplanes equipped with pistols and rifles, trucks, and a brigade of open-top Dodge touring cars, Pershing led the Americans on an eleven-month wild goose chase through Chihuahua and the Sierra Madre.

The Americans never came close to Villa. Even though he was reportedly wounded in the knee during an encounter with Carranza's forces, Villa managed to hide away and recover in a cave in the southern foothills of the Sierra Madre for two months.

In truth, Villa wasn't the only military exercise for Pershing's troops. Just as the Americans had used the Mexican shores for their first foreign amphibious assault and large-scale artillery practice during the War of 1846–48, followed by the Civil War, Pershing's forces essentially employed the Mexican battlefield as a training ground for the brewing First World War. The airplanes, several of which crashed, were the first to be used in combat by Americans. Twelve other planes, Gee Bee R-2s, eventually joined the First Aero Squadron in making 540 missions. Motorized vehicles were also operated for the first time on the battlefield, though with little success in traversing the craggy hills and sandy creek beds. In one of the daring raids on Villa's men, Pershing's young lieutenant, George S. Patton, engaged in his first military battle.

Only months before the States entered the First World War in 1917, Pershing led his defeated forces out of Mexico. He considered the expedition one of his great failures. He wrote to his father-in-law, "We are now sneaking home under a cover like a whipped cur with his tail between his legs." Even some of his beloved Buffalo Soldiers, for whom Pershing had earned his "Black Jack" nickname as their one-time commander in the Indian Wars, were slain and others captured in a mistaken battle with Carranza's forces.

Pershing didn't exit Mexico alone. He brought over a thousand Mormon settlers across the border with him, along with 427 Chinese refugees. Detested by Villa for reasons that still confound historians, the Chinese cooks, servants, merchants, and rail workers in Mexico sustained some of the worse atrocities by Villa and his northern rebels, especially during his final triumphant march in Chihuahua City in 1916.

As a cruel irony, the Chinese refugees, who had aided and supplied Pershing's Expedition, were not welcome in the States. Since 1882, Chinese had been refused citizenship. The refugees, hailed as "Pershing's Chinese," languished for years in military camps along the Texas border and in San Antonio until Pershing returned from the First World War as a hero and commander of the American Expeditionary Forces. The general finally came to the rescue of the refugees, gaining their admission as citizens. (Chinese exclusion laws weren't repealed until 1943.)

When researcher Carleton Gajdusek entered Creel in 1950, he encountered a Chinese Mexican who claimed to have survived the Villa purges and founded the site that became the town of Creel. Once a cook for railroad construction crews in the early part of the century, the man ran a hotel on the same site where he had pitched the first meal shack. He was defiant about his early role: "Primero yo, despues Creel."

Oddly enough, Villa possessed a strange admiration for the Japanese, an admiration that nearly killed him. The revolutionary and his brother maintained a Japanese servant, Gemichi Tatematsu. In a Shakespearean conspiracy concocted by an American captain, two other Japanese men were hired as secret agents to befriend Villa and poison his coffee. "And Dyo did put this dose of poison in a cup of coffee set in front of General Villa; but that Villa, having been suspicious that he might be poisoned through his food for a long time, poured half of the coffee that contained the poison into another cup and handed it to a Mexican who sat on his right."

Villa survived the assassination attempt. A specter of the American invasion still haunted him. In 1923, the retired revolutionary was gunned down in Parral while driving his own open-top Dodge touring car.

Over the course of our sojourn, one of my main sources of information was the wily Noreida, a feisty seven-year-old girl with Moorish eyes and a wide grin, who attached herself to Carla and made it her habit to stop by our cabin every morning before school and recount the village gossip. She eventually entered without knocking, wrapped in her rebozo, and took a seat in front of the fire in the corner. We always had a cup of hot chocolate waiting.

"My God," she once exclaimed. "You have chocolate AND milk AND sugar. What a house. I'm coming back here every morning."

And she did. Once she discovered a horde of children's books in Spanish in the back room (left behind by a government worker), she alternated her narrative on the village "saints and ain'ts" with a recitation of the books, page by page, word by word, letter by letter.

"Pancho," she would suddenly say in her bubbly fashion, "you're not paying attention. What's this word?" Then that smile would stretch. "They're going to dance matachines next week."

For all of my experiences among the adults, one of the most poignant events dealing with Rarámuri culture occurred among the children toward the end of our stay. Or rather, the children emerged from an adult-led ceremony as the keepers of the Rarámuri ways. A bantam corps of kindergartners became our guides into the future land.

Capped in red and orange crowns made from construction paper with strips of colorful streamers draping down the sides, the tiny kindergartners shuffled into their positions as matachin dancers on the cracked concrete floor of the basketball court. No more than five or six years old, the ten serious-faced dancers divided into their appointed roles: the matachines and monarchs faced off in opposite lines, with the two leaders standing at the front like partners. As anthropologist Robert Zingg noted in 1930, there was a vague similarity to the sashaying positions and steps of the Virginia Reel.

For the crowd of villagers who had arrived at the school for the graduation ceremony—of the kindergartners and half a dozen sixth-grade students—there was nothing ill-timed about the winter matachin dance taking place in May. They overlooked the lack of ornate crowns or costumes or capes. They were thrilled to see their kids taking part in a school activity related to their own culture. For the mestizo and ames-tizado Rarámuri teachers presenting the program, the matachines rep-resented one of several "folkloric" dances they hoped would entertain the crowd.

The distance between the teachers and the villagers was telling, es-pecially in terms of the role of the dances. None of the parents sat in the chairs arranged in the middle of the basketball court. The women re-fused to budge from their united wraps on the sidelines; the men stood under the backboard or leaned against the school walls like indifferent spectators. After fiddling with a static-ridden sound system for over an hour, the teachers launched their "show" to a polite but diffident audi-ence. They spoke only in Spanish to a crowd that had many monolin-gual Rarámuri speakers, especially among the mothers. After a comedy sketch and disco performance based on a Mexico City–based TV pro-gram (in an area where no one had electricity, let alone televisions), country swinging, and the swirling colonial Spanish dancers, the mata-chines took the stage.

Complete silence gripped the ball court. Then the sound system percolated the scratchy 6/8 rhythms of fiddles and guitars. Strangely, the local performers had not been asked to play by the teachers. Unlike any of the other stiff performances by the older kids, the kindergartners lightly stepped into the matachin cadence on their toes, rendering the movements with an intensity and a grace that immediately rooted them below the concrete and into their community. Even the principle mon-arch—Pato, an artful kid nicknamed the "Duck"—called out the orders to change positions with a keen alacrity, armed with his rattle and fan.

Originating in Europe (still today in northern Italy, matachin danc-ing takes place in a few mountain villages), the dance depicted the tri-umph of the Christians over Estevan's Moorish brethren. According to Jesuit priest Pedro de Velasco Rivero, in his classic text on the Rarámuri, *Danzar o morir, matachines* is synonymous with *matamoros*, that is, "to kill the moors." Other indigenous tribes in Mexico, Latin America, and the

American West also celebrate the dance; the Pueblos in New Mexico have their own interpretations. According to anthropologist Edward Spicer, the "dance of the *Matachinis* was introduced by Jesuit missionaries" to the Yaqui in Sonora "as a dramatization of the triumph of the Christians over the Aztec ruler Montezuma through Malinche, the first Christian convert in Mexico."

At first glance it seemed odd that the Rarámuri celebrated a ritual hauntingly close to their own conquest by the Spanish. But like all rituals in the Sierra, they had altered the dance for their own purposes. The kindergarten kids symbolized this reality. Instead of a folkloric act or the glorification of a battle of good over evil, the trancelike steps and rhythm of the music appeared to be more of an exhausting act of reconciliation. According to Bernabé, the matachin dancing in the winter represented the passing of the guard from one year or age to the next. Lasting until dawn, like all Rarámuri festivities, it finished with the birth of the sun. A large feast and tesguinada always followed. This transformation reminded me of the ruins in Carla's Italy: the Romans had celebrated their tumultuous winter solstice rituals long before Emperor Constantine was converted to Christianity in the fourth century and revised Western history and winter festivities.

Later that night, after the villagers had slaughtered a cow and feasted on a stew, the school continued the graduation fiesta under the stars. Accompanied by a blaring generator, a disco-mobile from Creel spun records, equipped with disco lights and a gregarious DJ, who introduced norteño polkas and romantic tunes with the exuberance of goading a sweaty hall of dancers. The few mestizo or amestizado couples took to the open-air basketball floor. The rest of the villagers watched the spectacle from the shadows for a few minutes, and then packed up their bundles of children.

"Are you coming?" a sixteen-year-old girl called to Carla. There was a sparkle in her eye; she was en route to her first tesguinada. A young man stood to her side.

They disappeared like the rest of the villagers into the forests and onto the plateau trails, leaving the teachers and mestizos behind. We followed. We all knew that the real graduation party—the tesguinada circuit—like those lurking Roman spirits of the past, had been summoned by the matachin graduates.

Sitting before the toasty glow of the calenton on the night before our departure, I decided to reread the last pages of *The Treasure of the Si-*

erra Madre while Carla made her final notes and packed her bags. I was actually ailing and suffering a lot of pain. Earlier in the morning, I had dislocated my shoulder while installing our solar panel on Bernabé's and Maria's cabin. When the pulley slipped while I was on the ladder, the panel had ripped my arm out of the socket. I was forced to climb onto the roof from the last steps of the ladder, dragging the panel along, and then I reached over with my other hand and snapped my shoulder back into place. There was a minute of sheer agony, but no revelation. In fact, despite the hair-raising pain, it had triggered more of a psychological reaction: Was this my final reckoning for swindling the evangelical solar salesman? Was nature itself punishing me for bringing electricity to this village?

My travails were not over. Later in the day, en route to visit a friend at the Rarámuri ejido of San Ignacio, we were nearly stuck in a muddy rut during a sudden torrential downpour. Still hurting on my left side, I jumped out of the Bronco to lock up the tires in order to shift the vehicle into four-wheel-drive. Mike, the visiting medical student from El Paso and doctor at the clinic, nonchalantly said we would be safe from the lightning, since our rubber tires were grounded. He was wrong. In the rush of the moment, I reached out my limp left arm and hand to turn the metal lock on the tire. Lightning struck the hubcaps at the same time my left hand touched the lock. My pain suddenly disappeared; my arm was numb for a full minute, until I shook off the shock and the throbbing shoulder returned. The villagers didn't know whether they should consider me a shaman or a fool.

No one in Mawichi, except for El Mudo, the village mute, said good-bye to us that final evening. He came by, knocked on the door, and then clapped and pointed at the road that cut out of the canyons like the Rio Urique, and for some reason I imagined him saying, "Pancho, there is the road you make, just as I make my road here."

When we returned to our cabin late that evening, delayed by the storm and lightning incident, we found that most of our village friends had given up on us and already departed for a distant tesguinada. It made me smile. My banjo may have already been packed, but I could still hear the sounds and laughter and verses from half-written songs. In this labyrinth of canyons and people, I knew the Rarámuri's tesguinada circuit would never end.

That quiet last night at our cabin, though, made me feel very much at home. I realized that I had never uttered a sigh of relief at the end of the day, which we had often felt in the suffocating crowds and arduous conditions in India, as if we had successfully endured another twenty-four hours in a foreign world. In fact, we felt the contrary; I think we could have eased into this rustic lifestyle for years. It pained us to go back to the other side.

Our sojourn had evolved into an indulgence we had often dreamed about: a year of study, reflection, and respite from the modern rat race. Mawichi brought us back to the dusty soil and the actuality of a land-based culture. Lumholtz, far from ever being romantic, was not far from the truth when he declared toward the end of his explorations in the Sierra Madre that the Rarámuri were "many times better off, morally, mentally, and economically than his civilised brother."

Beyond the calm and beauty of the canyon, we had lived a very healthy life in Mawichi. Neither of us fell ill all year, with the exception of a minor cold. The high altitude air was dry, fresh, and uncontaminated by the belch of industrial concentration or motor vehicles. The water came from a well that was clean. There were no piles of festering garbage or open sewers. With the exception of a few tins or packaged goods at the shop, the Rarámuri consumed very little that couldn't be thrown in a compost pile.

Arriving at the end of *The Treasure*, Traven declares, "The Indians living in the Sierra Madre, like all those living in the mountains of this continent, are a healthy lot. They reach ages which make old man Methuselah a poor runner-up."

Mawichi, in fact, was relatively free from diseases common in other areas in Mexico, despite the scourge of drought. Tuberculosis and meningitis had become rare. Infant mortality had been reduced significantly. The village struggled mainly with respiratory problems, along with seasonal bouts of dehydration and diarrhea, which had been exacerbated by the arid years.

"You can pass that gourd and drink tesguino in peace," the clinic doctor Mike had once joked, when I complained of a minor cough. "I'll let you know when tuberculosis reappears in the village."

Our valley darkened quickly that evening; the few cabins, even the mission and the school, blended into the caves at the foot the bluffs. The handful of kerosene or gas lamps transmitted a dull cast that dissipated in weakening increments over the night. Outdoor fires attracted more attention. Without electricity in the village, the night sky ruled, Orion's stars bleaching into a spread of rays and dark holes that we had followed across the world. I had often stood outside at night, listening to the custodial chorus of the village dogs, searching for the life struggles in Orion's circle of hunters and goddesses and jealous lovers struck by scorpions. The stars reminded me of the entangled dilemmas of mythos in every society.

At first, Bernabé had acted as if he wasn't interested in keeping our solar panel and lights.

"Why do I need light at night?" he said. "You're supposed to sleep at night."

I nodded. We had been cutting some boards at his work area behind the cabin.

"Javier," Bernabé suddenly said, stopping his work. "What do you do with those lights at night? Aren't you tired?"

It was true. After a day of hauling logs or digging ditches, I had often been too exhausted to accomplish much more than eat my dinner and crawl into bed with a book. The book on those nights would falter in my hands. I would envision the old character of Howard laughing at his partners' delusive obsession with the gold treasure—no less fervent than those of today's narcos, loggers, missionaries, tourist operators, and fellow travelers—an obsession that had been obliterated by the bandits.

"So we have worked and labored and suffered like galley-slaves for the pleasure of it," Howard said to Curtin when he finished his story. "Anyway, I think it's a very good joke—a good one played on us and on the bandits by the Lord or by fate or by nature, whichever you prefer. And whoever or whatever played it certainly had a good sense of humor. The gold has gone back where we got it?"

But Bernabé relented on the solar panel when Maria, forever with an eye to the future, intervened. She wasn't the only interested party. Earlier in the day, a man had come by our cabin as I was packing up the Bronco. We had worked together on the forlorn tourist cabin project. He cradled a car battery in his arms in that protective way I had seen Bernabé and others cart around lambs and goat kids.

"Pancho," Pedro said, "can you jump-start my battery?"

"Sure," I said, moving for the cables in the back of the vehicle.

As we locked the positives and negatives to their partners, it dawned on me that I had once visited Pedro's house. It was a tiny one-room hut, raised from decaying adobe bricks, covered with wood rafters. It possessed nothing more than a calenton stove and a mat for sleeping. A stone mano and a metate were in the corner. I didn't know he had a truck; I couldn't imagine where he had earned the money to buy one.

"So, what kind of car do you have?" I asked, as the battery charged.

Pedro grinned. "I don't have a car."

"Oh, so you're going to use the battery for light in your house," I said.

He had an old oil lamp. On special occasions or parties, some of the villagers rigged up electric bulbs connected to car batteries.

He shook his head.

"I just bought an old television from a mestizo in Creel."

Just as European diseases reached the Rarámuri before the arrival of the Spanish, television had arrived in this village before electricity. Pedro was the proud owner of the first television in Mawichi. On a clear night he said he could make out a hazy but acceptable reception from a station in Chihuahua City.

The televisions in the restaurants in Creel came to my mind, transmitting one sordid soap opera out of Mexico City after another. The televisions served as magnets for little Rarámuri kids, who stared outside the restaurant windows, their faces pressed against the glass.

Pedro thanked me and walked away, carrying the battery in his arms.

I watched him saunter down the dirt road, and then I looked at the pine-rimmed, boulder-walled hollows, partitioned by the creek and rock fences. The fields were buried three feet deep in brilliant shades of green corn. A crooked oak plow that Bernabé had used that morning to weed the furrows rested at the edge of his fields; he had sauntered off to *la junta* weekly meeting, matching his huaraches at the foot of the plaza walls with the rest of the community, just as his ancestors had done for centuries. Couched inside the cliff walls, divided by the creek, the Mawichi valley was one of the most beautiful settings I had ever inhabited.

My last sights that night settled on the blazing logs in the calenton, with the shadows flickering into the front room on either side of Carla, who sat at the table among a mound of papers and cassettes, writing her notes. *The Treasure of the Sierra Madre* finally faltered in my hands. I saw Howard, the old prospector, mounting a horse, heading back into the Indian villages in the mountains, forever in search of treasure.

Acknowledgments

Gracias a todos los Rarámuri de nuestro pueblo que compartieron conmigo sus historias, muy especialmente Bernabé, Tomas, Alfonzo, Margarita, Chemo, Galita, Javier, Martin, Cornelio, Chavela, Noreida, y Antonio "El Chapareke." Nateteraba! Wa'lu sukuira ya bitichi muchuwami. We a'la ku simiya buwechi.

This book would not have been written without the support of John and Jean Biggers, the generosity and postjourney haven of Doug and Katie Biggers, and the advice and tremendous assistance of Barney Burns and Mahina Drees. Eternal thanks to you all.

My work follows the well-worn paths of a lot of trailblazers, researchers, and writers in the Sierra Madre Occidental, most notably for me: Don and Marie Burgess, Padre Luis Verplancken, William Merrill and the Mexico-North Research Network, Andrew Darling, Luis Urias, John Kennedy, Jerome Levi, Romayne Wheeler, and the historical texts of Carl Lumholtz, among many others noted in the bibliography.

Grateful acknowledgment and thanks to the editors who helped improve excerpts that appeared in earlier forms in magazines, newspapers, and radio programs: Katie Bacon and the *Atlantic Monthly*, Celeste Wesson and PRI's Savvy Traveler, Sandy Close and the Pacific News Service, Michael Ondaatje and Michael Redhill at Brick Literary Journal, Marilyn Auer at the *Bloomsbury Review*, and editors at the *Arizona Republic*.

Thanks to the Illinois Arts Council for their timely support and Creative Nonfiction Award, and to John Morton. And special thanks, as always, to Judy McCulloh, my editor and literary shepherd.

Soprattutto grazie a Carla, mi compañera y my jo, che non solo mi ha guidato negli immensi canyon della Sierra Madre, ma mi ha anche ricondotto alla mia terra.

In order to protect the privacy of those mentioned in the book, the names of certain people and places, including the village where we resided, have been changed.

Bibliography

Artaud, Antonin. *The Peyote Dance.* New York: Farrar, Straus and Giroux, 1975.

Bancroft, H. H. *History of Mexico.* San Francisco: The History Co., 1886.

Bandelier, A. *The Gilded Man.* New York: Appleton and Co., 1893.

Basauri, C. *Monografia de los Tarahumaras.* Mexico, D.F.: Talleres Graficos de la Nacio, 1929.

Bennett, C. W., and M. R. Zingg. *Los Tarahumaras: Una Tribu india del norte de Mexico.* Mexico, D.F.: Instituto Nacional Indigenista, 1986.

Bonfiglioli, Carlo. *Fariseos y matachines en la sierra tarahumara. Entre la pasión de Cristo, la transgresión cómico sexual y las danzas de la conquist.* Mexico, D.F.: Instituto Nacional Indigenista, 1995.

Bourke, John. *An Apache campaign in the Sierra Madre; an account of the expedition in pursuit of the hostile Chiricahua Apaches in the spring of 1883.* New York: Scribner, 1958.

Burgess, Donald H. *Cuentos tarahumaras.* Mexico, D.F.: SEP, 1975.

Cardenal, Francisco. *Remedios y Practicas Curativas en la Sierra Tarahumara.* Chihuahua, Mexico: Editorial Camino, 1993.

Deeds, Susan. *Defiance and deference in Mexico's colonial north: Indians under Spanish rule in Nueva Vizcaya.* Austin: University of Texas Press, 2003.

de Velasco Rivero, Pedro. *Danzar o Morir: Religion y resistencia a la dominacion en la cultura Tahumar.* Coyoacan, Mexico: Centro de Reflexion Teologica, 1987.

Dunne, Peter. *Early Jesuit Missions in Tarahumara.* Berkeley: University of California, 1948.

DuToit, Brian. *Boer Settlers in the Southwest.* El Paso: Texas Western Press, 1995.

Fisher, Rick, and David Teschner. *History of Copper Canyon and the Tarahu-*

mara Indians: Unknown Mexico and the Silver Magnet by Carl Lumholtz and Grant Shepherd. Tucson: Sunracer Publications, 2001.

Flipper, Henry O. *Black Frontiersman: The Memoirs of Henry O. Flipper, First Black Graduate of West Point.* Fort Worth: Texas Christian University Press, 1997.

Flippin, J. R. *Sketches from the Mountains of Mexico.* Cincinnati: Standard Publishing, 1889.

Fontana, Bernard. *Tarahumara: Where Night Is the Day of the Moon.* Tucson: University of Arizona Press, 1997.

Gajdusek, Carleston. "The Sierra Tarahumara," *Geographical Review* vol. 43 (1953).

Geduld, H., and R. Gottesman. *Eisenstein and Sinclair: The Making and Unmaking of Que Viva Mexico.* Bloomington: University of Indiana Press, 1970.

González Rodríguez, Luis. *Crónicas de la sierra tarahumara.* Mexico, D.F.: SEP, 1987.

———. *Derechos culturales y derechos indígenas en la sierra tarahumara.* Ciudad Juárez: Universidad Autónoma de Cd. Juárez, 1994.

Goodwin, Grenville, and Neil Goodwin. *The Apache Diaries: A Father-Son Journey.* Lincoln: University of Nebraska Press, 2000.

Guthke, Karl. *B. Traven: The Life Behind the Legends,* Chicago: Lawrence Hill Books, 1991.

Harris, Arland. *Schwatka's Last Search.* Fairbanks: University of Alaska Press, 1996.

Ingstad, Helge. *The Apache Indians: In Search of the Missing Tribe.* Lincoln: University of Nebraska Press, 2004.

Jenks, Randolph. *Desert Quest: A Sierra Madre Odyssey.* Tucson: Patrice Press, 1995.

Karetnikova, Inga. *Mexico According to Eisenstein.* Albuquerque: University of New Mexico Press, 1991.

Katz, Frederick. *The Life and Times of Pancho Villa.* Palo Alto, Calif.: Stanford University Press, 1998.

Kennedy, John. *Tarahumara of Sierra Madre: Survivors on the Canyon's Edge.* Pacific Grove, Calif.: Asilomar Press, 1996.

Lange, Charles, and Carroll Riley. *Bandelier: The Life and Adventures of Adolph Bandelier.* Salt Lake City: University of Utah Press, 1996.

Lartigue, F. *Indios y bosques: Politicas forestales y comunales en la Sierra Tarahumara.* Mexico, D.F.: Ediciones del la Casa Chata, 1983.

Leopold, Aldo. *A Sand County Almanac.* New York: Ballantine, 1980.

Levi, Jerome. *Pillars of the Sky: The Genealogy of Ethnic Identity Among the*

Rarámuri-Simaroni (Tarahumara Gentiles) of Northwest Mexico. PhD dissertation, Harvard University, 1993.

Lister, F. C., and R. H. Lister. *Chihuahua: Storehouse of Storms.* Albuquerque: University of New Mexico Press, 1966.

Lowery, Woodbury. *Spanish Settlements within the Present Limits of the United States, 1513–1561.* New York: G. P. Putnam's Sons, 1901.

Lumholtz, Carl. *Unknown Mexico: Explorations and Adventures among the Tarahumara, Tepehuane, Cora, Huichol, Tarasco and Aztec Indians.* Glorieta, N.M.: Rio Grande Press, 1973.

Meed, Douglass. *They Never Surrendered.* Tucson: Westernlore Press, 1993.

Merrill, William. *Rarámuri Souls: Knowledge and Social Process in Northern Mexico.* Washington, D.C.: Smithsonian Institution Press, 1988.

Miller, Robert. *Shamrock and the Sword.* Norman: University of Oklahoma, 1989.

Nabhan, Gary. *Cultures of Habitat: On Nature, Culture and Story.* Washington, D.C.: Counterpoint, 1997.

Neuman, Joseph. *Historia de las rebeliones en la sierra tarahumara.* Chihuahua, Mexico: Editorial Camino, 1991.

Paciotto, Carla. *Bilingual Education for Chihuahua's Tarahumara Children: A Study of the Contexts of an Emerging Program.* PhD dissertation, Northern Arizona University, 2001.

Pennington, Campell. *Tarahumar of Mexico: Their Environment and Material Culture.* Salt Lake City: University of Utah Press, 1963.

Plancarte, F. M. *El problema indigena tarahumara.* Mexico, D.F.: Ediciones del Instituto Nacional Indigenista, 1954.

Porter, Eugene. *Lord Beresford and Lady Flo.* El Paso: University of Texas, 1970.

Raat, W. Dirk. *Mexico's Sierra Tarahumara: A Photohistory of the People on the Edge.* Norman: University of Oklahoma Press, 1996.

Roca, P. M. *Spanish Jesuit Churches in Mexico's Tarahumara.* Tucson: University of Arizona Press, 1979.

Rodriguez, Luis J. *Always Running.* New York: Touchstone, 1994.

———. *The Republic of East L.A.* New York: HarperCollins, 2003.

Rolle, Andrew. *The Lost Cause: The Confederate Exodus to Mexico.* Norman: University of Oklahoma, 1965.

Salmon, Robert. *Seventeenth Century Tarahumara: A History of Cultural Resistance.* Albuquerque: University of New Mexico Press, 1975.

Schwatka, Frederick. *In the Land of Cave and Cliff Dwellers.* Glorieta, NM: Rio Grande Press, 1977.

Sheridan, Thomas, and Thomas Nayler, editors. *Rarámuri: A Tarahumara*

Colonial Chronicle, 1607–1791. Flagstaff, Ariz.: Northland Publishing, 1979.

Shoumatoff, Alex. "Trouble in the Land of Muy Verde." *Outside* (March 1995), pp. 56–63.

Sinclair, Upton. *Autobiography of Upton Sinclair.* New York: Harcourt Brace, 1962.

Smith, C. *Emilio Kosterlitzky: Eagle of the Sonora and the Southwest Border.* Glendale, Calif.: Arthur Clark Publishing Co., 1970.

Spicer, Edwin. *Cycles of Conquest: The Impact of Spain, Mexico and the United States on the Indians of the Southwest, 1533–1960.* Tucson: University of Arizona Press, 1962.

Thrapp, Don. *General Crook and the Sierra Madre Adventure.* Norman: University of Oklahoma, 1972.

Toulmin, H. A. *With Pershing in Mexico.* Military Service Co., 1935.

Traven, B. *The Treasure of the Sierra Madre.* Cambridge, Mass.: R. Bentley, 1979.

Vallejo, C. *Noroi Raichara.* Sisoguichi, Mexico: Diocesis de Tarahumara, 1996.

Vatant, F. *La explotacion forestal y la produccion domestica tarahumara: Un estudio de caso, Cusarare, 1975–76.* Mexico, D.F.: Instituto Nacional de Antropologia y Historia, 1990.

Vea, Alfredo. *La Maravilla.* New York: Plume, 1993.

Wafer, Lionel. *A New Voyage and Description of the Isthmus of America.* Kila, Mont.: Kessenger Publishing, 2004.

Weisman, Alan. "The Drug Lords Versus the Tarahumara," *Los Angeles Times Magazine* (Jan. 9, 1994), p. 10.

Wheeler, Romayne. *Life Through the Eyes of a Tarahumara.* Chihuahua, Mexico: Editorial Camino, 1993.

Zingg, Robert. *Behind the Mexican Mountains.* Austin: University of Texas Press, 2001.

Index

Abee, Padre Juan Fernandez de, 95.
 See also Rarámuri
Agua Prieta, Mexico, 78, 83
Alaska, 32, 33, 95
Alexander, Grigori, 58
Alfonzo (Mawichi villager), xi–xiv, 2,
 53, 75, 85–86, 142
Almada, Francisco, 124
Alvarado, Carlos Mario, 152
America (Chicago newspaper), 31
Antigone (Sophocles), 129–30
Apache (Indians), 2, 40; and Ban-
 delier, 27; and cavedwellings, 21,
 23, 75; and Fimbres Expedition,
 82–84; and Goodwins, 77–84; and
 Navajo, 74–75. *See also* Geronimo
*The Apache Diaries: A Father-Son Jour-
 ney*, 77
Artaud, Antonin, 2, 16–18, 22, 33, 105

Bandelier, Adolph, 26–28, 31, 33, 48,
 118, 158
Basaseachi Falls, 23
Batopilas, 109, 130, 133. *See also*
 Shepherd, Alexander; Shepherd,
 Grant; Wheeler, Romayne
Bennett, Wendell, 95
Beresford, Lord Delaval James de la
 Poer, 138–40

Bermudes, Mexico, 154
Bern, Switzerland, 27
Bernabe (Mawichi villager), 11, 19,
 21, 25, 35, 45, 48, 49, 63, 96, 113,
 115, 127, 130, 169, 171; author's
 first contact, 4–9; and farming,
 141–43; and funeral ritual, 86; and
 logging, 109–10; and Rarámuri
 identity, 39; social interaction,
 29–31, 127–29, 135, 148–49, 169,
 171
Bernard, Claude, 53
Berry, Wallace, 163
Bierce, Ambrose, 163–64
Biggers, Doug, 9–10
Biggers, Katie, 9–10
Biggers family, 41–43
Bitsui, Erik, 74–77
Blake, Thomas, 112–13
Blood Meridian, 79
Bogart, Humphrey, 6, 12, 109, 124
Bosch, Hieronymous, 17
Bourke, John, 81
Brambila, Padre David, 4. *See also*
 Rarámuri
The Breakfast of Indians, 53
Breton, Andre, 17
Brocke, Alvin, 123
Browne, J. Ross, 32

Bryan, William Jennings, 139, 163
Brynner, Yul, 164
Buckeye, Arizona, 59–62
Buffalo Soldiers, 1, 80, 165. *See also*
  Flipper, Henry; Pershing, John
  "Black Jack"
Burns, Barney, 115; and Apache, 21,
  77; and author in Tucson, 10–11;
  and handicrafts, 10–11, 114
Burns, Robert, 109–10, 135
Burgess, Don, 40, 146

Cabeza de Vaca, Alvar Nunez, 41,
  147
Cabrera, Miguel, 105
Cajeme (Yaqui leader), 59, 158
Calles, Guillermo "El Indio," 53
Camilo, Antonio "El Chapareke,"
  34–37, 39, 86, 149
Carlota (Empress of Mexico), 156–57
Carranza, Venustiano, 164
Casas Grandes, Mexico, 27, 78, 103
Cash, Johnny, 85
Cepissak, Hubert, 106
Chico (Mawichi villager), 21, 25,
  63–67, 110
Chihuahua, xii, 3, 36, 39, 106, 117,
  130, 132, 146, 148; and Apache,
  78–80; and logging, 110; and
  Mennonites, 71, 72; and Mexican
  Revolution, 103, 136, 158, 159,
  160, 163–66; and North Ameri-
  cans, 122, 135, 136, 139, 156;
  and Rarámuri, 50, 66, 116, 141,
  143; and tourism, 119; and train,
  123–24
Chihuahua City, 85–86, 116, 119,
  165, 172
Churchill, Winston, 159
Ciudad Juarez, Mexico, 50, 66, 88,
  148
Clark (also Clarke) brothers, 153–54
Clinton, President Bill, 151
Cochise (Chihuaha leader), 79

Cochise, Nino, 81
Cocorit (Yaqui village), 59
Collier's Weekly, 159
Columbus, New Mexico, 164
Confederates, 1, 43, 153–54
Conn, Carole, 58
Conrad, Joseph, 132, 156
Copper Canyon, 6, 64, 75, 91, 118,
  119, 126, 132, 162
The Copper Canyon Conspiracy, 110
Coronado, Francisco, 148, 149
Correa, Miguel, 105–6
Coufral, Jan, 106
Creel, 7, 40, 46, 47, 58, 86; and Men-
  nonites, 71, 73; and Rarámuri, 50,
  66, 68, 69, 104, 105, 110, 115, 116,
  117, 127, 168, 172; Tarahumara
  Children's Hospital (*see also* Ver-
  plancken, Padre Luis), 89, 90, 94,
  133; and tourism, 24, 101, 117–20,
  122, 124, 134, 145, 146, 152
Creel, Enrique, 103, 117, 119
Creighton, Oscar, 163
Crook, General George, 27, 80–81,
  140
Cuahtemoc, Mexico, 71, 72. *See also*
  Mennonites
Curraghmore, Ireland, 140
Cycles of Conquest, 78

Darien Disaster (Panama), 111–13
Davis, Lieutenant Britton, 140
Death Day, 58
Diaz, Porfirio: as dictator, 23, 58, 59,
  123, 140, 158, 159; and films, 53;
  and Lumholtz, 22; and Mormons,
  102–3; and silver mines, 132
Dietrich, Marlene, 12
Douglas, Arizona, 82, 83
Dreben, Sam, 163
Drees, Mahina, 10–11, 114. *See also*
  Burns, Barney
Du Bois, W. E. B., 151
Dunne, Peter, 42

Eagle Creek, Illinois, 43–44, 143–45
Echeverria Alvarez, President Luis, xiii, 47
Edwardsville, Illinois, 28
Eisenstein, Sergei, 52–58
El Paso, Texas, 140, 160
Estevan: and Africans in North America and Mexico, 1, 147–48, 149; and Flipper, 150

Fall, Albert, 150
Fimbres, Francisco, 82–84
Fimbres Apache Expedition, 82–83
Flagstaff, Arizona, 8, 16, 74
Flaubert, J. B. E., 114
Flipper, Henry: as Buffalo Soldier, 80; as engineer and explorer, 150–51, 153; on Estevan, 151; and Kosterlitzsky, 158
Flippin, J. R., 150
FONATUR (tourism development agency), 119
Fonte, Padre Juan, 91, 94. *See also* Rarámuri
Fort Apache, Arizona, 27
Fox, Vicente, 136
Fuentes, Carlos, 60, 164

Gajdusek, Carleton, 165
Garibaldi, Guiseppi, 160
Geronimo: and Apache Wars, 80–81; in the Sierra Madre, 2, 21, 80–81, 140, 157, 158; surrender, 81. *See also* Apache
Goodwin, Grenville, 77–83
Goodwin, Neil, 77–83
Grand Canyon, 1, 16
Gran Vision (paved road), 3–4, 67–68, 73, 110, 117, 151
Greeley, Horace, 8
Greene, Bill, 150
"Green Go the Rashes, O," 135
"Green Grows the Laurel," 135
Grigsby, R. F., 79

Guachochic (village), 114
Guadalajara, Mexico, 7
Guarojio (Indians), 2
Guaymas, Mexico, 160
Guogochic (village), 79
Guthke, Karl, 13
Gwin, William, 155–56

Harper's Monthly, 22
Hearst, William Randolph, 73, 150
Highland, Illinois, 26
Hothschild, Adam, 156
Howells, William Dean, 22, 23
Hudson, Rock, 154
Huichol (Indians), 2, 23
Huston, John, 2, 12

Indian Relocation Act, 44
Insurgent Mexico, 163
In the Land of Cave and Cliff Dwellers, 33
Ivins, Anthony, 160. *See also* Mormons

Jackson, President Andrew, 44–45
Jenks, Pat, 152–53
Johnson, Lyndon, 62
Juarez, Benito, 154, 155

Katz, Friedrich, 103, 163. *See also* Villa, Francisco "Pancho"
Kennedy, John, 38
Kimbrough, Hunter, 54, 55, 56, 62
Kolata, Gina, 95
Korima, 50
Kosterlitzsky, Emilio, 157–58, 160

Lakota (Indians), 32
La Maravilla, 59, 60–63, 66
Lange, Charles, 27
La Tarahumara: Una tierra herida, 152
Leopold, Aldo, 128
Lesser, Sol, 57, 58
Levi, Jerome, 7–8
The Life and Times of Pancho Villa, 163

Life Through the Eyes of the Tarahu-mara, 132
Lillehammer, Norway, 22
Lincoln, Abraham, 137, 150
London, Jack, 53
"The Lone Ranger," 90
Los Ojitos, Mexico, 139
Lumholtz, Carl: and Apache, 79; and Bandelier, 27; on cavedwellers, 20, 75; early career, 22; on Mormons, 102, 103; on *rarajipari*, 124–26; and Rarámuri, 23–24, 30, 40, 170; on Rarámuri legends, 76; on *Semana Santa*, 96–97; on Sunday village gatherings, 19

Madero, Francisco, 158, 160
Malraux, Andre, 40
Manitoba, Canada, 72
Maria (Mawichi villager), 4–5, 7, 11, 29, 45–48, 50, 124, 130, 142, 171
Masters, Edgar Lee, 33
Mawichi (village), xiii, 44, 46–47; description, 3, 4, 16–17, 19, 21, 22, 28–31, 152, 169–73; drought and *yumari*, 141–42, 144; and films, 49; funeral, 85–89; *korima*, 50; and logging, 110, 161; *matachines*, 166–68; and *mestizos* (Mexicans) 69–71, 113–17; and missionaries, 42, 96–101, 104–7; *Muki Sekara* (shop), 113–17, 120; and outmigration, 66–67, 68; and outsiders, 74–77, 169–73; *rarajipari*, 124–26; *Semana Santa*, 96–101; Sundays, 24–26, 34, 74; and *tesguinadas*, 14, 66, 67–68, 168
Maximilian, Archduke, 155–57
Mayo (Indians), 10, 23
McCarthy, Cormac, 79
McComas, Charlie, 82
Mennonites, 71–74
Men with Guns, 113
Merino, Padre Felix, 104–5. *See also* Rarámuri

Merrill, William, 87, 106
Mexican Symphony, 58
Mexico City, 2, 17, 53, 54, 57, 66, 105, 118, 136, 138, 146, 148, 149, 154–56, 159, 172
Miles, General Nelson, 81
Moore, Clayton, 90
Morgan, Lewis Henry, 27
Mormons, 101–4, 165
Moscow, 157
Muki Sekara (shop), 120–21, 124

Nabhan, Gary, 11
National Institute for Indigenous People, 114, 116
Native Seeds/SEARCH, 11
Navajo (Indians, Dine), 40, 74, 81
Neumann, Padre Joseph, 95. *See also* Rarámuri
New Orleans Times, 156
A New Voyage and Description of the Isthmus of America, 111–13
New York Journal, 83
New York Times, 32, 132
New York Tribune, 8, 156
Noreida (Mawichi villager), 26, 96, 101, 168
Nostromo, 132

Obregon, Alvaro, 136
O'Conor, Hugh, 136
O'Donoju, Juan, 136. *See also* Rarámuri
O'Huighinn, Sean, 137–38
The Old Gringo, 164
O'odham, 30, 40, 60. *See also* Papago; Pima
Opata (Indians), 24
Oviedo, Padre Juan de, 149. *See also* Rarámuri
Owen, Albert, 122–24, 157
Owen, Robert: and cooperative principles; 120–22; in Mexico, 122, 123

Paciotto, Carla, 9, 71, 89, 91, 93, 119; with author in Mawichi, 2–5, 24–26, 34, 38, 51, 67, 101, 129, 168, 169, 173; and Flagstaff, 8; as Italian, 40, 46, 84, 152; and schools, 20–21, 28, 69, 92, 117, 134; and women, 38, 45–47, 65, 87

Papago (Indians), 40. *See also* O'odham

Papigochic (village), 42

Parral, Mexico, 4, 41, 72, 166

Pasqual, Padre Jose, 41, 95. *See also* Rarámuri

Patton, George S., 2, 73

Paz, Octavio, 107

Pershing, John "Black Jack," 2; and Buffalo Soldiers, 165; and Chinese,165; and Mormons, 104, 165; and pursuit of Villa, 73, 151, 164–65

The Peyote Dance, 16, 18

Phoenix, Arizona, 59

Pima (Indians), 2, 10, 23, 40. *See also* O'odham

Poinciana, Dona, 153

Porter, Eugene, 139

Porter, Katherine Ann, 54

Que Viva Mexico! 52–58, 59

Quinn, Anthony, 136

Raat, W. Dirk, 124

Rarajipari, 124–26

Rarámuri (also Tarahumara): agriculture, 28–29, 46, 70, 117, 140–42; as cavedwellers, 20–22, 31–33; and *chabochis* (non-Rarámuri), xiii, 14–15, 24, 25, 26, 30, 35, 66, 96, 99, 130–34, 135; and disease, 94–96, 170; geography, xi, 2, 19; history, 2, 19–20, 22–23, 24, 27, 33, 41–45; *hombre-mujer*, 65, 67; identity, xii, 39–40, 45, 47; *la junta* (village gatherings), 19–20, 24,

143; language and education, 64, 69–70, 134–35; and logging, 2, 3, 49, 51, 68, 110–13, 116, 118, 161; and missionaries (Jesuits, Franciscans, Protestant sects), 1, 7, 19, 36, 38, 41–43, 46, 89–91, 92–96, 104–7, 162; music, 14–15, 34–37, 38, 63, 68, 86–88, 145, 146; *narcotraficantes*, 2, 3, 51–52, 110, 120, 151–52; religion and rituals, 19, 36, 37, 38, 41–42, 86–91, 96–101, 142, 162, 166–68; shyness, 29–30, 38, 96, 122; *tesguino* and *tesguinadas*, 4–5, 9, 14–16, 36, 37–39, 64–65, 67–68, 100–101, 127, 140, 142–43, 168, 169; and tourism, 2, 3, 20, 25, 35, 47, 68, 99, 101, 110–11, 114, 117–20, 122–24, 126–30; and village life (*see* Mawichi); women, 46–48, 85–86, 129–30

Rarámuri Souls, 87

Reed, John, 163

Ribas, Padre Andre Perez de, 91, 94. *See also* Rarámuri

Riley, Carroll, 27

Riley, John, 138

Rimbaud, Arthur, 22

Rivera, Diego, 53, 54, 56

Rivero, Pedro de Velasco, 167

Rodriguez, Luis J., 39–40, 75–76

Rommel, General Erwin, 73

Samichique (village), 94

San Ignacio (village), 169

San Patricios (also Saint Patrick's Company or Battalion), 1, 136–38

Santa Anna, Antonio Lopez de, 121–22

Santa Fe, New Mexico, 27

Santa Rosalia, Mexico, 159

Sayles, John, 113

Schwatka, Frederick, 31–33, 79, 125

Scott, General Winfield, 138

Scribner's Magazine, 20

Shaw, George Bernard, 62
Shawnee (Indians), 43
Sheffel, Matthaus, 146
Shepherd, Alexander, 131–33
Shepherd, Grant, 133
The Silver Magnet: 30 Years in a Mexican Silver Mine, 133
Sinclair, Mary, 55
Sinclair, Upton, 52–58, 59–62, 123
Sisoguichic (village), 42, 46
Sketches from the Mountains of Mexico, 150
Snyman, W. D., 159
Sonoran Desert, 9–11, 59, 60
Sontag, Susan, 16
Spicer, Edward, 78, 168
Stalin, Joseph, 56, 57
Stilley, Stephen, 43–44, 93
Stilwell, Arthur, 123
Stout, John, 18
Stowe, Harriet Breecher, 43
"Such a Parcel o' Rogues in a Nation," 110

Tagore, Rabindranath, 69
Tarahumara Children's Hospital, 89–90, 94
Taylor, General Zachary, 136–37
Tecumseh, 43
Tejaban (village), 161
Tepehuane (Indians), 2, 77
Teporaca, 42, 43. *See also* Rarámuri: history
Terrazas, Juan, 117
Terrazas, Luis, 103
Terrell, General Alexander, 155
Thunder Over Mexico, 57
Tomas (Mawichi villager), 75, 142, 161–62
Topolobampo, Mexico, 122–23,
Traven, B., 6, 40, 109, 150, 170; early life and writings, 12–14

The Treasure of the Sierra Madre, vii, 2, 3, 6, 12–13, 39, 40, 52, 108, 124, 168–69, 170, 172
Trotsky, Leon, 56
Tucson, Arizona, 9–11, 46, 59, 78, 81, 93, 146, 148
Twain, Mark, 32

Vatant, Francoise, 19
Vea, Alfredo, 58–63, 158. *See also* Yaqui (Indians)
Verplancken, Padre Luis: and art museum, 104–7; and handicrafts, 114; origins, 89; and *Semana Santa*, 98, 101; service and work in Sierra Madre, 89–91, 132
Veyre, Gabriel, 53
Viljoen, Ben, 158–60
Villa, Francisco "Pancho" (Doroteo Arango), 2, 122; and death, 72; and Mexican Revolution, 102, 103, 104, 136, 150, 151, 158, 160, 162–66; and North Americans, 163–64; and use of airplanes, 162

Wafer, Lionel, 111–13
West, Don, 63
Wheeler, Romayne, 106, 132–33
Wilson, Woodrow, 163–64
Wolfe, Florida (Lady Flo), 138–40
Wray, Fay, 63

Xetar radio, 114

Yaqui (Indians), 51, 58–63, 66, 158, 160, 168
Young, Brigham, 102. *See also* Mormons

Zapata, Emiliano, 104
Zedillo, President Ernesto, 137–38
Zingg, Robert, 95, 167

JEFF BIGGERS has worked as a writer across the United States, Europe, Mexico, and India. He co-edited *No Lonesome Road: Selected Prose and Poems of Don West*, which won an American Book Award in 2005. He is the author of *The United States of Appalachia: How Southern Mountaineers Brought Independence, Culture, and Enlightenment to America.*

The University of Illinois Press
is a founding member of the
Association of American University Presses.

―――――――――――――――――――――――

Composed in 10/13 Janson Text
with Hoefler Historical Fell Type display
by Jim Proefrock
at the University of Illinois Press
Designed by Dennis Roberts
Manufactured by Thomson-Shore, Inc.

University of Illinois Press
1325 South Oak Street
Champaign, IL 61820-6903
www.press.uillinois.edu